Women, Business and Finance in Nineteenth-century Europe

"Through this collection of cutting-edge research, expertly framed by the editors, the analysis of both women's contribution to financial practice and gender relations in business in the European past is taken to a new level."
Katrina Honeyman, *University of Leeds*

Women, Business and Finance in Nineteenth-century Europe

Rethinking Separate Spheres

Edited by
Robert Beachy, Béatrice Craig
and Alastair Owens

BERG

Oxford • New York

English edition
First published in 2006 by
Berg
Editorial offices:
First Floor, Angel Court, 81 St Clements Street, Oxford OX4 1AW, UK
175 Fifth Avenue, New York, NY 10010, USA

© Robert Beachy, Béatrice Craig and Alastair Owens 2006

All rights reserved.
No part of this publication may be reproduced in any form
or by any means without the written permission of Berg.

Berg is the imprint of Oxford International Publishers Ltd.

Library of Congress Cataloging-in-Publication Data

Women, business and finance in nineteenth-century Europe : rethinking separate spheres / edited by Robert Beachy, Beatrice Craig and Alastair Owens.— English ed.
    p. cm.
  Includes bibliographical references and index.
  ISBN-13: 978-1-84520-185-2 (pbk.)
  ISBN-10: 1-84520-185-X (pbk.)
  ISBN-13: 978-1-84520-184-5 (cloth)
  ISBN-10: 1-84520-184-1 (cloth)
  1. Businesswomen—Europe—History—19th century. 2. Women employees—Europe—History—19th century. 3. Self-employed women—Europe—History—19th century. 4. Finance—Europe—History—19th century. 5. Family-owned business enterprises—Europe—History—19th century. 6. Retail trade—Europe—History—19th century. I. Beachy, Robert. II. Craig, Béatrice. III. Owens, Alastair, 1971-
    HD6053.W6294 2006
    331.4094'09034—dc22   2005029982

British Library Cataloguing-in-Publication Data
A catalogue record for this book is available from the British Library.

ISBN-13 978 1 84520 184 5 (Cloth)
         978 1 84520 185 2 (Paper)

ISBN-10 1 84520 184 1 (Cloth)
         1 84520 185 X (Paper)

Typeset by Avocet Typeset, Chilton, Aylesbury, Bucks
Printed in the United Kingdom by Biddles Ltd, King's Lynn.

www.bergpublishers.com

Contents

List of Tables vii

Contributors ix

Preface xi

1 Introduction
Béatrice Craig, Robert Beachy and Alastair Owens 1

ACTIVITIES OF WOMEN IN INVESTMENT AND FINANCE

2 'Making Some Provision for the Contingencies to which their Sex is Particularly Liable': Women and Investment in Early Nineteenth-century England
Alastair Owens 20

3 The Silent Partners: Women, Capital and the Development of the Financial System in Nineteenth-century Sweden
Tom Petersson 36

ROLES OF WOMEN IN DIRECTION OF FAMILY BUSINESS

4 Where have All the Businesswomen Gone? Images and Reality in the Life of Nineteenth-century Middle-class Women in Northern France
Béatrice Craig 52

5 Profit and Propriety: Sophie Henschel and Gender Management in the German Locomotive Industry
Robert Beachy 67

6 Artisan Women and Management in Nineteenth-century Barcelona
Juanjo Romero-Marín 81

INDEPENDENT OR SELF-EMPLOYED BUSINESSWOMEN

7 Women and Publishing in Nineteenth-century Spain
   Gloria Espigado — 96

8 Businesswomen in Austria
   Irene Bandhauer-Schöffmann — 110

WOMEN IN SHOPKEEPING AND RETAIL TRADE

9 Belgium's Tradeswomen
   Valérie Piette — 126

10 Limited Opportunities? Female Retailing in Nineteenth-century Sweden
   Tom Ericsson — 139

11 Retailing, Respectability and the Independent Woman in Nineteenth-century London
   Alison C. Kay — 152

WOMEN IN SERVICES

12 Hidden Professions? Female 'Placers' of Domestic Servants in Nineteenth-century Dutch Cities
   Marlou Schrover — 167

13 The Business of Sex: Evaluating Prostitution in the German Port City of Hamburg
   Julia Bruggemann — 182

Bibliography — 197

Index — 233

List of Tables

Table 2.1	Proportion of Male and Female Investments in Government Securities	29
Table 2.2	The Structure of Female Government Security Investment	30
Table 3.1	The Relationship between the Informal and the Institutionalized Credit Market in Three Swedish Cities during the Nineteenth Century	41
Table 3.2	Adult Depositors in Six Large Swedish Savings Banks	43
Table 3.3	The Growth of the Swedish Deposit Market 1860–1900, at 1860 Constant Prices	45
Table 3.4	The Ownership Structure in Eight Swedish Commercial Banks	47
Table 4.1	Lille Businesses according to the Sex of Owner	56
Table 4.2	Proportions of Women in Retailing in Lille	57
Table 4.3	Marital Status of Female Merchant Traders, Manufacturers and Retailers, Lille, 1831–90	58
Table 4.4	Female Retailers, Tourcoing, 1852–92	60
Table 4.5	Proportion of Female-run Textile Businesses in Tourcoing	61
Table 6.1	Independent Masters without Consanguineous Relatives Running Shops in the Same Trade's Workshops, Barcelona, 1823–60	84
Table 6.2	Women Running Artisan Workshops by Sector, Barcelona, 1823–60	91
Table 8.1	Self-employed Women and Men in Industry, Trades and Commerce in Vienna	116
Table 8.2	Viennese Trades with the Greatest Number of Self-employed Women in 1910, and the Average Number of Employees, Collaborating Family Members and Domestic Servants	117
Table 8.3	Marital Status of Self-employed Women in Industry, Trades and Commerce in Austria, 1890–1910	118
Table 8.4	Wives as Business Partners in Vienna and its Suburbs, 1869	118
Table 8.5	The Religious Affiliation of Self-employed Viennese in Industry and Trades in 1910	120

Table 9.1	Men and Women in Retailing in Belgium, 1890 and 1900	131
Table 9.2	Men and Women in Retailing in Belgium, 1910–30	131
Table 9.3	Sectors with a Majority of Women in Belgium, 1910	132
Table 10.1	Civil Status of Women Aged 15 years and over in Sweden, 1830–1900	143
Table 10.2	Women in Urban Retailing in Sweden, 1870–95	144
Table 10.3	Women in Retailing 1865–90: Sundsvall, Härnösand, Umeå	145
Table 10.4	Geographic Origin of Female Retailers, 1885	146
Table 12.1	Number of Placers in Utrecht according to Address Books and Census Data	175

Contributors

Irene Bandhauer-Schöffman is Lecturer in History and Gender Studies at the University of Klagenfurt, Austria. She is author of *Entzug und Restitution im Bereich der Katholischen Kirche* (Oldenbourg, 2004), co-editor *of When the War Was Over: Women, War and Peace in Europe 1944–1956* (Leicester University Press, 2000), *Nach dem Krieg: Frauenleben und Geschlechterkonstruktionen in Europa nach dem Zweiten Weltkrieg* (Centaurus, 2000), and *Unternehmerinnen: Geschichte und Gegenwart selbständiger Erwerbstätigkeit von Frauen* (Peter Lang, 2000).

Robert Beachy is Assistant Professor of History at Goucher College, Baltimore, MD, USA. His research focuses on early modern and modern German social, cultural and gender history. His publications include *The Soul of Commerce: Credit, Property and Politics in Leipzig, 1750–1840* (Brill Academic Publishers, 2005). He is currently working on two edited books: *Who Ruled the Cities? Elite and Urban Power Structures, 1700–2000* and *Pious Pursuits: German Moravians in the Atlantic World.*

Julia Bruggemann is Associate Professor of History at DePauw University in Indiana, IN, USA. She is currently finishing a book manuscript on prostitution in Hamburg during the Imperial period.

Béatrice Craig is Assistant Professor of History at the University of Ottawa, Canada. She is interested in the history of North American rural society and middle-class women in northern France in the nineteenth century. Her many publications include articles in *Enterprise and Society* and *Histoire Sociale*.

Tom Ericsson is Professor of History at Umeå University, Sweden. He is co-editor of *The Scandinavian Middle Classes 1840–1940* (Oslo Academic Press, 2004).

Gloria Espigado is Lecturer in History at the University of Cádiz, Spain. She is co-editor of *Pautas históricas de sociabilidad femenina. Rituales y modelos de representación* (1999); *Frasquita Larrea y Aherán. Europeas y españolas entre la*

Ilustración y el Romanticismo (2003) and *Mujer y Deseo. Representaciones y prácticas de vida* (2004), all published by the University of Cádiz Press.

Alison Kay recently completed her DPhil thesis on women engaged in small business in London (c.1740–1880) at the University of Oxford, UK. Her research interests include not only women as business proprietors but also women as investors and owners of property. She is particularly interested in women's work – life strategies in urban environments and the conflict between prescribed roles and the reality of women's working lives. She has published a number of journal articles and chapters on these themes.

Alastair Owens is Lecturer in Geography at Queen Mary, University of London, United Kingdom. He is co-editor of *Urban Fortunes: Property and Inheritance in the Town, 1700–1900* (Ashgate, 2000) and *Family Welfare: Gender, Property and Inheritance since the Seventeenth Century* (Praeger, 2004). He is currently researching women and investment in nineteenth and twentieth-century Britain.

Tom Petersson is a researcher at the Department of Economic History, Uppsala University, Sweden. He is co-author of *Both a Borrower and a Lender Be: Savings Banks in the Economic Development of Sweden, 1820–1939* (Uppsala University, 2000) and author of *Ägarstyrning under organisatorisk och institutionell förändring. Bank- och finanskoncernen Gota, 1985–1993* (Stockholm School of Economics, 2004).

Valérie Piette is Assistant Professor of History at Université libre de Bruxelles, Belgium. She is author of *Domestiques et servantes. Des vies sous condition. Essai sur le travail domestique au 19e siècle* (Académie royale de Belgique, 2000) and many other articles and chapters on women in business in the nineteenth and twentieth centuries.

Juanjo Romero-Marín is a research fellow at Barcelona University, Spain. His current research interests include nineteenth-century Spanish artisans, child labour, apprenticeship and domestic work. He has published numerous Spanish and English language journal articles and book chapters on these themes.

Marlou Schrover is a migration historian at Leiden University, the Netherlands. She has published books and articles on migration, ethnicity and gender. She is co-editor of *Women Workers and Technological Change* (Taylor and Francis, 1995).

Preface

The idea for this book originated from a session held at the fourth European Social Science History Conference that took place in Den Haag, the Netherlands, in spring 2002. That session brought together a number of scholars researching petit bourgeois and middle-class women's economic activities in different parts of nineteenth-century Europe. It quickly became evident that many of us were exploring similar issues and observing familiar trends. In spite of the prescriptive dictates of nineteenth-century bourgeois gender ideology, which frequently suggested that a woman's proper place was in the home, sheltered from the turbulent and potentially corrupting public world of trade, commerce and industry, we were each finding convincing evidence of middle-class women engaging in a wide variety of economic activities. Historical scholarship and debates all too rarely stray beyond national boundaries, especially where linguistic differences exist. As a consequence, while we all found parallels in each other's work, we were frequently ignorant of the substantive research agendas and revisionist trajectories of scholarship in countries where we were not specialists. Out of our dissatisfaction at this situation, the idea for this book was born. In it, we have attempted to bring together scholars working on the economic activities of petit bourgeois and middle-class women in different countries across Europe. We do this because we believe that much can be gained from learning by comparison.

The book aims to showcase, in an accessible manner, innovative research on these themes and to set this research within the context of the historiography of particular regions and countries of Europe. All of the essays were specially commissioned for the volume. We intend students and other researchers to use this book not only to discover something of the important work of the researchers included in the collection, but also as an introduction to historical scholarship on middle-class women's economic activities in these different countries and regions and as a platform for further study. Indeed, our hope is that this collection of essays will make a contribution to a growing revisionist scholarship that seeks to unsettle both some of the accepted – but intrinsically gendered – wisdoms of nineteenth-century European economic history, and some of the familiar analytical frameworks of gender history. In the same way that the contribution of working women to the commercial and industrial revolutions of nineteenth-century Europe has recently been re-evaluated, this book aims to reconsider the economic roles of females higher up the social scale. Additionally, we were keen to demonstrate some of the 'blood, sweat and tears' that studying the economic history of bourgeois women entails. Finding evidence of middling women's economic agency is no easy task. Women are frequently absent from conventional records, not least because of the inherent masculine bias of many historical sources. As the chapters in this book suggest, perseverance, an investigative nose, the skill to use sources innovatively and a willingness to read them against the grain are necessary qualities of researchers of middling women in nineteenth-century Europe.

The creation of the book has certainly been a pan-European if not global endeavour. With one editor in Canada, a second in the USA, another in the UK and a cast of contributors from across continental Europe, co-ordinating the production of this set of essays has not been an easy task. We would like to thank all of our contributors for responding so constructively and cheerfully to our demands, comments and suggestions. This is a collection of essays published in English, but not all the chapters were originally written in that language. Consequently, the crafting of this book has demanded more time, energy and good humoured communication than might normally be the case. Contributors to the book have acknowledged the assistance of a wide range of colleagues, critics and sponsors who helped them to prepare their contribution in their own chapters. Here we would like to thank the publisher's anonymous reader for the constructive comments offered on an earlier draft of the manuscript. Berg Publishers have been supportive throughout and we would especially like to acknowledge Kathleen May and Fran Martin, our editors, for their patience and encouragement. Finally, we would like to thank our partners and families, who bore the brunt of the stress and distraction that completing a project such as this one often entails.

Robert Beachy, Baltimore, MD, USA
Béatrice Craig, Ottawa, Canada
Alastair Owens, London, UK

–1–

Introduction

Béatrice Craig, Robert Beachy and Alastair Owens

Gender – what it means to be male or female – is key to our sense of identity. It is also central to the way we view others and our relationships with them. Most scholars would argue, however, that gender is not something that is biologically determined; rather it is a category of identity that has always been socially constructed. Masculinity and femininity, the gender identities usually ascribed to men and women, are not defined by anatomical differences between males and females – they are learned ways of acting, feeling and behaving.[1] Indeed, in Western societies, as Joan Scott has argued, gender has been a 'constitutive element of social relationships based on perceived relationship between the sexes'. It also expresses relationships of power.[2] In the nineteenth century, gender gained an increasingly important role in shaping access to material resources, and to economic and political power. More particularly, during this period a 'separate spheres ideology' emerged that functioned to restrict women's political and economic agency, albeit with uneven success, and not without challenges. The chapters in this book assess the significance of this ideology of separate spheres for understanding women's economic agency in nineteenth-century Europe. The aim is to highlight some of the ideology's contradictions, ambivalences and limits and to consider the ways it was resisted, refigured and transgressed in the everyday conduct of a variety of economic activities by petit-bourgeois and middle-class women across the continent. It focuses on women's activities as business owners and managers, as retailers and wholesalers, as entrepreneurs and innovators and as investors and creditors, to show how, in spite of the rhetorical force of the ideology of separate spheres, middle-class women played a central role in the economic transformations of nineteenth-century Europe.

From the Hierarchy of Gender to Opposite Sexes and Separate Spheres

Two distinct understandings of gender have co-existed in Western society, the origins of which can be traced back to the ancient world of Greece and Rome. One dominated most of the early modern period, while the other gained ascendancy in the late eighteenth and early nineteenth centuries.[3] While both were founded upon heterosexual understandings of the relationships between men and women, they are marked by important differences. In the former, gender signified a hierarchy. Men and women differed only by degree: men were stronger, braver, smarter and more rational than women. These qualities were desirable in men and women alike, but it went without saying that the only women who could display them at the same level as men were 'exceptional' – worthy of admiration, but clearly extraordinary. Ordinary women lagged behind. They could do almost everything men did, but rarely as well. Females were therefore best suited to serve men as helpers, and most women were expected to assist their husbands in his craft or occupation, whether merchant-trading, baking, weaving, farming or some other activity. Where such a gender ideology prevailed, a widow's continuance of her husband's trade after his death was usually tolerated (although within Europe this practice varied across time and space, as well as between different activities). However, this tolerance was often hedged with restrictions reflecting the notion that women were 'lesser males'. Craftsmen's widows were rarely allowed to take apprentices, for example. When gender signified a hierarchy, men and women therefore normally operated in the same 'joint sphere', but not on an equal footing.

In the second understanding of gender identities and relations, gender became the marker of binary oppositions between the sexes. Men and women were perceived as qualitatively different: a positive quality in one was a serious shortcoming in the other. Women displaying 'male' characteristics were 'mannish', 'unfeminine' or 'unsexed', and were depicted as deviants, if not monsters. Men who displayed stereotypical 'female' qualities were similarly objects of ridicule, dismissed as 'effeminate' and 'unmasculine'. Such ways of thinking stem from the conflation of gender with a particular kind of sexuality: heterosexual relationships between men and women were regarded as the norm and formed a basis upon which other dimensions of difference were built. Gender as a marker of opposition between the sexes justified a 'separate spheres' ideology which ascribed to men and women sharply differentiated social roles in accordance with their perceived natures. Considered strong, smart and rational, men deployed their talents in the public sphere, which encompassed political and economic activities. More generally, anything that required rational thinking, self control and competitiveness was thought of as male. Described as intuitive, sensitive, altruistic and emotional, women were intended to perform domestic duties. Public activities, including economic ones, were clearly unsuitable for women, not only because women were thought to lack the abilities to enter public life, but also because contact with the outside world would supposedly ruin their femininity. For their own good, women had to remain in the sheltered environment of the home, protected against the corrupting influence of the marketplace and dependent on the men who supported them.[4] The roles of men and women were not seen as merely different, therefore, but they were also regarded as complementary.

In the late eighteenth and early nineteenth centuries a renewed emphasis was placed on this perceived opposition between the sexes, and the 'separate spheres' ideology became a dominant European gender discourse. Historians have identified economic change, the emergence of new forms of political power and the rise of evangelical religious thought as important explanations for the appeal of the ideology at this time. On the one hand, the ideological shifts can be seen as a consequence of broader structural economic changes occurring across Europe – particularly industrialization – which saw the separation of production and consumption and of workplace and household, a process which had an inevitable impact on gender roles. However, the shifts can also be seen as a product of political changes. During this period, various groups constructed or reconstructed their identity in order to increase their political power – and they did so in gendered terms. In Protestant Europe, these processes were given moral force and divine sanction by a resurgence in evangelical Christianity which preached the virtues of a separation of gender roles and their centrality to a godly existence.[5]

Women's exclusion from the public sphere, economic activities included, would have been one significant strand in these shifts in gender identity. Leonore Davidoff and Catherine Hall's classic depiction of this process in *Family Fortunes*, for instance, asserted that in nineteenth-century England class and gender had been mutually constitutive. The ideology of domesticity and the notion that 'respectable' men supported their families (which implies that 'respectable' women had to be dependent on men) were central to the formation of middle-class identity. Middle-class women devoted their time and energy to creating and upholding the very bourgeois morals that cemented their social position ideologically, by raising children, and enforcing middle-class values in the community. Respectability made the middle class morally superior to the dissolute aristocracy, and justified bourgeois claims to a greater share of political power.[6] Working-class men soon developed their own version of this ideology. They redefined masculinity in terms of ownership of a skill and the ability to support one's dependants, and they objected to married women's working outside the house.[7] Many working-class families, where women had no option but to work, could not embrace this 'male breadwinner ideology', and it was followed unevenly across Europe.[8]

Later historians, interested in consumption as a cultural phenomenon, noted its role in class formation as well. The middle classes developed patterns of consumption that did not emulate those of their betters, and which became an important part of their class identities. They emphasized 'good taste', 'respectability' and prudent management of family resources. These qualities were also the creation of women, who decided how the house should be furnished and decorated, what kind of food should be served and how many servants were 'necessary' to meet class standards. Consumption, as much as moral behaviour, linked domesticity and class identity.[9]

Neither the separate spheres ideology nor the associated 'cult of domesticity' that marked bourgeois culture was uniquely a British phenomenon. Historians noted the disappearance of the economically active middle-class woman and the demise of older forms of gender ideology all over Europe and even North America.[10] In France, the issue had seemingly been settled several years before the appearance of *Family Fortunes*. Bonnie Smith published *Ladies of the Leisure Class* before gender had become prominent in the historian's analytical tool box, and before identity formation became a hot topic.[11] However, the book can be read retrospectively in the light of later theories. Smith described an early nineteenth-century France inhabited by petticoated captains of industry whose daughters and granddaughters turned their backs on the man-made world of capitalism. They retreated into a parallel world controlled by the natural and supernatural forces of reproduction and religion. Smith's late nineteenth-century world was unmistakably one of separate spheres, where women's lives became centred on domesticity.

Smith's findings may be one of the reasons why French historians, who developed an argument parallel to that of Davidoff and Hall, stressed the political rather than the economic dimension of women's exclusion. They paid less attention to the exclusion of middle-class women from the economic sphere (which they usually take for granted) than from politics. They argued that the celebrated Rights of Man and of Citizen underpinning the Revolution of 1789 and subsequent republican regimes referred exclusively to the rights of men. The universalist discourse of the French Revolution hid an intrinsically masculine definition of citizenship, which was never economically neutral. Implicitly, men were assumed worthy of active citizenship because they were expected to head a household, which included the support of dependants. A citizen was thus an individual who supported others, and represented them in the public sphere. The French Civil Code ensured that a dependant remained so. Children of both sexes were emancipated at the age of 21, but women lost all legal autonomy when they married and were reduced to the status of minor children. Among other things, a husband could forbid that his wife engage in a paid activity if he deemed this detrimental to the performance of her 'household' duties. If she did work outside the home, he could legally claim her earnings.[12] Economic liberalism, which also emerged in the late eighteenth and early nineteenth centuries, should in theory have facilitated women's economic activities, by removing all entrance barriers to the trades and professions and by allowing people to pursue an occupation of choice. Political liberalism, however, erected ideological, if not legal, barriers to women, especially if they were married.

Women in Central Europe did not fare better, and in most of the German states the separate spheres ideology gained ready acceptance, not least among civil servants and business elites.[13] Like elsewhere, the German states denied women rights of political participation. The barriers to women's economic activities were more ideological than legal (although in most German states, as in most of Europe, the economic activities of married women were subject to their husbands' control). Consistent with the 'cult of domesticity' evident in England, women were construed as the makers of culture and arbiters of good taste, and they could assume these roles because they did not have to 'work'.[14] In contrast, their husbands, as the responsible breadwinners, had less time for culture. Women's social activities were also key to their husbands' success. German civil service positions, for instance, have been described as 'two people careers'. Civil servants' wives were expected to create the networks and cultivate the connections that would facilitate their husbands' promotions. Similarly, German businessmen and industrialists viewed wives and daughters as the sponsors of social welfare and philanthropy, or the fine arts and cultural events.[15] Here too, then, the removal of barriers to women's economic activities (abolition of guilds or the elimination of gender guardianship for unmarried adult women) was counterbalanced by an ideology inimical to their taking advantage of new opportunities.

Far less is known about the situation in Mediterranean countries. As a research field, women's history developed later in those countries than in northwestern and central Europe or North America, and the historiography is still limited (and rarely translated). As in the earlier phases of English-language women's history, the interests of Spanish and Italian historians appear to have focused on female factory workers and the quest for equal rights. Mediterranean countries industrialized late, and their economies were dominated by family firms and family craft shops. Women were also always involved in agriculture. On the other hand, women's roles in crafts production was usually severely restricted by guild regulations. The abolition of guilds could have opened new opportunities for women, but, as Maura Palazzi has noted, 'the power to limit women's rights, previously contained in the statutes of cities and guilds was shifted to the male heads of families and to the rules of the "free" market'.[16] The abolition of formal restrictions on women's involvement in trades was sometimes accompanied by more rigid gender roles. However, another factor complicated the Italian situation: lengthy, but temporary, male emigration. Italy was, in Barbara Curli's words, 'a land of women left on their own', and the legal system increasingly treated emigrants' wives as temporary heads of family, while simultaneously branding the female businesswoman as an anomaly.[17]

The separate spheres ideology and its delegitimization of women's economic activities shaped the worlds of petit-bourgeois and lower middle-class groups. According to Geoffrey Crossick and Heinz-Gerhard Haupt, as the guilds lost their corporate legal status in early nineteenth-century Europe and retail enterprizes became part of the family patrimony, economic opportunities for petit-bourgeois women grew. However, Crossick and Haupt also show how ideological attitudes hardened as the century progressed, and that it became less acceptable for women to help their shopkeeper husbands or to run an establishment after his death.[18] Consequently, in up-scale shops women became invisible (although many probably worked as hard as ever behind the scenes). By century's end, the only women left in craft industries and retailing were those who had to work for a living – usually widows and spinsters – who were otherwise forced to work in a factory or enter domestic service. These women eked out a marginal existence in small, short-lived retail businesses. And whereas women at the beginning of the century could have been found in a wide range of crafts and trades, their granddaughters were confined to gendered economic ghettos (the needle trades, the provision of food, the hospitality industry and laundering), which were often an extension of household activities. This evolution may have been forced upon them in part from above: wealthy suppliers, often more ideologically wedded to separate spheres, were frequently reluctant to do business with women and either did not trust their business abilities or sought to distance themselves from those whose respectability was tarnished by a commercial pursuit.[19] But retailers and craftsmen may also have been aping their social superiors as they themselves became more bourgeois and adopted the male breadwinner ideology, which was spreading among skilled and unionized workers.

Separate spheres, in short, was a remarkably persistent ideology in nineteenth-century Europe. It was found from north to south and east to west, co-existing with a variety of legal, political, economic and cultural institutions. It was also a way of thinking about gender and the relationships between men and women that spanned a broad middle-class spectrum: from the wealthy bourgeoisie whose fortunes stemmed from new industrial and commercial opportunities, to the petit-bourgeois groups whose more modest economic activities met the growing consumption needs of Europe's expanding urban populations. The hegemony of bourgeois values and the dynamic of cultural emulation that influenced many parts of the continent also ensured that this was an ideology that shaped the lives of a working class and sometimes aspiring poor.

Masculinizing Work, Business and the Economy

The progress of the separate spheres ideology accompanied a redefinition of 'work', 'skills' and 'business', and a recategorization of which kinds of activities were deemed to be part of the formal economy. These processes all resulted in a reidentification of women as non-economic agents, even when they played a key role in the family economy.

First, the term 'work' came to be restricted to 'formal' market activities. The production of goods and services for intra-familial consumption was not 'work', despite the obvious economic importance of those activities for the family and the wider reproduction of society.[20] Housewives therefore did not 'work' but carried out their wifely and motherly 'duties' and their activities were defined as callings too hallowed to be priced.[21] Traditional female activities in family shops or farms, which had an even more obvious economic value, were also redefined by policy makers and judges as women's familial duties. These activities did not entitle women to financial compensation from fathers or brothers, and certainly not from husbands. Secondly, casual and part-time activities, even when labelled 'work', did not qualify the labouring individual as a 'worker', especially if the work was unskilled, done at home, or done by married women. Laid off male workers and single women were unemployed; laid off married women were housewives (and where unemployment insurance existed, they were rarely eligible for benefits). In France and England this allowed women who had engaged in a succession of paid activities for their entire married lives to claim they had 'never worked'.[22]

Work and workers were thus coded male and so were 'skills'. Thus women's work, almost by definition, could not be skilled. Women were not capable of learning the intricacies of a trade, and when they did, they were unable to learn new ways of doing old things. Women operated at an instinctive or reflexive level, not at a rational one. Their abilities were inborn, part of their feminine nature, and thus not 'skills'.[23] Sewing, for instance, became feminized in the course of the nineteenth century, and was demoted in the process from male skill to female innate ability.[24] On the other hand, what men did was often described in unmistakably male terms: if it was done by men, it was skilled, and if it was defined as skilled, it had to be reserved to men.[25]

This masculinization of economic activity has often been unconsciously reproduced by historians in their analyses of nineteenth-century Western economies. Angel Kwolek-Folland and Barbara Curli, for example, have noted that business historians have used concepts such as 'business', 'entrepreneurship' or 'profits' in narrow and highly masculinist ways.[26] Business is assumed always to have been a rational activity and businessmen to have been immune from emotionally driven decisions, a function of the neo-classical theoretical assumptions central to much business and economic history. The 'entrepreneur', as defined by the influential economist Schumpeter, was an Alpha-male.[27] As Wendy Gambers noted, in the United States 'businesswoman' meant white collar worker![28] On the other hand, women's leadership in voluntary or philanthropic associations, some of which handled considerable budgets and co-ordinated the activities of large numbers of volunteers, did not qualify as 'management', but was instead seen as a modest and natural extension of their domestic duties.

Finally, production, which was dominated by men, has been constructed as the quintessential economic activity. Reproduction, except among certain Marxists, takes place outside of the formal economy.[29] But so does consumption, and there can be no economy without consumers. Yet traditional economic models are supply driven, and economists have taken consumption for granted.[30] Contemporaries had an equally difficult time conceptualizing consumption – an activity orchestrated by women – as an economic process. More often than not, they described it as a parasitical activity that did little to enhance a country's productivity and that served as an outlet for women's irrational and irresponsible behaviour.[31]

The separate spheres ideology has therefore implicitly denied the economic value of many female activities. It has reinforced a perception of the economic world that reflected attributes and values deemed innately male and centred on male activities. This habit of obscuring women's economic activities was well established by the mid-nineteenth century. Politicians, public administrators, civil servants and statisticians, lawyers and even private businessmen ignored working women, overlooked their activities, and attributed their production to the nearest male. Some of the most significant sources for studying economic activity in nineteenth-century Europe, such as national decennial censuses, are marked by this careless disregard of women's contributions. The official construction of 'women' as wives and mothers who did not 'work' and who were 'naturally' unfit to acquire either production or management skills has therefore had profound consequences for historians. A recurrent theme in most of the contributions in this volume is the poverty of sources documenting women's economic activities, especially the activities of married and middle-class women. Whether in Britain, France, Belgium, Germany or Austria, women, especially those who married, are buried deep in the sources, and one needs to look hard to find them. As many of the contributors note, previous historians uncritically followed the lead of their sources, often replicating their masculine biases.

The second most recurrent theme in the contributions to this volume is the invisibility of middle-class women's economic activities in historical narratives. The separate spheres ideology was one of the dominant discourses of the nineteenth century – so dominant in fact that historians of women viewed it as a natural framework for interpreting women's past. Labour historians noted the existence of female factory workers;[32] historians of women documented the non-economic activities of middle-class women;[33] historians of the middle class were mostly interested in men;[34] and business and economic historians for their part, as we have seen, did not question the gendered nature of existing definitions of 'work', 'skills' or even 'economic activities'.[35] These studies presented a set of models in which it was difficult to locate women's activities. French business historians, for example, have emphasized the 'dynasticism' of French entrepreneurs, describing successions of fathers and sons (or sons-in-law), but also dismissing any thought that women could have played a significant role in the prominent family businesses of the long nineteenth century.[36] As Eliane Richard and Marlou Schrover have demonstrated for the Netherlands and Southern France, however, the alleged withdrawal of women from the world of business likelier reflected their erasure from historical sources than their departure from the economic sphere.[37]

Challenges

In recent years, the separate spheres paradigm has been forcefully challenged by English and German-speaking historians (though less so elsewhere, and in France it remains the unquestioned orthodoxy among women historians). Some, like Amanda Vickery, have reminded us that one should not confuse prescription with description. The separate spheres ideology was an ideal and may have corresponded poorly to the reality of women's everyday lives. Vickery makes the interesting point that a strident separate spheres discourse offers evidence that women were transgressing their 'proper sphere', rather than being increasingly confined to it. A more vigorous separate spheres discourse may reflect a higher level of contestation.[38] In addition, gender definitions and gender relations, including the definitions of male and female 'spheres', were never static, but constantly challenged, reshaped and rethought, in words and in action.[39] Gender is a dynamic social construct and the separate spheres ideology was but one among many forms of gender identity co-existing and overlapping in nineteenth-century Europe.[40]

Historians interested in the numerous female reform movements which developed in the nineteenth century concluded that women often used notions of a distinct feminine nature to stake out a place in the public sphere. Women carved spaces for themselves in the public sphere by capitalizing on the notion that they were innately different from men. They used contemporary understandings of 'women's nature' to get out of the house and engage in mass consumption and benevolent activities, and to participate in social reform movements.[41] They elaborated alternative definitions of citizenship which were not narrowly restricted to the franchise. Those who agitated for the franchise often did so on the basis of female essentialism: only the vote, they argued, could ensure that female values might influence policy making.[42] Others used the private sphere and domestic social networks to help to organize and co-ordinate early feminist campaigns.[43] Women thus challenged and redrew the boundaries of their sphere. Others questioned existing visions of sharply separated spheres, noting instead that the boundaries between the two were very porous indeed.[44] Gender history led to an interest in masculinity, and it became obvious that masculinity was constructed in the private as well as in the public sphere (an argument that can already be found in Davidoff's and Hall's *Family Fortunes*).[45] But one could also argue that femininity was constructed in the public sphere: 'good' middle class women were supposed to engage in reform or at least charitable activities. Moreover, as the century progressed and new forms of mass consumption emerged, women shoppers also became legitimate public figures, tramping the streets of metropolitan cities like London and Paris and visiting new department stores.[46]

None of this, however, undermined notions of the absence of middle-class women from the economic sphere. As recently as 1995, anyone surveying the writings of women, gender or business historians could have legitimately concluded that Smith or Davidoff and Hall had been right on one point: middle-class women had withdrawn, or been expelled, from the economic sphere, with one possible exception. The separate spheres ideology created commodities that could yield economic dividends, which women were particularly well positioned to sell: domesticity and femininity. Well documented for the United States, this allowed women to monopolize some trades like dressmaking and millinery. In the North American Mid-West, for example, businesses were strongly sex-typed; women accounted for at least 95 per cent of those engaged in activities defined as 'female'. Three-quarters of the businesses run by women catered to other women. Similarly, in Boston in 1876, 80 per cent of women listed in the city directories were selling food or clothing or offering lodging. More than half served their own sex.[47] Crossicks and Haupt's broad synthesis as well as Alison Kay's contribution to this volume suggest that the same process may have been at work in Europe alongside the emergence of a class of impoverished retailing widows. Millinery and fashion were the only forms of commerce catering to the higher end of the market in which women participated in significant numbers.[48]

The strong sexual segregation of the business world depicted by these authors, however, indicates that women were expected to restrict their economic activities to those deemed appropriate to their sex. Women were permitted to enter the public world of trade and commerce as long as their activities reinforced rather than undermined gender stereotypes. While the male/female and public/private dichotomies did not coincide, it was apparently good business to pretend that they did. The ideology of 'separate spheres', then, did not absolutely exclude women from the economic world, but allowed them to participate, though subject to constraints that did not apply to men. Or, as Joan Scott has suggested, one should not investigate the ways in which the spheres were separate, but the ways in which the economy was segmented and how gender was used for this purpose.[49]

Much more recently Eleanor Gordon and Gwyneth Nair have questioned the assumption of middle-class women's economic dependence on men.[50] They have found that in Victorian Glasgow – during the period when the separate spheres ideology was arguably strongest – a high proportion of women were not economically dependent on men and did not live in male-headed households. The notion that middle-class women were dependent on men, they argue, stems in part from an almost exclusive historiographic focus on married women. This led to a form of circular reasoning: women who did not fit the model were paid scant attention, and this reinforced the notion that married women's experience was the norm. Yet as others have shown for British cities, single women made up as many as half of the adult female population, a situation that was also true of many other parts of Europe.[51] For Gordon and Nair, the separate spheres discourse was one of several competing gender discourses that middle-class women could appropriate to justify their activities.[52]

Making the Economically Active Middle-class Woman Visible: An Outline of the Book

The presence of competing discourses helps to explain why some historians have managed to identify middle-class women who flouted the separate spheres ideology and even operated outside the 'segmented' female sphere of retailing. Throughout the nineteenth century, European women ran merchant trading houses or manufacturing concerns. Retail trade also appears to have been more 'feminized' and female retailers less marginalized than Crossick and Haupt have argued.[53]

Thus the contributors to this volume both affirm those who subscribe to the 'separate spheres' paradigm and support the revisionists who argue for the existence of a 'segmented sphere'. They additionally show that the pre-industrial concept of a 'joint sphere' was resilient and adaptable to new circumstances. Drawing on evidence of women's economic activity from a range of national and economic contexts, the chapters are grouped thematically into five general sections: 1) the activities of women in investment and finance (chapters two and three); 2) the roles of women in the direction of family businesses (chapters four, five and six); 3) independent or self-employed businesswomen (chapters seven and eight); 4) women in shopkeeping and retail trade (chapters nine, ten and eleven); and 5) women in services (chapters twelve and thirteen). Broader themes connect all of these chapters, of course, but those in sections two, three and four are especially interconnected since family firms often generated self-employed businesswomen, while retail trade was a widespread source of female self-employment as well as of family business. Spanning Western Europe, Britain, Scandinavia, Central Europe and the Mediterranean, these case studies share the common attribute of questioning whether the language of spheres, boundaries or gender divisions has any real analytical value for understanding female economic agency.

This is a central consideration in section one (chapters two and three), which documents the importance of female capital in underpinning the processes of wealth creation in the nineteenth century. Women were important players in financial markets, investing in order to generate an income for themselves and supplying credit and capital for others. Investment was one economic activity that could be harmonized with the prescriptive ideologies of separate spheres. Unlike running a shop or managing a business, it could be carried out with minimal visible economic activity. Whereas going out to work risked compromising a woman's gentility, investment offered a means by which to secure discreetly an income and accumulate a fortune. As one English investment guide addressed to women explained, while a wife 'cannot always share [her husband's] labours at the counter, and never at the office', she can save for 'the contingencies of both married and single life'.[54] Certainly, popular portrayals of financial markets were marked by assumptions about gender roles. Women were seen as best suited to low risk and consequently low income investments that provided them with a steady *rentier* income and that enabled them to remain relatively passive economic agents. Men, on the other hand, were judged to be more skilled at reading and interpreting financial information and, as a result, more suited to making speculative and higher risk investments.

While this gender-typing of investment markets clearly existed across nineteenth-century Europe, chapters two and three in this volume uncover the significance of female wealth in a variety of financial arenas and unsettle the notion that women's investment simply economically shored up the ideology of domesticity at the heart of separate spheres. Alastair Owens's contribution (chapter two) demonstrates the remarkable significance of single women as investors in British government securities. By 1840 he estimates that they comprised almost half of all personal investors in the British national debt. As holders of government securities, these women were creditors of the state and, as a consequence, at the heart of systems of public finance and the debates that surrounded them (a phenomenon noticed in other parts of Europe too).[55] He also shows how the income from these investments was used by these single women to support their own domestic wellbeing, ultimately illustrating the interdependence of public and private.

Tom Petersson (chapter three) considers female investment in nineteenth-century Sweden. Here women, especially widows, played a central and important role in urban credit systems. Younger women invested heavily in savings banks and managed their wealth independently of a husband or guardian, pre-empting later changes in the law. The investments of these women were significant for the Swedish economy as much of the wealth deposited by women was invested in local industry. Later in the century a modernized and institutionalized urban financial system emerged that was national in its reach, and here too women were significant, with commercial as well as savings banks becoming increasingly reliant on female capital. Finally, Petersson shows the importance of women in supplying capital for Swedish industrialization through participation in shareholding. While he concludes that Swedish women were more suppliers than demanders of industrial capital and never achieved 'fully fledged' economic agency, their contribution to economic life was far greater than a simplistic reading of the separate spheres thesis would suggest.

Section two focuses on the critical and often unrecognized roles that women played in family businesses. Mothers, daughters and wives made not only financial contributions to family firms but also provided labour power and management expertise. In her study of the textile centre of Lille in northern France, Béatrice Craig (chapter four) documents how women helped to finance and manage wholesale, retail and manufacturing businesses, and sometimes directed a family firm alone as a surviving widow. The economic contributions of these women have been overlooked, however, because their practical and even legal positions were systematically misrepresented in censuses, tax rolls and trade directories. Moreover, both nineteenth-century observers and contemporary historians have discounted the roles of these women in an effort to assimilate them to a 'separate spheres' ideology. Exceptions were sometimes made for a surviving widow, whose management of a family business might bridge male generations.

Even the direction of a manufacturing firm by the owner's widow could prove complicated or unseemly, especially in sectors of heavy industry that were vigorously gender-coded. Despite legal and proprietary rights, widows were sometimes forced to assume an inconspicuous role by manipulating management from behind the scenes. As Robert Beachy illustrates with a case study of the widow Sophie Henschel (chapter 5), some women in ownership positions effectively managed not only a family business but their own images as well. While maintaining absolute control of one of Imperial Germany's largest industrial concerns with an array of specialized engineering and production capacities, Henschel presented herself to the world as little more than the sponsor of welfare programmes for company workers. Ultimately, Henschel directed the family-owned conglomerate through the period of its greatest and most rapid expansion. Women's involvement in this crucial stage in a firm's life-cycle was hardly inconsequential, therefore, as some historians have suggested. Moreover, given the frequency with which women outlived men, such arrangements were common across European societies.[56]

Family business likewise trumped gender in the guild economy of Catalonia. As Juanjo Romero-Marín (chapter six) demonstrates, the abolition of guilds removed traditional ways of validating (male) skills, to which craftsmen responded by 'patrimonializing' their guild professions. In short, family patrimony and continuity came to replace guild structure. Women, who had been barred by guild rules from taking part in production, became central to the transmission of skills and the perpetuation of professional reputations: they provided capital, expertise, labour and a bloodline. Catalan artisan families, like German, Austrian, French or Belgian manufacturers, thus called on their women to ensure the survival of the family business, and with it the socio-economic status of the family unit.

Section three focuses on self-employed women who ran their own businesses. These contributions document female entrepreneurs who were active in traditional artisanal trades, as well as in newer business opportunities such as printing and publishing. As Gloria Espigado argues (chapter seven), Spanish women entered the publishing world as magazine editors and authors and often wrote exclusively for other women. Of course, writing and publishing were relatively new forms of economic activity that were increasingly opened to middle-class women beginning in the eighteenth century. Through publishing and authorship, Spanish women gained public roles, both as economic agents and through access to an incipient public sphere. Sometimes these women challenged existing gender norms with their writings; but more often than not, they promoted them. Here we have the paradox of women entering the public sphere to promote a gendered private one.

While middle-class women certainly did not retreat from the economy in the nineteenth century, as the discussion above has indicated, it would be wrong to suggest that the separate spheres discourse was not a real and powerful presence. As Irene Bandhauer-Schöffmann demonstrates for Vienna (chapter eight), the separate spheres ideology frequently influenced new legal restrictions. By the late nineteenth century, changes in Austrian commercial law increasingly restricted women to 'suitable' trades, which limited the economic latitude of many. Viennese businesswomen responded by entering new professions, by capitalizing on their femininity, and occasionally by challenging legal discrimination in the Austrian court system. On the whole, the challenge posed by gender discrimination was not insurmountable, and Viennese women learned to manipulate it to their advantage.

Section four examines different retail trades, exploring the activities and business networks of female entrepreneurs. It also considers the clientele of these retailers, focusing particularly on examples where women met the consumption needs of other women. Valérie Piette (chapter nine) shows how the nineteenth-century Belgian retail trade became increasingly 'feminized'; by 1900 fully 33 per cent of Belgium's retailers were women. While women remained scattered across all categories of trade, the higher the proportion of women in retailing, the more likely they were to dominate the food and textile sectors. This concentration might have reflected the entry of women of modest means into those retail sectors requiring little start-up capital. The feminization of retailing was also accompanied by an increase in the number of married women who maintained shops. Of course contemporary gender norms indirectly shaped their choices; women, rather than men, opened stores because it was better than the alternatives (factory work or domestic service) and could be combined with married life or motherhood. For both practical and ideological reasons, retailing became increasingly attractive to self-employed women by the end of the nineteenth century.

Sometimes, as in Sweden, the growth in the number of women retailers reflected government policy or design. As Tom Ericsson argues (chapter ten), by the middle of the nineteenth century Swedish government officials had concluded that shopkeeping was a proper activity for 'surplus' single or widowed females, who represented a potential burden to public welfare. Sweden's significantly larger proportion of women – a fairly widespread phenomenon in nineteenth-century Europe – posed a real conundrum to state bureaucrats who accepted implicitly the alleged female attributes of domesticity and dependency. For those middle-class women who never married or were left destitute by a husband's death, retail trade provided a respectable mode of self-employment and was promoted as a viable alternative to poor relief. Yet, as Ericsson demonstrates, women who did not 'need' to work because they were married also entered the retail trade in large numbers.

In chapter eleven, Alison Kay shows how women carved out a sphere of their own, catering to a mostly female clientele in nineteenth-century London's luxury retail trades. In order to attract clients these women emphasized their respectability, superior tastes and refinement. The vendors of luxury goods demonstrated these characteristics by revealing the high social status of some of their patrons, whom they mentioned on their business cards (an important source material for Kay's chapter). The separate spheres ideology, combined with the economic transformations of the nineteenth century, closed some economic opportunities to women but likewise opened others. And at the upper end of the retail spectrum (especially luxury fashion and millinery), self-employed women were able to manipulate this ideology to their own commercial benefit.

The final chapters, in section five, consider women who were engaged in 'service activities' and the 'segmentation' of certain service trades among women. As Marlou Schrover (chapter twelve) demonstrates for the Netherlands, the public activities of women preserved the privacy of both working-class domestics and the elite women who hired them. Women used their social capital to monopolize the position of intermediaries – or 'placers', as they were known – between other women seeking positions as servants and their would-be mistresses. Here women 'placers' earned the trust of middle-class and elite women seeking domestic help precisely because of their knowledge and social networks. In this manner, women were able to capitalize on widespread stereotypes about their nature to carve out a female niche in the economic sphere.

At the lower end of the economic spectrum, women sometimes fell into the 'oldest profession' or prostitution, especially the destitute, immigrants, or those without family or social networks. As Julia Bruggemann (chapter thirteen) demonstrates in her study of Hamburg, the state played an ambivalent role, sometimes sanctioning and sometimes criminalizing the sex industry, but always working to subject women to surveillance and control. Arguably, what little economic agency Hamburg prostitutes ever enjoyed was likely diminished with the implementation of the regulatory system and 'brothelization'. All the same, by the end of the nineteenth century, as Bruggemann demonstrates, many more Hamburg prostitutes worked illicitly than within the regulatory system. Certainly a small number of madams and procuresses enjoyed some measure of economic independence. Yet as Bruggemann argues, prostitution was never a source of empowerment for those women ensnared in the sex industry. And if the phenomenon of prostitution proved especially challenging to Victorian gender stereotypes, the sex workers themselves might well be considered the most aggrieved victims of the ideology of separate spheres.

Prostitutes, like small retailers and peddlers, simply coped and had neither the time nor the resources to justify or theorize their activities. They were unlikely to claim rights, *qua* women, for selling milk or haberdashery, as elite milliners or fashion merchants did. But since most (barring prostitutes) sold their wares from home and served other women, they faced little resistance, and sometimes encouragement, as in the Swedish case documented by Tom Ericsson. At issue among the petite bourgeoisie and the working class was the location of work, and not the phenomenon of female employment.

In the production trades (crafts and manufacturing), the situation was often different. Women were much less likely to be self starters and launch their own businesses. The experience of those who did resembled that of the retailers, but at a more profitable level. The women who inherited businesses were also less likely to be limited to 'female' sectors, and the two phenomena were linked. In France, Belgium, Germany, Austria and Spain, women in production trades were usually successors, and the businesses they directed were not gender coded. A female manufacturer might inherit a business from her father (or in Belgium from a female relative); more frequently she received it from her husband. But what mattered here was not the type of business, but the legitimacy – or legality – of a woman's claim to ownership.

Although some successors fitted the stereotype of the widow as bridge between a prematurely departed husband and sons too young to assume control, many business widows were more than genealogical stopgaps as Robert Beachy demonstrates with the example of Sophie Henschel. In some cases, there were no sons, but often social norms and the law considered the widow a part owner of the business alongside the heirs, allowing her to act as the senior partner. Transmission through the female line could also be a means to counter legal changes judged detrimental to the family, or the occupational group.

Conclusion

The separate spheres ideology that emerged fully formed after 1800 clearly played a formative rhetorical role in the cultures and societies of nineteenth-century Europe. It was, however, as Gordon and Nair have argued, just one among several discourses through which petit bourgeois and middle-class men and women organized and made sense of their lives.[57] Older understandings of gender relations co-existed alongside the separate spheres model, while alternative ways of constructing gender identities and relations were played out in the everyday activities of making a living. A diverse continent, Europe provided a setting in which competing gender understandings encountered each other and clashed, but also co-existed harmoniously. Accordingly, it is possible to witness a range of social formations and economic arrangements, with women variously operating in 'separate', 'segmented' and 'joint' spheres. To some extent, individuals (men and women), different social groups and other 'actors', like the state, might pick and choose from a complex and varied collection of gender discourses, appropriating whichever seemed most suited to specific situations and goals. While the constraints that women faced in carrying out economic activities were frequently very real, as an analytical framework for studying bourgeois women's history the separate spheres model is too restrictive, as it appears to deny such women any real economic agency.

Indeed, the chapters in this book are united in their insistence that the separate spheres thesis cannot serve as the 'mistress narrative' of European bourgeois women's economic history. In a variety of ways, and often deploying innovative research techniques that identify female economic agency within a sparse historical record, these chapters unsettle and challenge the view that middle-class women were creatures of domesticity and strangers to the marketplace. Focusing particularly on urban occupations, the volume explores enterprising women in Spain, France, Austria, Germany, Belgium, the Netherlands, Sweden and Britain in a broad range of economic pursuits and sectors. The comparative framework fostered by this approach adds force to growing revisionist literatures on women's economic roles within different national European historiographies. Likewise, the volume should inspire others to continue identifying enterprising women in other parts of the continent.

Notes

1. While the distinction between sex as a biological category and gender as a socially constructed identity has been an important conceptual dichotomy in writing on these themes, scholars have questioned the simplicity of this binary opposition. See, for example, Butler, 1990 and 1993, on how biological sex is itself a gendered social construct.
2. Scott, 1987, p. 42.
3. Tuana, 1993; Laqueur, 1990.
4. Kerber, 1988.
5. Davidoff and Hall, 1987; Vickery, 1993.
6. Davidoff and Hall, 1987. The book was republished with a new prefatory essay in 2002.
7. Rose, 1992; Canning, 1992, 1996; Horrel and Humphries, 1993; Creighton, 1996; Abram, 2002; Clark, 1995.
8. Frader and Rose, 1996; Janssens, 1998.
9. Brewer and Porter, 1993; Weatherill, 1988; Thirsk, 1990; Coyner, 1977; Breckman, 1991; Whitney, 1986; Tiersten, 1993; Gordon and Nair, 2003.

10. Simonton, 1998, pp. 155–9.
11. Smith, 1981.
12. Fraisse, 1995; Landes, 1988; Hufton, 1992; Bock, 2002; Scott, 1996.
13. Brunner, 1968; Duden, 1977; Hausen, 1981; Frevert, 1988; Gray, 2000.
14. Frevert, 1995; Quataert, 2001.
15. Augustine, 1994; Evans, 1991; Kaplan, 1991; Frevert, 1991; Meyer, 1987.
16. Palazzi, 2002, p.21.
17. Curli, 2002, p. 651.
18. Crossick and Haupt, 1995, especially chapters 2–5.
19. Crossick and Haupt, 1995.
20. Snell, 1981; Humphries, 1990.
21. Robert, 1984.
22. Burdy, Dubesset and Zancarini-Fournet, 1987.
23. Sinclair, 1991; Simonton, 1998, pp. 76–83; Tilly and Scott, 1978; Valenze, 1991.
24. Coffin, 1996.
25. Abram, 2002, p. 195; Rose, 1992, pp. 24–9; Hafter, 1995, pp. vii–xv; Canning, 1996.
26. Kwolek-Folland, 1998; Curli, 2002; Lewis, 1995. In a North American context, Lamoreaux, 2003, has recently challenged this view of the entrepreneur.
27. Bandhauer-Schöffmann, 2003.
28. Gamber, 1998, p. 190.
29. The classic account is Engels, 1884.
30. A fact noted by the pioneers of the history of consumption, McKendrick, Brewer and Plumb, 1982.
31. See, for example, Vickery, 1993; Kowaleski-Wallace, 1996; or Finn, 1996.
32. Tilly and Scott, 1978; Simonton, 1998; Abram, 2002.
33. See, for example, Abram, 2002; McMillan, 2000; Frevert, 1989.
34. See, for example, Crossick and Haupt, 1984 and 1995, on the European petite bourgeoisie. See also Kocka, 1996.
35. Curli, 2002.
36. Chassagne, 1991; Verley, 1994; Daumas, 2004.
37. Richard, 1996; Schrover, 1997.
38. Vickery, 1993; for Germany see Trepp, 1996; Habermas, 2000; and Beachy, 2001.
39. Kerber, 1988; Gordon and Nair, 2003.
40. Gordon and Nair, 2003; Nead, 2000.
41. Rappaport, 2000; Prochaska, 1980; Reagin, 1995.
42. Evans, 1977.
43. Caine, 2001; Richardson, 2000; Walker, 2000.

44. Tosh, 1999.
45. Davidoff and Hall, 1987; Tosh, 1999.
46. Rappaport, 2000; and the essays in Crossick and Jurmain, 1999.
47. Murphy, 1991; Khan, 1996; Lewis, 1992; Gamber, 1992 and 1997.
48. Crossick and Haupt, 1995. See also the chapter by Alison Kay in this volume.
49. Scott, 1998.
50. Gordon and Nair, 2003.
51. See Green and Owens, 2003, for Britain; the chapter by Ericsson in this volume for Sweden; and Hahn, 2002, for other parts of Europe.
52. Gordon and Nair, 2003.
53. Craig, 2001a, 2001b, 2001c. See also the special issue of *Histoire Sociale*, Volume 34 (2001); Guy, 1997; Palazzi, 2002; Kurgan-van Hentenryk, 1996; Van Molle and Heyrman, 2001; Richard, 1996; Schrover, 1997.
54. A Lady, 1854, p. 32.
55. Lincini, 2004.
56. See the situation for England outlined in Owens, 2002b.
57. Gordon and Nair, 2003, chapter 1.

–2–

'Making Some Provision for the Contingencies to which their Sex is Particularly Liable'
Women and Investment in Early Nineteenth-century England

Alastair Owens

> When an inexperienced person comes into possession of her fortune, and especially if it be a small one, her first enquiry is, "How can I invest my money so as to get the highest possible interest?" Let her rather seek to place it where her Capital be safest ... The Duke of Wellington used to say "High interest is another name for bad security."[1]

This quotation, taken from a book offering advice to women on 'everyday matters relating to property and income', is typical of mid-Victorian attitudes towards female investors. Women are cast as individuals who 'come into' wealth rather than generate it and who are financially inexperienced and naïve; consequently, they need male advice to find a secure outlet for their money. This characterization of female investors was part of a now very familiar ideology: middle-class men's and women's economic roles were antithetical but complementary. Men were active in the public world of work, business and finance, taking risks in order to generate family income: women's activities were to be confined to the domestic sphere. There they steered clear of the 'stormy seas of commerce' and, financially dependent on their husbands, focused their 'natural' talents on maintaining the household and reproducing the family unit.[2]

Like other contributions to this book, the aim of this chapter is to problematize this picture of women operating in a 'separate sphere' and playing a limited and passive economic role. It considers the case of female investment, examining the reasons for and the consequences of women's decisions to place their wealth in certain outlets, especially government securities. It suggests that the financial sphere was a highly gendered arena, but that the paradigmatic idea of '*separate* spheres' fails to capture the complexity of female investment activity which linked rather than separated public and private.[3]

The 'separate spheres thesis' has found its most powerful exposition in English historiography in the influential work of Leonore Davidoff and Catherine Hall – especially their 1987 book *Family Fortunes*.[4] In it, they argued that the separation of the feminine domestic realm from the masculine public sphere in the late eighteenth and early nineteenth centuries was key to English middle-class formation. Their work foregrounded gender alongside class as an analytical category that explained patterns of social change during an important period of English history. Moreover, in demonstrating how the separation of spheres worked at an ideological level, they provided a compelling framework for understanding the unequal distribution of power between men and women. *Family Fortunes* was therefore significant as it offered both an historical and conceptual foundation that could account for female constraint and subordination and the origins and persistence of modern bourgeois patriarchy.

Davidoff and Hall's book provoked a lively debate. Critics argued that they overemphasized the significance of the division of the world into private-feminine and public-masculine realms, both as a product of the late eighteenth and early nineteenth centuries and as a feature solely of middle-class life.[5] Furthermore, while plausibly explaining why economic, social and political life was so deeply gendered, the separate spheres model was politically disempowering when applied rigidly: it seemed to deny women historical agency. In part, this stems from the different ways that historians have conceptualized 'public' and 'private'. Some critics read *Family Fortunes* as an account of the confinement of middle-class women to the domestic sphere and their total exclusion from the public world.[6] Detailed empirical studies of men's and women's lives have, of course, challenged the view that the public and private spheres were cast iron containers occupied solely by one or other of the sexes.[7]

Such a reading also distorts Davidoff and Hall's thesis. Although the gendered categories of 'public' and 'private' were central to their understanding of men and women of the middle class, Davidoff and Hall were attentive to the fragile and unstable nature of such divisions. Boundaries were unclear and were frequently crossed, and their demarcation mattered in some arenas, some places and at some times more than others. But more crucially for this chapter, their book showed 'how "autonomous" male actors were embedded in families [and] how "dependent" women provided the contacts and capital ... which made countless enterprises possible'.[8] In other words, 'public' and 'private' could never really be separate; they were interwoven, relied on one another and were mutually constitutive. Whatever the apparent force of nineteenth-century rhetorics of gender division, it is empirically and conceptually impossible to separate public from private.

Some of Davidoff and Hall's critics have, however, taken a different stance. Their concern has been less to demonstrate how public and private were interwoven and more to claim a role for women in the public sphere (or, less frequently, to establish a space for men in the private sphere). This is especially the case for those interested in examining women's economic roles in industrialising Britain. Recent studies of women's business activities and engagement with credit markets have optimistically portrayed middle-class females as active wealth creators.[9] They argue that the legal constraints on female economic activity were often circumvented in practice and that the ideology of domesticity at the heart of the 'separate spheres' thesis was, for most women, more an ideal than a reality. Considerable attention has also been paid to women without husbands, who were often forced to be more resourceful than their married counterparts.[10] These studies provide an important counterbalance to the view that middle-class women in later eighteenth- and early nineteenth-century Britain were confined to a life of domesticity. However, there is a danger, in spite of the many caveats that accompany their conclusions, that these scholars overemphasize the degree of female public autonomy and entrepreneurship while underplaying the extent of their subordination. In sometimes giving the impression that men and women were equal in economic affairs (and often in other arenas too) these studies run the risk of diverting historical attention away from the complex questions of patriarchy, power and inequality at the forefront of gender studies.

Women, Economic Change and Investment in Industrializing Britain

In recent years there has been a growing recognition of women's economic contribution to the industrial revolution in Britain. While the work of pioneering economic historians such as Ivy Pinchbeck and Alice Clark provided an important early account of women's economic roles in the eighteenth and nineteenth centuries, this more recent interest has largely been prompted by the development of women's and gender history and by a broader reassessment of British economic growth in the age of industry.[11] Historians now agree that economic change was more gradual than hitherto thought and that factory-based mass manufacturing was only one aspect of a more complex pattern of industrial and commercial change where older methods of production continued and where smaller firms proliferated alongside larger mills and factories.[12] While econometricians have cast doubts over whether Britain ever experienced the level of sustained economic growth required to justify the use of the label 'industrial *revolution*',[13] others have emphasized the social and gender dimensions of industrial growth as a reason to retain the idea of revolutionary change.[14]

Women's work during the industrial revolution has been extensively studied, highlighting in particular the exploitation of female labour through factory or domestic piece work.[15] There is also a growing, but less well developed, literature on women's business activity – those females who owned or managed firms, rather than those who worked for others.[16] While these studies have raised questions about female involvement in credit networks, often demonstrating a surprisingly active engagement within them, the role of women in financial markets has received more limited attention.[17] This is surprising since during the nineteenth century middle- and upper-class England is supposed to have become 'a nation of shareholders'.[18] The period was one that saw the 'rise of the popular investor' and one where new ways of writing about finance began to distinctively shape a vibrant culture of investment.[19] But historians' interest in investors focuses on men, as in the long running debate about the propensity of wealthy businessmen to invest in land.[20]

Women and Investment

In broad terms, women's demand for investments was constrained by the law. Until the late nineteenth century, the legal limitations on married women's rights to administer or dispose of their property limited their economic powers. The common law doctrine of coverture held that upon marriage a woman surrendered almost all her property rights to her husband.[21] Whatever a wife owned became her husband's and, in theory, she was unable to obtain credit or contract debts in her own name. Consequently, married women's ability to engage in any economic activity, including investment, was severely limited. However, historians are divided on the actual impact of coverture on married women. On the one hand, it has been seen as an overarching legal framework that denied women power and was clearly 'conducive to the elaboration of the ideology of separate spheres'.[22] On the other hand, revisionist studies have stressed that 'the law of coverture is best described as existing in a state of suspended animation ... [and that] ... wives' legal inability to contract and litigate debts was often ignored or attenuated in practice'.[23] While such an observation applies mostly to married women's day-to-day consumption activities, it is possible that legal constraints did not entirely prevent women from making investments. Recent research on other aspects of English property law has demonstrated that married women used the law of equity to escape coverture. Personal trusts were frequently used to that effect, and trustees were significant players in investment markets.[24] Moreover, common law did not impede the financial dealings of widows and spinsters.[25] In many cities single women made up between 40 and 50 per cent of the adult female population and sex differentials in mortality rates meant that most married women spent some of their later life as widows.[26] It would therefore be inaccurate to suggest that women were entirely absent from nineteenth-century finance.

Research is beginning to show that women were active in a variety of spheres of investment.[27] Studies of wills and related documents suggest that considerable numbers of middle-class women owned real estate. Land, other real property and mortgage loans had long been important outlets for capital, especially among the upper class. While at the end of the Napoleonic Wars in 1815 the price of land generally stagnated, real estate located in towns and cities became more profitable. Ownership of small-size properties, especially urban cottages and houses, was common among both males and females. In early nineteenth century Stockport, for example, 55 per cent of females who left wills owned real estate – a figure that broadly corroborates the findings of a similar study of Birmingham and Sheffield.[28] Even in smaller towns, such as Ashby de la Zouch and Hinckley in the English Midlands, around 40 per cent of women who left wills possessed real estate.[29] The relative ease with which such property could be acquired and disposed of, coupled with the growing demand for urban land and housing, workshops and factories in the early nineteenth century, provides an obvious explanation for the apparent popularity of real estate investment.

Women also played an important but rarely examined or explained role in financing transport infrastructure. Widows and spinsters provided around 6.5 per cent of the total capital invested in canal building between 1755 and 1815, although their contributions varied between different schemes and across different parts of the country.[30] Women also constituted about 18 per cent of the investors in West Midlands canals in the eighteenth and early nineteenth centuries, although the value of their holdings in the 1820s was around 30 per cent lower than that of male shareholders.[31] Nevertheless such capital was important to the development of canal companies and often provided healthy rates of return.[32] Profits on railway investments were often more modest, but here too women provided important contributions to the financing of railway development. In the West Midlands they formed around 11 per cent of those who bought railway shares.[33] Studies of other companies confirm this finding, suggesting that women formed between 5 and 20 per cent of investors in early railway schemes across the country. An exception was the Liverpool and Manchester Railway, where women account for almost a third of all investors in 1845, although their holdings were equivalent to only around 16 per cent of the total share value.[34] While women's investments in railways were generally small, the invention of 'safe' investment products such as 'railway debentures' was particularly attractive for females who wanted a secure outlet for their wealth.

Potentially lucrative financial opportunities were also emerging in the industrial and commercial sectors. Typically, investment might be made by entering into a business partnership or by purchasing shares in a joint stock company. Alternatively, capital might be invested in industry or commerce in a less formal way, perhaps in the form of a loan offered at a modest rate of interest to a family member or through the agency of a local broker or solicitor. Various evidence suggests women had long been important in providing capital for industry, while later in the century it is clear that they were also becoming corporate shareholders.[35]

Finally, it is also evident that women had an active involvement in life assurance markets. Life assurance appeared in the eighteenth century in part from a desire by men to provide financially for their wives after their death. But while many middle-class men insured their lives for the benefit of their wives, evidence from a study of eighteenth-century Norfolk demonstrates that women also took out life assurance in significant numbers, often for the benefit of other women.[36] By the nineteenth century, life assurance was well established. Investment literature such as the *Ladies' Guide to Life Assurance* (1854) depicted life contingency products as a way of preparing for old age and widowhood, of creating a bequeathable inheritance or as a protection from a financially incompetent husband.[37]

Making Investments: Gender, Information and Risk

Collectively, these studies of female investors would seem to challenge the view that women were absent from the public world of wealth accumulation. Although researchers have indeed been quick to claim this, it remains the case that the field of investment was markedly gendered.[38] Women were more active in some investment arenas than in others. A recent survey of women investors in Britain before 1914 concluded that 'women do appear to have preferred the role of shareholders to that of the risk-taking entrepreneur'.[39] Most of the evidence suggests that females chose low risk options and remained relatively passive in relation to their financial dealings. Analysts make a distinction between 'financial' investors, primarily seeking a *rentier* income, and 'economic' investors who derived additional commercial benefits from their investment, such as a reduction in a firm's transaction costs.[40] Women are frequently considered to be more common among the former than the latter. They minimized risk and sought income security.[41]

Indeed, the question of risk is central to understanding gendered patterns of investment.[42] Investment implies the placing of capital with an individual, institution or agency in anticipation of receiving some kind of return. It acts as both a mechanism for storing wealth and as a means for generating new wealth. In making an investment the risks are therefore twofold, relating firstly to the uncertainty of the capital value of the asset acquired and secondly to uncertainty of the value of the income generated by that asset. Most investors would wish to preserve or enhance the capital value of the asset acquired while maximising their income from it. Before investing one must therefore evaluate the risks involved, a process that depends upon access to and interpretation of information. This information can take many forms, from personal knowledge of the credit-worthiness of the individual or institution with whom the investment is being placed, to an understanding of trade cycles and patterns of demand for a particular commodity upon which the fortunes of an investment may rest. Interpretation of that information is a combination of personal skill and luck, but is also significantly shaped by existing patterns of knowledge circulation and the broader culture of information evaluation. At the core of understanding women's and men's investment activities is the issue of the different ways in which they accessed and interpreted information.

Generally, historians have argued that women were less able than men to access and interpret financial information.[43] Much financial information passed through male social networks, such as trade associations and other clubs and societies that flourished in nineteenth-century towns and through male-dominated business communities.[44] Solicitors, appraisers, brokers, auctioneers and other advisers made it their business to seek out investment opportunities and secure the best returns.[45] A good deal of information about investments also appeared in newspapers and an emerging financial press. Local newspapers provided endless commentary on the state of markets, published advertisements promoting different investment opportunities and listed prices of securities and other commodities traded on stock exchanges. They also carried news of the hazards of financial speculation, extracting the names of local bankrupts and insolvents from commercial publications like the *London Gazette*. Investment handbooks, such as G. M. Bell's *Guide to the Investment of Capital* (1846), also began to appear in the nineteenth century, offering authoritative knowledge on where it was safe to place one's money.[46] Finally, much information about economic opportunity and the financial probity of individuals and investment schemes would pass through more informal family and kinship networks, and would be the focus of speculation at domestic soirées and other such social occasions.

Women could certainly access some of this information – they read newspapers and, as in the example of the *Ladies' Guide to Life Assurance*, other kinds of financial literature too.[47] Moreover, even if they were excluded from the male business culture that was developing in towns and cities, they were often at the centre of domestic and kinship networks where discussion and gossip ensured knowledge of economic opportunities as well as of financial mishaps. Nevertheless, accounts of women as investors in nineteenth-century literature and other writing about finance tend to emphasize their ignorance of investment risks and lack of financial skill. Such depictions of financially innocent spinsters and naïve widows, which form part of a complex moral discourse about Victorian markets and money, undoubtedly exaggerate women's inexperience as investors.[48] However, they also point to the ways in which financial markets in nineteenth-century England were seen in gendered terms. A combination of custom, cultural expectation and direct barriers to information access meant that women were not in as good a position to assess the risks and uncertainties of some speculative ventures.

Consequently, we might expect to find women in investment arenas where access to information was good, investments were secure, and where returns might not be spectacular, but were nevertheless reliable. These, it might be argued, are the key characteristics of early nineteenth-century female investments. The remainder of this chapter will explore a type of investment that appears to fulfil all these criteria: government securities. But while the ownership of government securities would seem to reinforce gender ideals about the economic and domestic roles of women, the very act of investing in the state linked the realms of public and private so that the two were interdependent.

Money in 'the Funds': Women's Investment in Government Securities[49]

Government securities, issued by the Bank of England (founded in 1694), emerged as a popular investment product in the early eighteenth century. An important function of the Bank was to provide the British government with the financial means to fight wars. Over the course of the eighteenth century, the British Empire expanded dramatically and, in order to support this frequently violent process, the government borrowed heavily.[50] While many contemporaries were concerned by the burdens that the 'national debt' placed on the state, historians have pointed to the importance of this 'financial revolution' in state borrowing in enabling Britain to get ahead in the 'scramble' for empire.[51]

The Bank of England borrowed money by selling government securities. Individuals who purchased them became creditors of the state. In return, the government paid the investor a dividend on his or her capital, usually around the rate of 3 to 6 per cent per annum. Government securities were, however, an unusual type of loan since there was no obligation to repay the capital. Instead, most securities were issued 'in perpetuity', meaning that the annual return would, in theory, be paid for ever. When purchasing securities, investors were therefore buying the right to receive a dividend and could not demand that the government refund the capital value of the loan. Nonetheless securities could be sold on the stock exchange through a broker. They could also be given away, passed on as financial assets to someone else, perhaps as a bequest.[52]

Different issues of securities were distinguished by different rates of return and not all securities were perpetual. Sometimes they paid out dividends only for a specified period of years (annuities for years); on other occasions they paid out only for the duration of the purchaser's life (life annuities). By the end of the Napoleonic Wars in 1815, government borrowing ground to a halt as the sheer scale of the state's indebtedness began to cause panic. By this time the value of the national debt was somewhere around £750 million and the costs of paying out dividends (effectively the interest on the debt) was almost half of total government expenditure.[53] But while the scale of the debt was of concern in the early decades of the nineteenth century, demand for 'the funds', as government securities were often known, was buoyant. In 1823 there were almost 284,000 individuals who received dividends on government securities of various types, the most popular being the 'three per cent consolidated annuities' (often abbreviated to the 'three per cents' or, more simply, 'consols').[54]

Government securities were therefore not simply a popular and attractive investment; they were part of a complex financial system that supported the British imperial state. This point did not escape contemporaries, especially those who were not in favour of government borrowing. They believed that the state was enfeebled by the debt and that the long-term financial burdens that it created would one day ruin both government and empire.[55] Investors in securities were sometimes seen as economic 'parasites', sucking the financial life blood of the British Empire, instead of using their wealth for more productive purposes.[56] But who were the government's creditors and how significant were women as investors in the national debt?

Who Invested in the State?

It is possible to trace who owned government securities by analysing a set of sources known as the Bank of England Will Registers. This series of records lists all the investments owned by those individuals who died leaving a will specifically mentioning government securities. While the registers are not without some problems – for example, they only record a person's assets at the point of death – they provide a reasonably representative sample of individuals who invested in 'the funds' (the national debt was also the focus of investment for many other organizations and institutions such as savings banks, friendly societies and insurance companies).[57] Each of the registers for the years 1810, 1820, 1830 and 1840 was examined in order to analyse the characteristics of investors and the nature of their holdings.

Over the thirty years covered by this study, both the proportion of the personal investor population and the total value of the invested wealth accounted for by women grew. In 1810 women comprised around 35 per cent of investors and held roughly 23 per cent of the total value of the invested wealth (Table 2.1). By 1840 the proportions had risen to 47 per cent and 32 per cent respectively. While the sizes of women's holdings ranged widely and were, on average, a little over half of those of men, they were far from insubstantial. Table 2.2 demonstrates that by 1840 the average holding was a little under £5,000, a figure that would have generated an annual return of around £150, a sum equivalent to the yearly wage of a salaried 'white collar' worker. By the middle decades of the nineteenth century, women formed almost half of the personal investor population in government securities and financed a significant proportion of the national debt.

Table 2.1 Proportion of Male and Female Investments in Government Securities (%)

	1810	1820	1830	1840
Ia Total investors				
Men	65.3	63.3	58.4	52.8
Women	34.7	36.7	41.6	47.2
Ib Total female investors				
Widows	56.6	54.5	52.2	49.4
Spinsters	41.2	44.5	46.0	49.1
Other	2.2	1.0	1.8	1.5
IIa Total market value of investments				
Men	76.9	79.0	79.4	68.0
Women	23.1	21.0	20.6	32.0
IIb Total market value of female investments				
Widows	55.2	50.0	54.0	34.9
Spinsters	41.3	47.7	45.0	59.7
Other	3.5	2.4	1.0	5.4

Note: The 'market value' refers to the value of each individual's holdings at the time of death, calculated by the Bank for the purposes of probate. In the few instances where no market value was recorded, one was estimated using a multiplier. This multiplier was calculated by working out the average market value of the given investment type as a percentage of its purchase value for the whole sample year.
Source: The Bank of England Will Registers, 1810 Volumes: 4 L-Z, 5 A-K, 5 L-Z, 6 A-K; 1820 Volumes: 12 K-Z, 13 A-I, 13 K-Z, 14 A-I, 14 K-Z, 15 A-I; 1830 Volumes: 32 K-Z, 33 A-I, 33 K-Z, 34 A-I, 34 K-Z; 1840 Volumes: 53 A-I, 54 A-I, 54 K-Z, 55 A-I, 55 K-Z, 56 A-I.

Given the legal constraints that married women faced, these findings probably underestimate the significance of female capital in financing the national debt. It is likely, as has been pointed out in studies of eighteenth-century securities markets, that many male investors were trustees who invested on behalf of legally incapacitated married women.[58] Indeed, virtually all of the female investors among the Bank of England Will Register records were single women. A notable trend over the period was the growing significance of spinsters as investors in securities; by 1840 they were equal in proportion to widows and owned the greatest share of female invested wealth (Table 2.1).

Why did women invest in government securities and what is the consequence of their doing so for the theory of separate spheres? The very label which contemporary commentators used to describe such investors – 'public creditors' – underlines the fact that women's financial dealings in government securities

Table 2.2 The Structure of Female Government Security Investment (%)

I Number of investors

Size of holding (£s)	1810	1820	1830	1840
0–99	3.5	3.9	2.4	2.6
100–499	27.9	26.3	23.0	23.4
500–999	18.1	17.2	15.8	17.0
1,000–4,999	33.2	36.4	36.1	35.5
5,000–9,999	10.2	7.5	11.3	11.7
10,000–24,999	4.9	6.5	8.7	4.9
25,000–49,999	1.3	1.9	2.1	2.6
50,000 and over	0.9	0.3	0.6	2.3

II Market value of investments

Size of holding (£s)	1810	1820	1830	1840
0–99	0.1	0.1	0.0	0.0
100–499	2.3	2.3	1.5	1.5
500–999	3.4	3.7	2.5	2.6
1,000–4,999	21.1	22.4	19.1	16.7
5,000–9,999	18.6	16.9	17.1	17.4
10,000–24,999	18.8	30.7	29.3	15.8
25,000–49,999	13.9	18.6	15.1	16.5
50,000 and over	21.9	5.3	15.3	29.4
Average holding	3,662	3,395	4,515	4,894

Note: See note under Table 2.1.
Source: See Table 2.1.

cannot easily be accounted for by the 'separate spheres thesis'. Even accepting that most women who invested in 'the funds' were passive in their financial dealings – 'strangers to the manoeuvres of the stock exchange', as one contemporary put it – it is difficult to think of an investment that could be more 'public'.[59] Women's investment in the national debt tied them into a financial system that had been at the heart of the nation's strategies of warfare and territorial expansion. Moreover, they bought, sold and collected the dividends on their securities through some of the most established and prominent public financial institutions: the Bank of England and the Stock Exchange. The willingness of women (and men) to loan their capital to the state and participate in these institutional markets for government securities enabled imperial expansion and the country's drive for European military supremacy. The early nineteenth century was also a period when the legitimacy of the national debt as a means of financing the British government's activities was subject to the greatest public scrutiny and debate.[60] In short, even if their financial presence was not widely noted, through investing in government securities, women were central to emergent systems of public finance and the political arguments that surrounded them.

Yet, if women's investment in government securities had such important consequences for the financial ambitions of an expansionary state, it also served more private needs of financial security, personal welfare and domestic well-being. Public and private were linked, and the priorities of one fulfilled the needs of the other. Contemporary accounts of 'the funds' suggest that it was, in fact, the public nature of government securities that made them so attractive for women.[61] Information about the funds was widely available. Prices were quoted in most national and local newspapers and fluctuations in values were reported on. To recall the arguments made earlier in this chapter, female investors therefore had easy access to information that they could readily understand and interpret, enabling them to assess financial risk. Moreover, the very fact that government securities were guaranteed by the British state, gave investors a degree of confidence that was rarely afforded other investment opportunities. In the nineteenth century the state came to be viewed as a powerful guarantor of personal liberty and protector of private property, in part because its activities could be subject to surveillance and because its actions could be held to account.[62] This was embodied in the methods of buying and selling securities and of collecting dividends at the Bank and Stock Exchange, where strict rules of conduct made investment a publicly ritualized and scrutinized activity. As one contemporary investment guide summed it up, 'the British Funds are a description of security that are sought after in consequence of their superior safety, as founded upon the national credit and the punctuality with which the dividends are paid ... investments are made more from these weighty considerations than from the temptation of a high dividend.'[63]

Accordingly, as Francis Playford noted in 1849, many women 'hasten[ed] to invest in the secure asylum of the public funds'.[64] Indeed 'the funds' were widely depicted as a dependable source of financial support. Dividends from government securities provided respectable single women with the income they needed to maintain a genteel lifestyle without the need for work. The investments themselves required little effort to maintain, save a trip to the Bank of England to collect the dividends. The majority of securities were issued as annuities – 'the classic form of income provision for the dependant: female kin "friends" and ex-servants' – and the holders received a guaranteed fixed income twice yearly.[65] This offered certainty in an otherwise financially turbulent world and, as other studies have demonstrated, could be effectively used for personal welfare and for the maintenance of single women.[66] Twice-yearly dividends of £75 (the approximate income derived from the average female investment in 1840), would cover the rent on a house or tenement and support a life of modest comfort.

In short, investment in government annuities, while playing an important role in legitimating a public financial system, also helped to maintain the domestic

32 • *Alastair Owens*

worlds of single women and the gendered notions of gentility and economic dependency that shaped these worlds. Women's investment in low risk outlets like 'the funds' is testimony to the gendering of financial markets in early nineteenth-century Britain and the way in which ideologies of domesticity shaped the economic behaviour of males and females. The crux of the argument here, however, is that women's investment activities did not simply enable their retreat to domesticity. Rather, their behaviour also had important public consequences, effectively linking the fortunes of the state with the private needs of individuals. Women's investment in the national debt tied them into the production of both public and private spheres.

Conclusion: Between Public and Private

This chapter has attempted to problematize the view that in nineteenth-century England the ideology of separate spheres denied women financial agency. However, female investors did not participate without restriction in the public world of wealth creation; an examination of investment in government securities shows how the generation of 'private' domestic security and a system of 'public' state finance were linked. The emphasis has therefore been on the relationships between public and private – recognizing their interdependency and mutual entanglement – rather than on the distinctions and differences between them. By its very nature, capital creates relationships and dependencies between people, institutions and social groups. The relationship between creditor and debtor that characterizes investment is a case in point. Thinking about the relationships created by economic processes offers a way of recovering the financial agency of nineteenth-century women without completely dismissing the idea of separate spheres which had an undeniable rhetorical presence in contemporary culture and ideology. The single women who invested in the national debt may have acted in ways that fulfilled expectations that female investment should be risk averse, seek modest returns and require minimal effort to support private domestic priorities, but the consequences of their actions were of profound importance to the finances of the British state.

Evidence of women's increasing significance as holders of government securities adds to a growing body of literature that seeks to uncover the economic agency of middle-class women and to highlight their contributions to Britain's commercial and industrial revolutions. Nevertheless, the argument here is that it is not necessary to discard or ignore bourgeois ideologies of domesticity as an important contemporary discourse, or as a framework that can help historians to make sense of women's economic lives in the past. Seeing public and private as separate distorts reality. Recognizing the connections between the two spheres, so clearly evident in women's investment in government securities, helps in understanding how such ideologies came to be constructed and how they operated. In short, it is just as possible to provide critique of the 'separate spheres thesis' by examining its intra-discursive contradictions and instabilities as it is to look for alternative ways of conceptualising the discursive terrain of gender identity in nineteenth-century England.

Acknowledgements

Some of the research discussed in this chapter was carried out in conjunction with David R. Green of King's College London. I am grateful to him for allowing me to draw upon this material and for his constructive sharing of ideas. I also thank Mark Paddon, Gideon Abate and Craig Bailey for their research assistance and Christine Wiskin for her comments.

Notes

1. Banker's Daughter, 1864, p. 9.
2. For further discussion of this ideology see Poovey, 1988.
3. Vickery, 1993, provides a discussion of 'separate spheres' as a paradigm of English women's history.
4. Davidoff and Hall, 1987. The book was reissued with an additional prefatory essay in 2002.
5. See, for example, Gordon and Nair, 2003; Vickery, 1993; Wahrman, 1993.
6. A point noted in Davidoff and Hall, 2002, p. xvi.
7. See, for example, Gleadle and Richardson, 2000; Gordon and Nair, 2003, and other literature discussed below.
8. Davidoff and Hall, 2002, p. xvi.
9. Berg, 1993 and 1996; Green, 2000; Lane, 2000; Wiskin, 2000. Although mainly focusing on the early modern period, Erickson's 1993 study of women's property ownership has been particularly influential.
10. Gordon and Nair, 2000, 2002 and 2003; Green and Owens, 2003.
11. Clark, 1919; Pinchbeck, 1930.
12. See, *inter alia*, Crafts, 1985, and Sabel and Zeitlin, 1985. For an overview see Berg and Hudson, 1992, and Daunton, 1995.
13. Crafts, 1985, provides a broadly 'anti-revolutionary' view.
14. Berg and Hudson, 1992.
15. See, for example, August, 1999; Lown, 1990. Overviews are provided by Honeyman, 2000; and Sharpe, 1998.
16. See, for example, Gordon and Nair, 2000; Hill, 2001, chapters 3 and 4; Wiskin, 2000.
17. Wiskin, 2000, provides the most extensive discussion of women's credit networks.

18. Quoted in Maltby and Rutterford, 2005 (no pagination).
19. Preda, 2001; Poovey 2002 and 2003.
20. For a taste of these debates see Rubinstein, 1992; Thompson, 1992.
21. For further discussion see Holcombe, 1983; Shanley, 1989; Staves, 1990.
22. Finn, 1996, pp. 704–5.
23. Finn, 1996, p. 707.
24. Berg, 1993; Morris, 1994, 1998.
25. Hill, 2001; Gordon and Nair, 2002 and 2003.
26. Green and Owens, 2003; Maltby and Rutterford, 2005.
27. A contemporary overview of investment opportunities can be found in Bell, 1846. *Victorian Studies* volume 45(1), 2002, contains a number of useful essays discussing Victorian investments. Poovey, 2003, pp. 1–33, provides a useful outline of the nineteenth-century British financial system.
28. Owens, 2000, p. 92; Berg, 1993, p. 241.
29. Lane, 2000, p. 186.
30. Ward, 1974, pp. 23, 74.
31. Hudson, 2001, pp. 195, 201.
32. Hudson, 2001, chapter 5.
33. Hudson, 2001, p. 195.
34. Reed, 1975, p. 125.
35. Davidoff and Hall, 1987, chapter 6; Maltby and Rutterford, 2005.
36. Clark, 1999, p. 177.
37. A Lady, 1854.
38. For revisionist claims see, for example, Hudson, 2001; Lane, 2000.
39. Maltby and Rutterford, 2005.
40. See Hudson, 2001, pp. 1–2.
41. For critical discussion see Maltby and Rutterford, 2005.
42. Hudson, 2001, pp. 7–13.
43. For critical discussion see Hudson, 2001, pp. 14–15, 194–205; Wiskin, 2000, chapter 1.
44. The associational culture of towns is discussed by Morris, 1983.
45. Miles, 1981.
46. Bell, 1846.
47. A Lady, 1854.
48. Maltby and Rutterford, 2005; consider also Poovey, 2002.
49. A fuller discussion of the material in this section of the chapter can be found in Green and Owens, 2003.
50. For further discussion of this 'financial revolution' see Dickson, 1967.
51. Brewer, 1989; Cain and Hopkins, 2001; O'Brien, 1988.
52. For an overview see Fairman, 1824.
53. Green and Owens, 2003; Mitchell and Deane, 1962, pp. 389–91.

54. Playford, 1864, p. 35; Levi, 1862, p. 333.
55. See, for example, Levi, 1862.
56. For a discussion of contemporary political debates about the national debt see Daunton, 2001, chapters 2 and 5.
57. Green and Owens, 2003, pp. 519–24, 532, has further discussion of the sources.
58. Dickson, 1967. See also Carter, 1968, on investment in the eighteenth century.
59. Lowe, 1823.
60. See Daunton, 2001, p. 112, for further discussion.
61. See, for example, Bell, 1846.
62. For a recent discussion of this see Joyce, 2003.
63. Bell, 1846, p. 26.
64. Playford, 1864, p. 29.
65. Davidoff and Hall, 1987, p. 275.
66. See Owens, 2001, pp. 304–13, for further discussion of annuities as a form of support for single women and a means by which to achieve domestic security.

–3–

The Silent Partners
Women, Capital and the Development of the Financial System in Nineteenth-century Sweden

Tom Petersson

Introduction

By 1900 Sweden had one of Europe's most modern and efficient financial systems, providing crucial support for the industrialization process and the country's economic development. Previous research on the emergence of this financial system has been concerned mostly with the changing legal frameworks of financial markets and the close connections between the development of commercial banks and large-scale industrial companies.[1] The roles of women and of female capital in the growth of the banking and financial system have received far less attention. This reflects a wider historical ignorance of the financial contribution of women to the industrial revolution in Sweden. Drawing upon evidence from estate inventories and the internal accounting books of savings and commercial banks, the aim of this chapter is to examine women's investment activities in order to assess their contribution to the emergent financial system.[2] A wider goal is to demonstrate the significance of female capital to the development of the nineteenth-century Swedish economy.

In recent years, the literature on female capitalists and businesswomen in industrializing Sweden has grown rapidly. One of the key insights of this new historiography is that women were very active as small-scale entrepreneurs within urban commercial and traditional handicraft sectors.[3] Studies have also shown that women played an important role in several of the great industrial companies that were established in Sweden beginning in the 1850s. They not only supplied these companies with necessary venture capital; firms often exploited their personal networks and social abilities as part of their economic strategies.[4] Such perspectives challenge the view of contemporary bourgeois gender ideology that women were financially passive and unable to exercise economic power. Men and women *did not* occupy 'separate spheres', where males were active in the public world of wealth creation, while females were shielded from the market in the sanctuary of the domestic realm.[5] As Davidoff and Hall have shown in their study of industrializing England, women within capitalist families frequently provided businesses with indispensable resources that ensured their economic welfare and success.[6] In Sweden, too, both small and large capitalists had to rely on women for capital, credit, co-operation and support.[7]

However, despite the clear involvement of women in industrial enterprises, their direct influence on the management of firms and on strategic decision-making is difficult to analyse. Female shareholders, for example, nearly always delegated the authority that stemmed from their financial interest in a firm to agents. Indeed, there can be no doubt that legal restrictions and social and cultural conventions meant that female capitalists frequently faced problems in publicly exercising their economic power. In evaluating women's contribution to the Swedish financial and industrial revolutions, it is therefore necessary to assess carefully their various economic agency. The traditional, stereotypical, masculinist concept of economic agency as being publicly active and profit-maximizing would seem an unfair and anachronistic yardstick against which to view women's (and most men's) economic roles. As this chapter will argue, other economic roles that were more passive and less publicly visible – such as long-term investment in banks and other financial institutions – were just as important in facilitating economic growth and the development of financial institutions in nineteenth-century Sweden.

The Legal Context

The extent to which women could act as independent economic agents was constrained by legal and other institutional arrangements that regulated different types of economic activity. Swedish law, like that in most other parts of Western Europe, was built around the concept of the household, since men and women were envisaged working together in what has generally been called 'the family economy'.[8] Established by law, property rights arguably formed the most significant determinant of personal independence in economic and financial transactions, as they established the claim to possession and alienation. In the early nineteenth century, the Swedish Code of 1734 provided the legal framework that defined property rights throughout the country. Important within the context of this chapter is the fact that the Code placed women and children under their father's, brother's or husband's legal guardianship. This severely limited their property rights, with the consequence that the only women with full legal power in economic matters were widows.[9]

However, in the first half of the nineteenth century the law was extensively reformed. Many of the reforms constituted the first steps towards legal equality between men and women. In the early nineteenth century the right of inheritance was cognatic but still not equal. Amongst the nobility and peasants in the countryside, sons inherited twice as much as daughters, while the inheritance rights between the sons and daughters of burghers and clergymen were equitable. In 1845 daughters, regardless of their parents' economic or social status, were granted the right to inherit an equal share of the family estate. Between 1846 and 1864 women's rights to conduct commerce were also greatly extended. From 1858 to 1884 unmarried women were gradually released from the legal incapacity bestowed by guardianship. In 1884 the age of majority for unmarried women became 21 years – the same as that for unmarried men. Legislation passed in 1874 even made it possible for married women to control their property; it could be withdrawn from their husbands' control either by making a premarital settlement or through a division of the joint property of husband and wife. Under the same conditions, a married woman also gained the right to dispose of her own income.[10] Collectively these reforms significantly extended the economic powers of Swedish women.

The motives for these seemingly radical changes were partly economic, partly political. The peasants and burghers in the Swedish Parliament initiated the reform of 1845 which gave women equal rights of inheritance. They aimed to undermine the nobility's superior economic position by attempting to force them to divide their property upon death. Many of the later reforms that strengthened women's legal status were motivated by economic incentives. Swedish economic and industrial development was generating new demand for capital and land. Much of this was owned by women, but because of the law of guardianship – part of the 1734 Swedish Code – it was difficult for females to act as independent economic agents. These laws were placed under even greater pressure with the rapid growth in the number of unmarried women during the first half of the nineteenth century. In order to get access to female capital and to provide a means by which these women could become self-supporting, reform of the legal system was seen as necessary. These commercial priorities drove reformers to change the law, not a desire to make women and men equal.[11]

It is important not to exaggerate the impact of these legal changes on the economic rights of females. Women in general, and wives and minor women in particular, remained in a subordinate position, both in relation to men and within the socio-economic system. However, alongside these legal reforms, a number of institutional changes reshaped the Swedish financial and banking system over the course of the nineteenth century. The remainder of the chapter will consider how institutional change and legal reform enabled women to make a significant contribution to the emergent financial system that underpinned Swedish economic growth.

The Early Financial System, 1800–70

In the first decades of the nineteenth century the National Bank of Sweden dominated the institutional credit market. Through government discount companies and private discount houses, the National Bank channelled capital to selected sectors of the economy. A limited range of financial services was also offered to the public. The discount houses not only discounted bills, they also took deposits of cash and offered different kinds of loans. However, the economic crisis of 1815 led to all the private discount houses becoming insolvent. By 1818 the National Bank was the only intermediate financial agency in the Swedish institutional credit market.[12]

In 1820 the first savings bank was established in Göteborg, Sweden's second largest city and an important channel for trade with Britain and other Western-European countries. Over the following twenty years, more than sixty savings banks were founded in major cities around the country. The first commercial banks, the so-called 'Enskilda banks', were established during the 1830s. The Enskilda banks were founded on their owners' unlimited liabilities and they had the right to finance their business by issuing their own notes. The Enskilda banks contributed to the creation of liquidity in Swedish capital markets, and they also promoted economic growth. In comparison with the savings banks, however, their growth was less rapid. Nevertheless, by the mid-nineteenth century a nationwide banking system was beginning to develop.[13] What role did women play in this emergent financial system? How did the situation vary between town and country?

The Financial System's Agrarian Inheritance

Although the modernization of the banking and financial system was initiated in the larger cities, agricultural production dominated the Swedish economy for much of the nineteenth century. Research on the agrarian financial system has concentrated on the question of how the commercialization and general development of Swedish agriculture were financed. In the 1830s large-scale farmers and estate owners began to form regional mortgage associations. These were male-dominated institutions. Individual landowners, initially the wealthiest individuals, could obtain credit for land reclamation, the purchase of new farming implements and other productive investments by mortgaging their own land. The National Bank of Sweden, the first commercial banks and some of the larger city savings banks also actively loaned capital to wealthy agriculturalists with large estates.[14] Middle-sized and small landowners sought capital through small loans raised from others within the agrarian sector. Extensive studies of the agrarian capital market between 1800 and 1870 have shown that almost 90 per cent of the total value of all loans raised were economic transactions between private persons, thus bypassing the new financial organizations.[15]

Whether informal or institutionalized, the agrarian credit market was dominated by men who borrowed from other men. Women were few in number and, in general, borrowed smaller sums. Considering the character of the agrarian household-based socio-economic system, this is not surprising. The household was usually headed by a man. Women were not readily accepted as independent economic agents – only a few ran their own farms. It was thus almost impossible for female landowners, except those with very large landholdings, to get access to credit. However, the fact that some rural women were allowed to take out mortgage loans in the new financial organizations is confirmed by institutional records. A significant and interesting change was the increase in the number of loans – almost 40 per cent of all mortgage loans after the middle of the century – granted to husbands and wives together.[16] It was sometimes an advantage to have a spouse when negotiating with creditors. Nevertheless, this does not alter the general picture of the agrarian credit market before 1870: it was a closed market, open almost exclusively to men, and aimed at meeting the needs and demands of male creditors and borrowers.

Cities as Centres of Financial Innovation

The transformation of the Swedish banking and financial system had its origins in the larger cities. As in the countryside, informal credit markets remained important in the supply and circulation of urban capital throughout the nineteenth century. In recent years, researchers have examined extensively the relationships between informal and modernized, institutionalized credit markets during Sweden's transition from an agricultural to an industrial economy.[17] By analysing large numbers of estate inventories – and in Lindgren's case debt records – it has been possible to reconstruct the key characteristics of urban credit markets. This research suggests that a large but diminishing share of total credit provisions in the cities occurred outside the scope of the modern, institutionalized financial system (see Table 3.1). Investigation of the sources of capital in such informal urban credit markets has revealed a large number of wealthy women acting as lenders of money and as private bankers. The majority were widows, some of them relatively old, but young unmarried women sought to make their capital more productive through local, informal credit markets. In light of the legal changes in the mid-nineteenth century, which allowed women to enter into businesses and crafts previously open only to men, it is perhaps not that surprising that there was a greater acceptance of women as independent economic agents in the cities than in the countryside.

Table 3.1 The Relationship between the Informal and the Institutionalized Credit Market in Three Swedish Cities during the Nineteenth Century

City	Year	Informal credit market, %	Institutionalized credit market, %
Falun	1820–22	80	20
	1860–62	65	35
	1900–02	10	90
Kalmar	1841–45	81	19
	1871–75	76	24
	1901–05	45	55
Sala	1860	90	10
	1880	70	30
	1900	20	80

Source: H. Lindgren, 2002, p. 827, K. Lilja, forthcoming, H. Hellgren, 2003.

One of the most striking examples of a woman acting as a private banker can be found in Lilja's study of the capital market in nineteenth-century Falun. Helena Catharina Renström became a widow in 1840 at the age of 52. She had been married to her husband, Adolph Renström, who was fifteen years her senior, since 1821. Adolph had run a well-known restaurant in the city. At the time of his death in 1841, he was not only a very successful restaurant-keeper, he also had the second largest capital share in one of Sweden's oldest and biggest mining companies, Stora Kopparberg. This made Adolph one of Falun's most important local notables. Helena Renström inherited not only assets worth nearly 100,000 Swedish crowns, but also more than 50,000 crowns in financial claims, distributed among numerous debtors. When Helena died twenty years later, the estate inventory reveals that she had administered her inheritance in a very successful way. Moreover, she had increased the value of her total assets by a considerable sum, quadrupling her financial claims to more than 200,000 crowns. Obviously, Helena Renström continued to act as a private banker in Falun's local credit market for a long time after her husband's death. This example, alongside several others in Lilja's study, demonstrates that local financial and credit markets were not always gender-typed. It is also obvious that, due to the size and relative complexity of these financial transactions, and the numerous parties and legal questions involved, many wives had taken an active role in family businesses before they became widows.[18]

Thus, despite the establishment of hundreds of savings banks, commercial banks, mortgage associations and other financial institutions, traditional, informal channels for accessing and investing capital were still widely used. Within these local, informal credit markets, which were based on trust, reputation and personal knowledge – often derived from family, kin or other social relationships – wealthy widows were important intermediaries. Not only did they support themselves through such financial activities, they also made their own capital available for productive investments, thereby contributing to the economic development of Swedish towns.

Savings Banks as Market-makers and Intermediates of Women's Capital

The first savings banks were mostly established in the larger cities. As institutions for the depositing of surplus capital, they were an instant success. An important reason for this was that they were non-profit organizations; the lack of a profit motive instilled confidence in public investors. They were intended to reduce public expenditure on the poor and to promote desirable economic behaviour by the public at large, encouraging people to save for sickness and old age. The savings banks were thus founded with a strong sense of moral purpose and sought to promote investment from those lower down the social scale.[19]

While savings banks were mostly set up and managed by adult males, the social structure of the depositors was quite different. Approximately one-third of all depositors in the savings banks were under the age of 16. Of the adult depositors, the proportions of men and women were equal. A very large quota – between 70 and 75 per cent – of female depositors were young and unmarried, aged between 16 and 25 years.[20]

The investment behaviour of women depositors in savings banks differed considerably from that of their male counterparts, something which strengthens the argument that women's capital was of immense importance in the modernization of the Swedish banking and financial system. Women in general saved a lot more than men, both in absolute and relative terms. The balances on women's savings accounts were often 20–30 per cent higher than those of men. The most diligent savers were young, unmarried women in their twenties, who saved more than twice as much as men of the same age and marital status. More significantly, women depositors in savings banks invested continuously, on a long-term basis. This meant that once their savings had been deposited in the bank, the capital could be transformed into productive investments – savings banks re-invested their capital in a range of different outlets. There is also considerable evidence suggesting that once young female depositors married, investments that were made within the family or household were directed to their husbands' accounts. Women over the age of 55, most of whom by this stage were widows, also saved considerably more than male depositors of the same age.[21]

Another important reason for the success of the savings banks in attracting deposits was their flexible and liberal attitude towards women depositors. Several savings banks stipulated in their bylaws that adult depositors, independent of sex

Table 3.2 Adult Depositors in Six Large Swedish Savings Banks

Savings bank	Year	Number of depositors	Women %	Widows %	Wives %	Unmarried %	Servants‡ %
Stockholm	1821	644	47	7	13	28	52
	1832–41*	865	52	11	16	34	39
	1842–61*	1,709	52	9	20	32	39
	1862–75*	3,605	59	9	21	42	28
Falun	1830–33*	231	32	10	8	22	45
	1855†	96	58	16	18	11	50
	1880†	106	49	6	23	6	43
Borås	1831–32*	135	51	6	13	29	52
	1841†	541	47	2	10	58	30
	1855†	1,216	49	10	11	19	60
Nyköping	1832–62*	2,115	44	19	9	29	43
Jönköping	1839	1,165	50	17	0	34	49
Sölvesborg	1860	662	52	17	7	26	50

Notes:
* Average annual number of new depositors
† New depositors
‡ Also unmarried
Source: Stockholm's savings bank 1946, Accounting records of Nyköping's savings bank, Monographs of Jönköping's, Borås' and Sölvesborg's savings bank, K. Lilja, 2000.

or socio-economic status, had the right to make withdrawals from their own accounts. Hence, even married women could dispose of their own savings without consent of a legal guardian (i.e. their husband). This progressive practice was introduced by savings banks decades before the reforms of 1874, which formally allowed married women to dispose of their own income.[22]

Investing Women's Capital

As well as procuring money from individuals seeking to deposit surplus capital, savings banks also invested the collected funds. Recent studies have revealed how banks that were active in several large Swedish cities invested the majority of their capital in the expanding urban, industrial and commercial sectors. In this respect the early savings banks followed the practice of many of the commercial banks.[23] Hence, the savings of women were channelled through the savings banks to the capital-hungry sectors of the urban economies. As many scholars have previously concluded, women's capital, both directly and indirectly, contributed to the financing of new businesses in the transition to a new industrial society.[24]

In sharp contrast to the gender structure of depositors, there were almost no women at all amongst the borrowers in the savings banks. Considering the loan structure of the banks and the lack of acceptance of women in other contemporary financial organizations, this is not surprising. Broadly speaking, women were also not accepted as borrowers in the discount companies or in the commercial banks. Their investments were not based on women's capital, and the financial services they offered were intended almost entirely for men.[25]

In the 1850s, however, things began to change – gradually discount companies and commercial banks began to compete for women's personal savings and capital. When Stockholm's Enskilda bank opened for business in 1856, it was the first of the Swedish commercial banks to obtain a considerable proportion of its capital from deposits made by the public. Their foray into the deposit market had an immediate effect upon the savings bank in Stockholm. The savings bank lost a large number of depositors to the Enskilda bank, including many thrifty maids and wealthy widows. As a consequence, the total number of savings bank deposits fell. Other commercial banks soon followed the example of Stockholm's Enskilda bank and opened up deposit accounts for the public.[26]

Between 1800 and 1870 women, especially urban women, therefore played a significant role in the modernization of the Swedish banking and financial system as suppliers of venture capital. In the next phase of development, when the system was consolidated, the roles of women and their capital increased.

The Modernized Financial System, 1870–1900

The emergence of a truly modern banking system in Sweden is usually dated to the early 1870s. This was due both to the growing number of banks during this period and to some important institutional changes that occurred during the 1860s. In 1863 the usury law, which had limited interest rates to 6 per cent annually, was abolished. A year later, in 1864, legislation made it possible for joint stock banks to be established. Another important institutional change was the banking act of 1864, which in practice allowed for free establishment of Enskilda banks.[27]

Relative to the general level of European financial development, these changes meant that by 1870 Sweden had an exceptionally advanced and diversified banking system. Alongside nearly 40 commercial and 250 savings banks, over 40 local and regional mortgage associations had been established. Confidence in the new financial organizations and the system as a whole was very high. The relative sophistication of this banking system has been seen as pivotal to the simultaneous industrialization of Sweden.[28]

The new financial organizations gradually squeezed out the old merchant houses, wealthy capitalists and the private banking companies, which had earlier dominated the local credit markets. The large cities, notably Stockholm and Göteborg, continued to strengthen their positions as regional and national centres for financial innovations and transactions. A growing share of the public's savings and capital in Sweden was thus channelled through the financial institutions based in the country's most important cities. The agrarian credit market was more conservative, still highly influenced by old traditions and norms, and thus totally dominated by men.[29]

As discussed above, the legal status of women was reformed in the late nineteenth century. For example, in 1884 unmarried women received full legal capacity at the age of 21 – the same age as unmarried men. Together with other reforms, it seems that women's legal status and their potential to act as independent economic agents were gradually strengthened. But did institutional reforms lead to an actual change in women's roles as capital owners? Did the legal changes alter women's activities within the banking and financial system?

The Expansion of the Deposit Markets and Growing Competition for Women's Savings

The commercial banks' decision to enter the deposit markets at large had an immediate effect on the growth of an institutionalized Swedish financial system. In 1880 the total deposits in the commercial banks exceeded those in the savings banks and, by the turn of the century, the deposits were almost twice as large. Financing, lending and other activities made as a consequence of deposits from the public were not entirely voluntary decisions, based on economic rationality. The National Bank of Sweden announced in the 1870s that the Enskilda banks' note-issuing rights would be revoked, forcing such banks to seek out new ways of financing their lending activities.[30]

Table 3.3 The Growth of the Swedish Deposit Market, 1860–1900, at 1860 Constant Prices

Year	Total deposits, millions Swedish crowns		No. of accounts, thousands		Average balance, Swedish crowns,	
	Savings bank	Commercial bank	Savings bank	Commercial bank	Savings bank	Commercial bank
1860	27	18	188	n/a	145	n/a
1880	159	268	753	128	177	1,416 (151*)
1900	466	824	1,201	446	334	1,608 (478*)

Note:
* Average balance on savings accounts
Source: Statistics of Swedish commercial banks, K. Lilja, 2000, p. 33 and T. Petersson, 2001, p. 73.

When the commercial banks entered local and regional depositor markets, they automatically appealed to savings banks' traditional segments of depositors. Business enterprises of all sizes also turned to the commercial banks to manage their short-term cash balances, something which partially explains the higher average balances on the deposit accounts of such banks. When commercial banks introduced their own versions of savings accounts in the 1890s, modelled on those offered by the savings banks, the competition for women's savings increased further.

Stockholm's Enskilda bank was initially the most successful commercial bank operating in the deposit market. Their strategy was to 'steal' depositors not only from the agents who worked in the informal deposit markets, but also from savings banks. As market makers in local deposit markets, the savings banks had shown that it was possible to raise considerable amounts of capital from customer groups that previously had been neglected. By the late nineteenth century the commercial banks were also targeting these groups, especially women. For example, in Stockholm's Enskilda bank 40–50 per cent of the individual deposit accounts were held by women.[31]

In the savings banks, women continued to constitute the most important group of depositors. They also carried on investing larger sums of money for a longer period of time than their male counterparts.[32] Hence, both the savings banks and, from the later nineteenth century, the commercial banks were becoming more and more dependent on women's wealth for financing loans. The growing competition for women's savings was, however, not the only change concerning females in the Swedish financial market.

Women and Ownership

As the Swedish economy underwent a more intense industrial transformation beginning in the 1870s, new financial innovations and instruments were introduced to the public. The breakthrough of the joint stock company as a modern form of corporate organization, was one such innovation. However, older kinds of company organization based on the principle of personal responsibility continued. In the late nineteenth century, shareholding in both types of companies became more and more popular. In many large, industrial companies women owned considerable portions of the shares. Kerstin Norlander, who has studied middle-class women as capital owners and entrepreneurs, concludes that both the legal and the educational systems functioned as structural obstacles for women. Consequently, men became capitalists in the sense that they controlled capital, while women did not.[33] Ylva Hasselberg and Tomas Matti's analysis is somewhat different. In their study of ownership changes and ownership influence in Stora Kopparberg, Sweden's oldest and biggest industrial company at that time, women formed approximately 20 per cent of the largest shareholders. These females were often central to family networks and played a crucial strategic financial role in making alliances with other owners. In this sense, women were excluded neither from the networks of key corporate shareholders nor from the right to exercise (indirect) ownership.[34]

An enquiry into the shareholders of commercial banks in the late nineteenth century reveals a similar picture. In small, strictly local and regional banks as well as in larger, nationwide commercial banks, a large number of women can be found among the shareholders. Moreover, in general women shareholders owned as much as their male counterparts. Two categories of female shareholder naturally dominated: young, unmarried women and widows. These two categories of females owned 30–40 per cent each of all shares owned by women. The ownership of shares in commercial banks, like the ownership of shares in other kinds of companies, was a key component of many families' economic strategies. Shares were transferred within the family in order to provide financial security for future generations and surviving relatives. Many women derived a *rentier* income from their investments that ensured their own well-being.

Table 3.4 The Ownership Structure in Eight Swedish Commercial Banks

Bank	Year	No. of shareholders	Women, %	No. of shares	Women, %
Smålands Enskilda bank	1878	990	30	6,000	*23*
Kristinehamns Enskilda bank	1889	247	37	1,340	*28*
Gotlands Enskilda bank	1893	254	25	1,000	*27*
Norrköpings Enskilda bank	1898	227	43	1,600	*25*
Östergötlands Enskilda bank	1899	558	41	2,600	*36*
Sundsvalls Enskilda bank	1900	817	39	6,000	*22*
Södermanlands Enskilda bank	1900	344	35	1,500	35
Skaraborgs läns Enskilda bank	1904	624	38	3,000	34

Note: Figures in italics are estimated values
Source: Annual reports.

What were the consequences of women's owning significant numbers of shares in the Swedish commercial banks? Could women make use of their position as major shareholders, or were they merely passive investors, constrained by their gender and social status, as some previous research has suggested? When it comes to the long-term management as well as the day-to-day operations of the banks, both in the commercial and savings sectors, not a single woman was appointed as board member or as any kind of manager before the turn of the century.[35] As in many other companies, women frequently did not attend the annual shareholders' meetings and instead delegated their voting rights to a male relative or authorized agent. They were largely absent from shareholder politics and corporate governance. Women were not excluded by formal obstacles, but by tradition and contemporary customs within this field of economic activity.

Women as Borrowers?

One of the most notable features of the lending activities of Swedish banks during the entire nineteenth century was the prevalence of insider loans. As Naomi Lamoreaux has pointed out, granting loans to insiders was not merely a way to increase the bank's information on the borrowers and thereby reduce risks connected to lending, but also an economic benefit for the managers, owners and other insiders.[36] It was not unusual for insider loans to constitute more than half of the total value of loans made by the more substantial Swedish commercial banks.[37] Given their prevalence as investors in the banks, it would not be unreasonable to expect large numbers of females to be insider borrowers from savings banks. However, there is little evidence to suggest that this was the case. According to the reports from a government banking inspection and the extensive literature on nineteenth-century commercial banks, women borrowers were practically nonexistent.

The situation in the savings banks was similar. Despite the fact that their entire business was more or less based on the savings of women, a very small portion of the loans in the savings banks were granted to female borrowers. Before the 1890s, only 1–2 per cent of annual, new loans were made to women. In the 1890s this share rose considerably, but still never exceeded 4 per cent. Again, the widows' relatively strong position is striking, as they formed the largest group of female borrowers. It was often harder for women to borrow money from the banks. A prerequisite for getting a loan in a savings bank if you were a woman was thus the possession of some kind of real estate, which could be used as collateral. Male borrowers could make use of their personal networks in order to borrow money and were often granted signature loans – an opportunity that did not exist for women.[38]

In summary, after 1870 women continued to play a very important role in the modernized Swedish banking and financial system. They provided the large amounts of capital that were transferred to the expanding sectors of the economy and thereby significantly contributed to Swedish industrialization. Nevertheless, there were some informal restrictions which circumscribed women's possibilities to act as independent and fully fledged economic agents. Female owners of capital in general, and shareholders in commercial banks in particular, could not exercise their ownership directly, due to the informal, invisible restrictions that limited their potential to participate in shareholder politics and the management of the banks. Women were in the paradoxical situation of providing much of the capital for the modernization of the Swedish financial system, but of having little power to influence directly its development.

Conclusions

During the nineteenth century the Swedish banking and financial system was transformed. New organizations were established and new financial instruments were presented to the investing public. However, it is important to acknowledge the fact that active and viable financial and credit markets existed long before the emergence of modern banking organizations. In these localized urban credit markets, it was not unusual for women, particularly wealthy widows, to act as private bankers and money lenders. The complexity of many of the financial transactions made at this time, coupled with evidence of the nature and organization of the household economy, suggest that women had experience of credit markets long before they became widows. At the centre of familial, kinship and community relationships, these females had access to specialized knowledge and information and understood the networks of trust and reciprocity that were essential components of economic success in an age of uncertainty.

Nevertheless, the modernization of the banking and financial system was highly dependent on some essential contributions made by women. The savings banks successfully managed to recruit large numbers of female depositors. Women not only saved more than male depositors, they also invested for a considerably longer period, and their capital was redirected by the savings banks to investments in the expanding sectors of the economy. Women's wealth was seen as both stable and reliable and therefore perfectly suited to one of the essential prerequisites of economic development – long-term investment.

The transition from the informal to the institutional credit market accelerated in the last decades of the nineteenth century. The competition amongst the financial organizations to attract female capital increased. It was not only women's inherited capital that the financial markets sought. In addition, growing numbers of economically independent working women chose to invest their income in new ways. Both savings and commercial banks sought a share of, and became increasingly dependent on, female capital. Indeed, in the commercial as in the savings banks, women constituted a major category of shareholders. However, despite their contributions to the financing of the banks' investments and their role as shareholders, women's wider economic and political rights were limited. Crucially, few were able to borrow from the banks.

The legal reforms that occurred in the nineteenth century, which formally equalized the status of men and women, had very limited effects on the banking and financial system. It is true that some of the financial organizations preempted the reforms by allowing all women to manage their accounts without a legal guardian. However, when it came to the management and control of the financial organizations, it was only the men who exercised power and authority. Thus nineteenth-century Swedish women were important but mostly silent actors in the country's financial and economic development.

These findings suggest a need for mediation between historiographical viewpoints. On the one hand, acting in large numbers as key investors in an evolving financial system, nineteenth-century Swedish women do not easily fit into the roles ascribed to them by the separate spheres thesis and the associated rhetoric of bourgeois gender ideology. Women were far from economically inactive, and without their savings and investments the development of the Swedish economy would undoubtedly have been delayed. On the other hand, women's agency as participants in financial markets and as decision makers within financial institutions was clearly different from that of men. Accordingly, this study has demonstrated that there is a need to recognize that economic agency can be asserted in a number of different ways. The publicly active, profit-maximizing male entrepreneur represents just one kind of economic agency, while the 'silent' investment activities of middle-class women represent another. In judging their contribution to the industrial revolutions of nineteenth-century Europe, it is therefore important to be wary of measuring women's (and men's) behaviour against a definition of economic agency which is itself a product of the very ideology that this book calls into question.

Notes

1. See, for example, Lindgren, 1997, and Olsson, 1997.
2. Recent research on Swedish banking and financial history has shifted away from consideration of the macro development of the financial system to examine the various credit and savings institutions that comprised regional and local financial markets. Detailed studies have been concerned with identifying the economic roles and behaviour of men and women within such institutions. See Petersson, 2000; Lilja, 2000 and forthcoming, Hellgren; 2002 and 2003; and Lindgren, 2002. I am deeply grateful to Kristina Lilja, Hilda Hellgren and Anders Sjölander for allowing me to see their unpublished research.
3. See Tom Ericsson's chapter in this volume.
4. Göransson, 1993; Norlander, 1994 and 2000; and Hasselberg and Matti, 2002.
5. See further arguments in Scott, 1998.
6. Davidoff and Hall, 1987.
7. Göransson, 1990, and Ulvros, 1996.
8. Tilly and Scott, 1978.
9. Qvist, 1980, and Norlander, 1994.
10. Qvist, 1980, Göransson, 1990, and Ågren, 1999.
11. Ighe, 2004; Qvist, 1980; Sjöberg, 2001, pp. 14 and 171–4. See also Tom

Ericsson's chapter in this volume.
12. Andersson, 1983.
13. Petersson, 2001, pp. 61–89.
14. Magnusson, 2000, pp. 3–31; and Petersson, 2001.
15. Martinius, 1970, p. 164; and Svensson, 2001, p. 239.
16. Svensson, 2001, pp. 211–20.
17. Lindgren, 2002; Hellgren, 2003; Lilja, forthcoming.
18. Ulvros, 1996; Hellgren, 2003; and Lilja, forthcoming. For examples of eighteenth-century widows as private bankers, see Fagerlund, 2002.
19. Lilja, 2000, pp. 29–36; Petersson, 2001, pp. 62–3. See McCants, 1997, pp. 17–18, for a theoretical discussion on non-profit organizations.
20. The savings banks considered depositors older than 16 to be adult, although the formal age of consent was 21 for men and 25 for women up to 1884. Results from a large number of investigations on the structure of depositors in Swedish savings banks are summarized in Lilja, 2000.
21. 'Stockholm's savings bank', 1946; Lilja, 2000.
22. For example the savings bank in Falun, which from 1852 allowed married women to dispose of their own savings, Lilja, 2000.
23. Nygren, 1983; Petersson, 2000; and Petersson, 2001, pp. 157–203.
24. Göransson, 1990; and Davidoff and Hall, 1987.
25. Petersson, 2001.
26. Financial Committee of 1852, 'Stockholm's savings bank', 1946; Gasslander, 1962, p. 45.
27. Sandberg, 1978; Nygren, 1983; and Ögren, 2003.
28. Goldsmith, 1969, pp. 209–12; Sandberg, 1978; Nygren, 1983; Petersson, 2001; Lindgren and Sjögren, 2002.
29. Gasslander, 1962; Nygren, 1983; Petersson, 2001.
30. Petersson, 2001, pp. 72–3.
31. Frölander, 1906, p. 64; Brisman, 1923, p. 92; and Gasslander, 1962, pp. 46–8.
32. Sjölander, 1995; and Lilja, 2000.
33. Norlander, 1994 and 2000.
34. Hasselberg and Matti, 2002.
35. Register of employees and directors in Swedish financial organizations.
36. Lamoreaux, 1994.
37. Petersson, 2001, pp. 78–9.
38. Nyköping's savings bank, accounting records and Sjölander, 1996. See also Hellgren, 2002, for similar results.

–4–

Where have All the Businesswomen Gone?
Images and Reality in the Life of Nineteenth-century Middle-class Women in Northern France

Béatrice Craig

The presence of women, especially widows, at the head of early modern European trading or manufacturing firms has been well documented.[1] Most gender historians, and even business historians, agree that those women would have disappeared between the end of the eighteenth and the middle of the nineteenth century, pushed out by the combined impact of the separate spheres ideology and of structural changes, such as industrialization, the use of extra-familial capital and the 'managerial revolution'.[2]

Not all historians concur however. Eliane Richard, in a short article on Marseilles, argues that the disappearance of the businesswoman may have been more apparent than real. Businesswomen would have been erased from historical memory in two successive steps; first, contemporary documents overlooked them; second, historians accepted uncritically the image conveyed by those sources and equated the absence of evidence as evidence of an absence.[3] Marlou Schrover encountered the same problem in the Netherlands: Dutch historians assumed there were no business women left in the nineteenth century, with the exception of impoverished widows running *winkeltjes* (small shops). Dutch tax registers, however, tell a different story and reveal women managing large and small businesses alongside their husbands, or on their own.[4]

Over the past fifteen years, historians have increasingly become critical of the separate spheres 'paradigm' and its claim that nineteenth-century women were confined to the domestic sphere. Some challenges are theoretical, like Amanda Vickery's article which asks whether the public/private distinction ever really reflected reality.[5] Most criticisms do not focus on women's relationship to the economy. Nonetheless, some historians are uncovering various instances of women remaining at the head of businesses in the nineteenth century, or playing significant financial roles in emerging capitalist economies.[6] American historians have uncovered an even more interesting phenomenon: women manipulated the separate spheres ideology to carve their own niche in the realms of production and retailing. They specialized in trades catering to an exclusively female clientele (dress making or millinery), or drew on stereotypical 'female' skills (food and drink retailing, boarding-house keeping, education, entertainment and publishing popular literature).[7] This led Joan Scott to wonder whether one should not talk of 'segmented' rather than 'separate' spheres.[8]

Through her study of the Lille area of northern France, Bonnie Smith has contributed to this image of the middle-class woman estranged from business. She concluded that at the beginning of the nineteenth century large numbers of women were actively involved in business. Their daughters and granddaughters, on the other hand, were completely alienated by capitalism and turned their backs on it. Instead of managing or helping to manage the family business, they devoted their time to family reproduction and religious practice.[9] But it seems that Smith, like the historians of Marseilles or the Low Countries, was misled by her sources. She too accepted a discourse that was at odds with the reality. In the Lille area there were fewer businesswomen at the beginning of the century than she suggests, but they did not desert the family office or the family store over the following decades.

Sources and Methods

Lille is an old textile centre, annexed to France in 1668. It successfully adapted to the emerging industrial order in the nineteenth century. Its economy, however, was not limited to cloth production, but also included the transformation of local agricultural products into sugar, oil, flour, beer and distilled alcohol. It was also a trading and administrative centre and housed several garrisons. Tourcoing, a hinterland village fifteen kilometres north east of Lille, had also been involved in textile production since the Middle Ages. It experienced spectacular growth in the second quarter of the nineteenth century and became one of the country's major wool-combing centres and a key site for the production of fabric for the fashion industry. In both cities, production and trade remained dominated by family firms until at least the First World War. Increased production and population growth also fuelled the expansion of the retail sector, especially in Lille where many luxury stores were located.[10]

Three types of sources provide us with information about women in trade and manufacturing in both cities: censuses, tax rolls (*matrices de patentes*) and trade directories. Each source has shortcomings which result in an underestimation of the number of women in business. However, their collective use can compensate for some of their individual deficiencies. All reflect a vision of a society organized around nuclear households with 'appropriate' economic roles for male and female spouses, prevalent among those who decided how the document should be constructed and among those who participated in its elaboration. For instance, the census reports people's occupation, but this information is based on the person's answer. Manufacturers may claim they were landowners or *rentiers* (living off their investments). Censuses are also notorious for underreporting married women's occupations. Either the husbands, who usually filled out the questionnaires, or the census takers did not bother reporting it. Worse, at the end of the century, official instructions directed census takers to list women assisting their husbands as having no occupation. This erased married women from the labour force. Moreover, the higher up the socio-economic ladder a woman was, the less likely she was to have an economic activity distinct from her husband; wives of manufacturers were less likely to have an occupation than wives of craftsmen.

The business tax rolls (*matrices de patentes*) are more precise and more reliable. All manufacturers, merchant traders and retailers had to pay this tax. Craftsmen were exempt if they had no employees (a working wife or child did not qualify as an employee), and at the end of the century the tax was waived for widows who took over their husband's craft shop. Assessment took place on a yearly basis and the rolls indicate the name, address and occupation of all the individuals liable for this tax. In addition, they indicate the address of the business, the type of activity it engaged in, its size, the name and address of the manager if different from the owner, the tax category, and the amount to be paid. Retailers were distributed in eight different categories depending on the presumed volume of activities. Wholesalers were always put in class one and two.

Women had to pay the tax like everyone else, but two factors made married women invisible. First, when a husband and a wife were both liable for the tax, they only had to pay the higher of the two assessments (unless they were married 'in separation of property', in which case they both had to pay their own tax on their own business; this was rare in northern France). If the highest tax was the husband's, the wife disappeared from the record.[11] Secondly, men were known to take the *patente* in their name even when their wife was running the business, and the phenomenon is not always as obvious as in the case of the mechanic who paid the tax on a dressmaking shop! Single women and widows, on the other hand, did not escape the clutches of the tax collector, even if they were mere partners in a firm, because for most of the century all partners had to pay this tax.

Censuses and tax records are available for Tourcoing, but not for Lille where they were destroyed in a fire.[12] For Lille evidence can be taken from trade directories. From 1829 to 1856 the printer Vanackère published the *Almanach annuel du commerce, des arts et des métiers des villes de Lille, Armentières, Roubaix et Tourcoing*. Ravet-Anceau commenced publication of his *L'annuaire de l'arrondissement de Lille* in 1853, which was followed by *L'annuaire du commerce, de l'industrie, de la magistrature et de l'administration de l'arrondissement de Lille* in 1860. These directories are difficult to use. Their aim was to inform the public of the various services and industries existing in the area, but we do not know under what circumstances a specific provider or producer was included. It seems that both printers used existing lists, such as the tax rolls, as a starting point and improved upon them by visiting the businesses and asking the public to inform them of errors and omissions. Vanackère, for example, claimed his 1850 edition had been thoroughly revised following a visit to all businesses listed. This procedure could explain why the printers' 'database' visibly improves over time, and why the proportion of women increases in both series as years go by. A further problem is that the two printers did not necessarily group listings by occupation, but in broader trade categories, which varied from year to year. One year, for instance, all cotton wholesalers, spinners and weavers may be listed together; in another year, the wool, cotton and linen spinners might be merged into a general 'spinning' category. It is also not always possible to distinguish retailers from manufacturers. What can one do with an entry which reads 'tarpaulins' for instance? Is this a manufacturer that also sells to the general public or a store selling ready-made goods?[13] Finally, both printers presented their information as if the business person was a male: they listed only the last name and occasionally a Christian name. Some women were given a courtesy title (Delle, Dame, Veuve) and occasionally their Christian name was recorded. It is thus possible women are hidden among individuals listed without a title or Christian name. One should thus assume that the directories, like all other sources, underreport women.

The results that follow are based on an analysis of a sample of the 1820, 1851 and 1886 censuses for Tourcoing, and of directories for specific years (every ten years starting in 1830), and of tax rolls (1840 and every five years, beginning in 1852). In addition, data were collected for *all* the retailers listed in the tax rolls of 1852, and for the northern section of the city listed in the tax rolls of 1886. The information pertaining to those households was then cross-referenced with the 1851 and 1886 censuses.[14]

Counting Heads

Lille

Beginning with Lille, we are immediately faced with the problem mentioned above: the fewer the directories a printer had published, the smaller the number of women in the directory (see Tables 4.1 and 4.2). It is doubtful that the proportion of female-headed businesses would have dropped by half between 1850 and 1860, to regain 1840 levels within ten years. The drop is most likely a source artefact, caused by the shift from a series published by an established printer, to one put on the market by a newcomer. It is therefore prudent to deal with both series independently. They both suggest either that the proportion of female-headed businesses was on the rise in each half of the century or that the printers got better at identifying women, or both. Regardless, the data in the two tables really cannot support the notion that middle-class women played a lesser economic role at the end of the century than at the beginning. In 1890 the women of Lille were more likely to run a store than their grandmothers. At worst the trend line was flat.

Table 4.1 Lille Businesses according to the Sex of Owner

	I Almanachs Vanackère								
	1831			*1840*			*1850*		
	Total	F	%	Total	F	%	Total	F	%
All[a]	3,961	377	9.5	4,914	535	10.9	4,545	631	13.9
Wholesale trade and manufacturing[b]	982	63	6.4	1,121	63	5.6	943	34	3.6
Retail[b]	1,253	173	13.8	1,714	324	18.9	1,875	455	24.3

	II Annuaires Ravet-Anceau											
	1860			*1870*			*1880*			*1890*		
	Total	F	%	Total	F	%	Total	F	%	Total	F	%
All[a]	6,654	492	7.4	9,630	999	10.4	10,340	1,080	10.4	16,209	2,028	12.5
Wholesale trade and manufacturing[b]	1,197	80	6.7	2,009	149	7.4	2,052	156	7.6	1,574	132	8.4
Retail[b]	1,912	202	10.6	3,543	615	17.4	3,869	709	18.3	5,387	959	17.8

Notes:
a. All figures exclude the trade in alcohol.
b. Only businesses clearly identified as wholesale trade, manufacturing or retail are included in those categories; hence totals are much higher than the sum of the two categories.

Women were never equally distributed across all retail categories (Table 4.3). They remained rare among butchers and bakers, while their number appears to have considerably increased in textiles and clothing. There was no ghettoization of women in 'female' sectors, as in the United States or, as some of the chapters in this book show, in other European countries.[15] In Lille the only feminized sectors were those listed under a feminine term: *lingère* (seamstress), *tailleuse* (female tailor – the masculine is *tailleur*, and they are listed separately), ironers and midwives. Laundresses were not listed. Men continued dominating many sectors deemed 'feminine': in 1831, 86 per cent of food, clothing or textile stores were kept by men, against 78 per cent in 1890. In 1831, 42 per cent of the female retailers sold textiles and clothing, as opposed to 34 per cent of the men. In 1890, 49 per cent of the women sold these commodities, but a quarter of the male retailers were still active in this sector. The feminization of retailing thus remained limited. The range of goods sold by women did not narrow over the course of the century either. Contrary to what happened in the United States or in Germany, women sold everything and anything in the 1830s and continued to do so in the 1890s.[16] Craft industries displayed the same characteristics. At the century's end,

Table 4.2 Proportions of Women in Retailing in Lille

| | *I Vanackère* |||||||||
| | | 1831 ||| 1840 ||| 1850 |||
	Total	W	%	Total	W	%	Total	W	%
Bakers, butchers, colonial groceries	288	24	8.3	326	30	9.2	296	29	9.8
Other food	375	28	7.5	535	62	11.6	648	84	13.0
Textiles and clothing	438	107	24.4	661	209	31.6	739	323	43.7
Others	152	14	9.2	192	23	12.0	192	19	9.9
Total	1,253	173	13.8	1,714	324	18.9	1,875	455	24.3

| | *II Ravet Anceau* ||||||||||||
| | 1860 ||| 1870 ||| 1881 ||| 1890 |||
	Total	W	%	Total	W	%	Total	W	%	Total	W	%
Bakers, butchers, colonial groceries	367	21	5.7	529	32	6.0	600	33	5.5	564	38	6.7
Other food	826	76	9.2	1,167	118	10.1	1,296	186	14.4	1,858	357	19.2
Textiles and clothing	413	90	21.8	1,285	415	32.3	1,363	438	32.1	1,664	479	28.8
Others	306	15	4.9	562	50	8.9	610	52	8.5	1,301	85	6.5
Total	1,912	202	10.6	3,543	615	17.4	3,869	709	18.3	5,387	959	17.8

Sources: Vanackère's Almanach, 1831, 1840, 1850; Ravet-Anceau's Annuaire, 1860, 1870, 1881, 1890.

Note: Taverns and other alcohol retailers are not listed individually in 1831; subsequently, the distinctions between estaminets, cabarets and débits de boissons are inconsistent. I eliminated those retailers from the totals.

one could find Lille women who were gunsmiths, watchmakers, printers, makers of glass eyes, bookbinders, harness makers, coopers, blacksmiths, lime makers, roofers, painters and contractors of public works. Many of these women had probably taken over their role from a deceased husband. They probably did not do the work themselves but supervised employees, dealt with customers and kept the books. The above list comprises trades requiring extensive, if not expensive, equipment, in addition to the mastery of a skill. Women needed to maintain a fully equipped shop as well as a clientele. Continuing the trade required both practical and theoretical knowledge in order that craftsmen and other employees could be effectively managed.

The proportion of women in wholesale trades and manufacturing declined slightly in the middle of the century (and at the end of the Vanackère series, where numbers should be going up). However, the secular trend line is almost flat, displaying a slight rise at the end of the century. Female manufacturers, like female merchant traders, could be found in all sectors: spinning, weaving, machine toll manufacturing, sugar refining and chemical making. The type of activity seems to have had no impact on a woman's ability to take the helm.

The directories indicate women's marital status, but one cannot draw very firm conclusions from these data (Table 4.3). Married women were often overlooked or

Table 4.3 Marital Status of Female Merchant Traders, Manufacturers and Retailers, Lille, 1831–90

Manufacturers and merchant traders

	1831 N	1831 %	1840 N	1840 %	1850 N	1850 %	1860 N	1860 %	1870 N	1870 %	1881 N	1881 %	1890 N	1890 %
Single	11	17.5	15	23.8	5	14.7	19	23.8	40	26.8	37	23.9	26	19.7
Married	3	4.8	5	7.9	2	5.9	11	13.8	37	24.8	38	24.5	39	29.5
Widowed	48	76.2	38	60.3	26	76.5	42	52.5	63	42.3	73	47.1	59	44.7
'Sisters'	1	1.6	5	7.9	1	2.9	8	10.0	9	6.0	7	4.5	8	6.1
Total	63	100.0	63	100	34	100.0	80	100.0	149	100.0	155	100.0	132	100.0

Retailers

	1831 N	1831 %	1840 N	1840 %	1850 N	1850 %	1860 N	1860 %	1870 N	1870 %	1881 N	1881 %	1890 N	1890 %
Single	29	16.8	51	15.7	101	22.2	46	22.8	189	30.7	214	30.2	217	22.6
Married	51	29.5	31	9.6	161	35.4	11	5.4	141	22.9	177	25.0	198	20.6
Widowed	79	45.7	103	31.8	143	31.4	86	42.6	200	32.5	259	36.5	397	41.4
'Sisters'	14	8.1	23	7.1	30	6.6	21	10.4	38	6.2	31	4.4	26	2.7
Not specified	0	0.0	116	35.8	20	4.4	38	18.8	47	7.6	28	3.9	121	12.6
Total	173	100.0	324	100.0	455	100.0	202	100.0	615	100.0	709	100.0	959	100.0

hidden behind their husband's identity, but they become more visible as the accuracy of the printers' data improved. Among merchant traders and manufacturers, the business was always listed in the name of the husband, even when women played a very active role. Married women who ran their own business were rare in the first half of the century and more common in the second. Many of them headed garment or household linen making businesses. This sector, however was not fully feminized, and at best half of the businesses were run by women (the highest proportion was found among the *confection pour dames* – manufacturers of women's clothing – where in 1890 thirty-seven out of sixty-five manufacturers were female). The proportion of married women in the retail sector went up in both series, rising from 29 per cent to 35 per cent in the Vanackère directories and from 6 to over 20 per cent in the Ravet-Anceau series. The Lille data suggest therefore that women, and more particularly married women, took advantage of the expansion of retailing, especially the ready-to-wear garment industry. The growth and diversification of the local economy appears to have been especially beneficial to them.

At this time Lille was characterized by fairly stable proportions of women in the wholesale and retail trades and in manufacturing. The proportion of female-headed manufacturing or wholesale firms dropped slightly in the middle of the century, but then recovered. In retailing one witnesses an increase in the proportion of shops run by women, but this did not lead to a fully fledged feminization of any sector, nor to a narrowing of the range of activities pursued by females. Most women were in food and textiles, because most stores retailed food and textiles, and the food and textile sectors were the ones experiencing the greatest growth over the course of the century! It also seems that the increased level of female activity was the result of the greater participation of *married* women in the retail sector.

Analysis of the directories therefore provide an overall view of the evolution of the activities of the women from the various layers of Lille's middle class. The data for Tourcoing offer a finer grained and more detailed picture.

Tourcoing

Women did not disappear from retailing in Tourcoing. The proportion of retailers who were women in the tax rolls remained almost constant between 1852 and 1892: 13.6 and 14.2 per cent respectively. The linkage of the tax records and the censuses for 1852 and 1886 allows us to identify an important number of female retailers whose businesses were taxed under their husband's name. These women are recorded as running a store in the census, while their husband reported a different occupation. Correcting the *patente* data in light of the information provided by the census yields percentages of 22.3 per cent female retailers in 1851–52 and 31.5 per cent in 1886. This shows that the women of Tourcoing were no more excluded from retailing as the century progressed than their sisters in Lille (Table 4.4). The large difference between the raw figures derived from the *patentes* and the corrected figures also underlines the extent to which married women's activities could be hidden in the sources.

Table 4.4 Female Retailers, Tourcoing, 1852–1892

	1852, entire town		1886, Canton Nord agglomeration	
	Reported in patentes N	Corrected figures N	Reported in patentes N	Corrected figures N
Male-run stores	548	493	500	402
Female-run stores	86	141	85	183
Total	634	634	585	585
% of women	13.6	22.2	14.5	31.3
Number of women retrieved from census		55		98
% of women retrieved		39		54

Crossick and Haupt concluded that, at the end of the nineteenth century, female retailers were restricted to a narrow range of activities and concentrated at the lower end of the retail ladder.[17] The typical end-of-century female retailer would have been a widow eking out a scant living from the sale of basic groceries and haberdashery. But in Tourcoing, as in Lille, women were not excluded from any kind of trade. Most were retailers of food or textiles as these were the largest sectors of the retail economy. All retail sectors remained dominated by men. Most women also kept 'low end' stores (classified as category 6 to 8 in the tax rolls). Indeed, the proportion of women who kept such stores increased from 75 to 80 per cent between 1852 and 1886. This is not because they were pushed out by men, however. If we look at the matter from a different angle, one notes that, in 1852 17 per cent of the 'high end' stores (class 3 to 5) were kept by women (compared with 22 per cent in 1886). Women simply became even more prevalent in 'low end' retailing (24 to 34 per cent). There were more and more women in all levels of retail, but, as low end retail was growing faster, women were more likely to operate a small store selling basic necessities than a fancy store on Tourcoing's prestigious Grand Place.

Most retailers were married, and their spouse's occupation suggests that running a store was part of a family strategy little concerned with the 'male bread winner ideology'. Female retailers rarely belonged to the poorest layers of society. They were married to men engaged in traditional crafts (such as hand weavers), to skilled workers (such as wool sorters, mechanics or boiler operators), or to foremen. They were the workers most likely to be able to support a wife and children on their wages alone. But those were also the working-class households most likely to have the resources needed to open a small shop. A small store may not have made much profit, but, as female wages were low, the store could easily have been more remunerative. In addition, shopkeeping could be combined with housework and child care. When the male breadwinner was laid off, the store would keep the family going.

By the end of the century, the standard of living of the workers in the Lille area had increased slightly.[18] The wives of the better paid workers took advantage of a growth in consumer demand for basic necessities and opened stores catering to women from their own social class. The growth of small-scale retail outlets run by women was therefore less the consequence of women's immiseration than of the economic ambitions of the upper echelons of the working class.

The information about Tourcoing textile factories contained in the tax rolls corroborates the conclusions drawn from the Lille directories (Table 4.5).[19] Among

Table 4.5 Proportion of Female-run Textile Businesses in Tourcoing

	Spinners and spinner-twisters		Manufacturers[5]		Preparation and finishing[6]		Combinations[7]		Total	%
1814[1]							17		17	11.8
1818[2]			21		65	7.7	7	14.3	93	7.5
1820[3]	15	6.7	46	6.7			6	16.7	67	11.9
1833[4]	26	15.4	61	15.4	52	3.8	15	13.3	154	9.7
1840	37	8.1	74	8.1	23	8.7	6	16.7	140	10.0
1852	50	6.0	53	6.0	18	5.6	15	13.3	136	5.9
1857	55	1.8	43	1.8	21	9.5	15	6.7	134	4.5
1862	59	6.8	43	6.8	32	15.6	15	20.0	149	8.1
1867	54	3.7	41	3.7	49	14.3	11	0.0	155	7.7
1872	52	7.7	39	7.7	44	22.7	16	0.0	151	9.9
1877	47	8.5	45	8.5	76	13.2	13	7.7	181	9.4
1882	43	14.0	40	14.0	78	14.1	17	17.6	178	11.2
1887	56	5.4	61	5.4	70	14.3	21	28.6	208	10.6
1892	42	7.1	51	7.1	78	17.9	24	4.2	195	10.8
1897	49	6.1	49	6.1	50	20.0	26	3.8	174	9.2
1911	36	8.3	42	8.3	36	16.7	41	9.8	155	9.7

Notes:
1. Spinners and putters out to weavers only.
2. Putters out to wool combers, and putters out to weavers employing at least five weavers.
3. Spinners and putters out to weavers employing at least five weavers.
4. From report to the *prefet* dated 27/2/1833. Includes spinners and putters out to weavers and wool combers.
5. Putters out to weavers; carpet and fabric manufacturers, alone or combined with yarn seizing; hosiery; manufacture of knitted garments.
6. Wool sorting; wool washing; cotton beating; wool carding or combing; yarn twisting, doubling and seizing fabric or yarn dying; fabric bleaching; ribbon making; sewing.
7. Two or more of the preceding activities, for instance spinning and manufacturing, or spinning and carding; also any of the above combined with wholesale trade.

Sources: *Patentes* for Tourcoing 1814–1911; the figures for 1833 are derived from a report to the *prefet* on the state of manufacturing in the town.

manufacturers, there was a similar trend line: a slight rise at the end of the century following a slight drop in the middle. Wholesale trades followed the same pattern with a small time lag. The proportion of female manufacturers is also higher than in Lille, but this may be a false difference stemming from the nature of the sources.

The censuses and the tax rolls report similar proportions of textile firms run by women in 1851–52 (4.3 and 4.4 per cent) and 1886–87 (9.75 and 9 per cent). Considering that censuses undercount women, and that small numbers are easily distorted, the fact the figures are so close is remarkable. The sources also suggest that it was common for a widow to take over a firm from a deceased husband. In 1851, 14 per cent of the households in the census were headed by a widow. Around 4 per cent of the textile firms were headed by a widow, suggesting a succession rate of about 25 per cent. In 1886 widows still headed 14 per cent of households, and 9 per cent of the textile firms were headed by women, which would correspond to a succession rate of about 2/3 (unmarried female business heads are rare). Accordingly, women must have been involved in the running of the business when their husband was alive; between one- and two-thirds of females from the entrepreneurial class were active in the family business. It is clear therefore that women did not disappear from manufacturing and wholesale trades. Moreover, after 1882 unmarried women without a male business partner began to make their entry onto the economic stage: they usually paid the tax on new niche production activities, like hosiery. The increased presence of women in business at the century's end was also due to the proliferation of workshops specializing in preparatory and finishing processes. These were more likely to be headed by a woman than the more mainstream spinning and weaving mills.

Firms run by women were not necessarily smaller than those run by men. The largest industrial complexes were usually headed by males, but this was not always the case. The Masurel family were one of the most prominent textile families in Tourcoing (and one of the first to turn the family firm into a share holding society in the early twentieth century). In 1897 the business was run by François Masurel's widow. It was composed of a wool combing and wool carding plant, a spinning mill, a twisting mill producing yarn for weaving and for knitting, a plant for manufacturing knitted garments and a dye works. With almost 50,000 spindles, the spinning mill accounted for a quarter of all the wool spindles in town. It was also the largest of its kind. Employing eighty-eight individuals, the dye works was also the largest in the town. Female-owned spinning mills were usually slightly smaller than the ones owned by men, but they were far from marginal businesses. Preparation and finishing included very tiny plants, but also very large ones like wool combing factories or dye works. One of the longest lasting was the Fouan-Leman wool combing firm, which 28-year-old Catherine Fouan-Leman took over from her husband in 1867, and which she ran until the First World War (her oldest son and designated successor died in the early twentieth century). One finds the same phenomenon in sectors where the male–female comparison is possible: women are underrepresented among the very big and very small businesses. One also notes that, in business cycle downturns, the proportion of firms headed by women increased as if women had better staying power!

The situation in Tourcoing therefore parallels the one in Lille. Women's involvement in manufacturing and wholesale trades decreases slightly in the middle of the century, but then recovers. The recovery seems to be due to the greater growth of the preparatory and finishing sectors, which were more feminized than spinning and weaving, which in turn were themselves less masculine than the wholesale trade (in other words, the older a sector was, the fewer the women). Simultaneously, the growth of the retail sector was accompanied by an increased feminization of that sector, particularly as a consequence of skilled workers' wives entry into this line of work. In short, economic growth, the emergence of new modes and new sectors of production, and the expansion of retailing did not have a negative impact on women's abilities to run their own business.

Cultural Shifts

Not all middle-class women had been economically active at the start of the century. Their granddaughters did not swap the account book for the prayer book. Female retailers, manufacturers and merchant traders remained important in the regional economy, but they were players that many forces conspired to hide, especially if they were married. The following is a good example of a 'hidden' business woman whose existence would have completely escaped us but for the survival of a document which did not directly concern her. In the late 1860s Auguste Allain, a merchant trader from Paris, formed an unlimited liability partnership with François Destombes, a merchant trader from Roubaix (immediately to the south of Tourcoing). One of the 'articles of association' forbade each partner to engage in any activity not related to the association – this was a customary clause. The article, however, continued thus:

> It is well understood that Mme Destombes may continue the trade in spinning mill equipment which she is currently carrying out under her husband's name. The latter owes the partnership his full commitment and will not get involved in his wife's business. The same clause applies to Mme Allain. The association will not be liable for the ladies' debts.[20]

If Mme Destombes ceased her activities before becoming a widow, or died before her husband, she probably left no other traces of her activities. Widows could go into business without raising eyebrows and so could unmarried women once they reached a given age and it became unlikely that they would ever marry. Younger women also helped in the family business, but they were even less visible than their mothers. But they too sometimes emerge unexpectedly from the sources.[21] In 1870 Désiré Darras-Lemaire, a spinner from Tourcoing, negotiated a 200,000 franc line of credit with the Caisse d'escompte de Lille. His wife was allowed to endorse financial instruments under the same conditions as him. But it was also agreed that 'Melle Victorine Darras, without occupation, residing in Tourcoing, is also granted the signature by her father and mother and authorized to obtain credit. Mr. and Mrs. Darras grant her all necessary power and authorization to that effect.' *No occupation?* It is hard to believe Melle Darras spent her days doing *petit point*! Moreover, the Darras-Lemaire spinning mill was no small factory; in 1867 it boasted 14,420 spindles.

These women, half hidden in administrative sources, are even less visible in contemporary written discourse and subsequent histories of the region. Pierre Legrand, a local writer and father of a member of parliament in the region was regretting in 1851 that the middle-class women of the time were disdaining the trades which their mothers had embraced.[22] Late nineteenth and early twentieth-century regional authors systematically mention the women pioneers of the industrial revolution in the area, but they have little to say about female activities after the arrival of the railways and the gas lights in the 1840s and 1850s. In the twentieth century the existence of these enterprising foremothers practically became an embarrassment. The non-involvement of middle-class women in family business appears to have become associated with 'modernity'. Jean Lambert-Dansette, a native of Armentière and member of a textile family, made a point mentioning these economically active female ancestors in the doctoral thesis on the textile entrepreneurial class that he defended in Paris in the early 1950s – but without any illusions about the reaction such a mention would provoke:

> The most remarkable characteristic of intra-familial solidarity was the role played by the women in the business, women who could genuinely be called 'enterprising women'. Their activities, which nowadays make the *more advanced members of the bourgeoisie smile condescendingly*, were almost universal in the previous century.[23] (my emphasis)

To be 'advanced' a mid-twentieth-century, middle-class woman did not have to bother with business. It was as if businesswomen belonged to a glorious, but definitively past, age in the region's history. This phenomenon is not specific to northern France. Kolleen Guy, who studied the Champagne industry in the nineteenth century, noted that several Champagne firms had been run by widows. These women took over the businesses in the first half of the nineteenth century, before the 'separate spheres' ideology had become established. But she also found that when late nineteenth-century scholars wrote the histories of the Champagne businesses, they refused to acknowledge these widows as independent businesswomen.

They systematically described them as sorrowful widows who piously preserved the legacy of their husbands.[24] These sources therefore seem to document the inexorable march of the 'separate spheres ideology' and the equally inexorable departure of middle-class women from the economic sphere, when in fact, as the evidence presented in this chapter has demonstrated, they merely construct a discourse at odds with everyday economic practices.

Notes

1. See, for example, Clark, 1919; Filton and Wadsworth; 1973; Clark, 1981; Chassagne, 1981; Prior, 1975; Butel, 1986; Davidoff and Hall, 1987; Collins, 1989; Hunt, 1996; Hafter, 1997; Musgrave, 1993; Rabuzzi, 1995; Beachy, 2001 and 2004.
2. Smith 1981; Davidoff and Hall, 1987; Alter, 1988; Crossick and Haupt, 1984 and 1995; Frevert, 1991; Chassagne, 1991; Verley, 1994; Sweets, 1995; Rabuzzi, 1995 and 2001; Hall, 1992; Hausen, 1981; Gray, 2000.
3. Richard, 1996.
4. Schrover, 1997.
5. Vickery, 1998.
6. Lemmens, 1987; Jaumain, 1993; Piette, 1996; Richard, 1996; Vickery, 1998; Van Molle and Heyrman, 2001; Beachy, 2001; Palazzi, 2002; Romero-Marín, 2001; Kay, 2001, and 2003a; Kurgan-van Hentenryk, 1996; Lane, 2000; Wiskin, 1999; Owens, 2001, 2002a and 2002b.
7. Murphy, 1987 and 1991; Lewis, 1992; Gamber, 1992 and 1998; Kwolek-Folland, 1998.
8. Scott, 1998.
9. Smith, 1981.
10. Trénard, 1977; Lottin, 1988; Pouchain, 1980 and 1998; Daumas, 2004.
11. Loi du 1er Brumaire an VII, Loi sur les finances du 25 Mars 1817, Loi du 25 avril 1844, Loi du 26 Juillet 1860, Loi du 15 Juillet 1880.
12. Archives municipales de Tourcoing AMTg, Matrices de patentes, 1814–51, G1C1–G1C2, Matrices de patentes, 1852–97, G1C3–G1C46, Recensements de 1851 et 1886 F1A4–5 et F1A 12–15, Table de population 1821–36 F1D1–2.
13. The consequence of this is that in Table 4.1 and 4.2 the numbers of wholesalers, manufacturers and retailers are far short of the total number of businesses listed in the directories. I included in 'retail' only categories which were unmistakably retail ones (grocers, fashion shops, for instance), and in manufacturing equally unambiguous entries (spinning mills, makers of chemical products, for instance).
14. The Matrices de patentes are incomplete before 1852, except for 1840. There

were too many retailers in 1886 to work on the whole town, therefore I limited myself to canton Nord, which comprises the northern half of the city and included half of the town centre and Grand Place.
15. Murphy 1987 and 1991; Lewis, 1992; Gamber, 1992 and 1998; Kwolek-Folland, 1998.
16. Crossick and Haupt, 1984 and 1995.
17. Crossick and Haupt, 1984 and 1995.
18. Codaccioni, 1976; Craig, 1998.
19. Partnerships where women are the main partner are counted among the female-headed businesses, and the ones where women are not the main partner among the male-headed firms. Almost all those female patente holders are widows.
20. Archives départmentales du Nord (ADN), Tribunal de commerce de Lille, Actes de sociétés, 6U2 650.
21. AND Enregistrement, enregistrement des hypothèques, 4Q38 674 1870.
22. Legrand, 1852.
23. Lambert-Dansette, 1954, p. 594.
24. Guy, 1997.

–5–

Profit and Propriety
Sophie Henschel and Gender Management in the German Locomotive Industry

Robert Beachy

Introduction

The year 1910 marked an important anniversary and production milestone for Imperial Germany's largest locomotive manufacturer, Henschel & Sohn. Located in Kassel, the enormous industrial complex, owned and managed by Widow Sophie Henschel and her son Carl, traced its 100-year history to the machine tool factory founded by earlier Henschel generations. The centennial also coincided, auspiciously, with the completion of the Henschels' 10,000th locomotive, an achievement that placed the firm far ahead of its closest German competitors.

Private family celebrations began on 14 August with a memorial service at the family gravesite for Sophie Henschel's husband, Oskar, who had died in 1894. Public festivities commenced the next day with a ceremony in the factory, attended by German and foreign dignitaries representing all corners of the globe. The day was capped by a banquet held in Kassel's city courthouse and attended by 200 invited guests. In his speech to the assembled guests, published the following day in the local newspaper, Kassel's ruling burgomaster honoured the 'restless energy and untiring activity of Herr Henschel [Sophie's son Carl]'. He also commended the 'quiet activity of a woman [Widow Henschel] who has worked for decades to ameliorate the sickness and need of the Henschel employees, making the work of compassion and charity her life's mission'.[1]

The occasion was given a more lasting memorial with the publication of an oversized glossy book or *Denkschrift*. Replete with drawings, photos, blueprints and documents, the *Denkschrift* presented a carefully constructed image of Henschel & Sohn, intended for public consumption. Detailed bird's-eye paintings captured the production complex in Kassel, a nearby factory in Rothenditmold, and the firm's own steel mill. High-quality photographs showed Henschel workers in shop and assembly rooms, as well as engineers, managers and salesmen working at drafting tables and desks. The centrepiece of these images was some thirteen pages of photographs presenting the dozens of different locomotives constructed by the Henschel firm for a range of German, European, South American and Asian railways.[2]

The complex engineering of these powerful machines symbolized not only the accomplishments of the family firm but also the industrial might and global economic reach of Imperial Germany. Befitting the national role of such an important business, the *Denkschrift* recounted the history of the entrepreneurial Henschel family and lionized its achievements. The introduction included a full-page portrait of Sophie's son Carl, suggesting his prominence in the firm. According to the *Denkschrift*, Carl entered the business in 1896 following the death of his father Oskar – Sophie's husband – two years earlier. Just as Carl's father had been forced to assume control in 1860 upon *his* father's death, the *Denkschrift* explained, now 'the burden of the business rested on the shoulders of a still young man [Carl Henschel], who with courage and resolve began his life's work'.[3] This account further praised young Henschel's energetic leadership and expansion of the business, which kept to the vision of his father.

In this official firm biography, Sophie Henschel played a significant role but not one that directly involved the management of Henschel & Sohn. Much like the encomium delivered by Kassel's burgomaster, the *Denkschrift* applauded her philanthropic work. Boasting of Henschel & Sohn's excellent labour relations, the commemorative volume attributed the manifest satisfaction of the Henschel employees, the 'good working conditions and salaries' and the firm's welfare institutions to the 'unwavering engagement of the widowed *Frau Geheimrat* Sophie Henschel'.[4] Of course, a paternalistic labour policy represented an important element of Henschel & Sohn's public image, and the *Denkschrift* devoted its closing chapters to the many services enjoyed by Henschel employees. Health and accident insurance and old-age pensions, as well as emergency funds for invalids, widows and orphans, were among the philanthropic projects funded and directed by the Widow. Sophie Henschel was also credited for the range of company institutions, including schools, social housing and recreational facilities, that the Henschel Firm had developed over the years.[5] While her husband and son were depicted as firm patriarchs, Sophie Henschel appeared as a benevolent mother who monitored the well-being of her extended factory family.

The firm history was extremely misleading, however, and not least for ignoring the entrepreneurial contributions of Widow Henschel. Before his death in 1894, Oskar Henschel conferred sole ownership and control on his wife. Only later could their only son Carl begin formal employment, and not until 1900 did Widow Henschel finally allow her son, now 27 years old, a formal partnership with signing privileges. Despite suffering a stroke that same year, the Widow-proprietress maintained her position as director until 1912, when at the age of 70 she finally retired and ceded control to Carl. But both the 1910 *Denkschrift* and the public ceremonies misrepresented Widow Henschel's leadership. If Sophie Henschel was both proprietor and chief executive, why would she allow her own contributions to go unrecognized?

These representations of Sophie Henschel (and of her son) offer a perfect illustration of the work of a powerful 'separate spheres' ideology.[6] Leadership of an industrial concern like Henschel & Sohn was scarcely suited to an elite bourgeois widow. Not only was it inappropriate for Sophie Henschel to assume credit for her family's phenomenal business success. It was likewise unseemly that a woman be seen to direct the largest company in a major German industrial sector.[7] Henschel & Sohn, an industrial behemoth with national economic importance, could ill afford to present itself as a firm owned and operated by a woman. Viewed as the provisional owner-director, Sophie Henschel might bridge male generations, assuming a temporary role in her husband's stead. The 1910 *Denkschrift* suggested as much, explaining that the 'administration of the inheritance went first to the widow' after 1894.[8] But as the *Denkschrift* implied, Sophie Henschel's service was a stopgap measure until her son could assume his rightful place. Not appropriate for management, Widow Henschel was instead assigned a more gender-appropriate function as the patroness of charity.

As much recent feminist scholarship has proposed, the ideal of 'separate spheres' was truly ideological, a prescriptive set of norms often defied by social and economic realities.[9] Like most contributions to this volume, this chapter questions the ability of 'separate spheres' to account for the complex and often contradictory economic roles played by nineteenth-century bourgeois women; the case of an industrial magnate like Sophie Henschel is especially difficult. Widow Henschel not only managed her marital patrimony for nearly twenty years. She also determined when and how her own son might participate in his father's business. Well after Carl Henschel had reached his majority, Widow Henschel continued holding the reigns of power. Even the formal terms of her retirement in 1912 included an established legal right to review any major decisions affecting the business.

Yet public images of Sophie Henschel, at least those projected during her lifetime, were so misleading that we can only assume that she managed them as effectively as she managed the firm itself. As I will argue, Sophie Henschel actively participated in a phenomenal charade. Instead of openly acknowledging her power, Henschel assumed a less public role – one that kept her out of the limelight – and promoted instead the perception of her son's leadership. She carefully cultivated her reputation for philanthropic work and pursued 'appropriate' forms of female civic activism, including membership of the 'Patriotic Women's Association' (*Vaterländischer Frauen-Verein*), a German-nationalist women's philanthropic organization whose Kassel chapter she helped to organize in 1869.

This clever combination of civic involvement and charitable work projected the perfect image of bourgeois feminine propriety. Arguably, it also obscured the fact that Henschel never ceded control of Henschel & Sohn and was primarily responsible for the firm's tremendous growth in the decades following the death of her husband. For the sake of her own business interests, Sophie Henschel negotiated and manipulated the cultural parameters of a 'separate spheres' ideology. Her discreet 'gender management' – of both Henschel & Sohn and her own public image – illustrate the social and cultural faultiness of late nineteenth-century business elites.[10]

Henschel & Sohn, a Family Firm

The firm Henschel & Sohn claimed 1810 as its founding date, the year Georg Christian (1759–1835) and his son Carl Anton (1780–1861) formally opened a machine-tool factory. However, the Henschels proudly traced their metalworking tradition as far back as the seventeenth century and had received exclusive Hesse patents for casting bells and firearms in the 1780s. Carl Anton began experimenting with the design and construction of steam-powered carriages in the early nineteenth century, and his son Carl (1810–60) investigated English locomotive manufacturing and railway construction as a student travelling in England in the 1830s. By 1848 the firm had produced its very first locomotive for a railway line in the state of Hesse.[11]

By this point Henschel & Sohn already employed over 200 workers, reflecting the growth fostered by several Henschel generations. This successful family management naturally shaped the expectations of Oskar Henschel, who was born in Kassel in 1837. The young industrial scion attended school in Kassel and was later tutored at home. In 1855 he travelled to the Parisian World's Fair with his father and then began studies at a vocational and engineering school (*Polytechnikum*) in Karlsruhe. Oskar Henschel entered the family firm in 1857, and by 1859, at the age of 21, was made a formal partner. Following his father's death one year later, Oskar became the firm's director. The year 1860 also marked the completion of the 50th Henschel locomotive, and the firm now employed some 350 workers. Still a very young man, Oskar Henschel married Sophie Caesar in 1862.[12]

Sophie Henschel's own background was one of privilege and social distinction. Her paternal grandfather Friedrich Wilhelm Caesar was a successful wholesale merchant in Bremen. Her father Clemens Theodor, in contrast, purchased an estate in Westphalia, trading a commercial vocation for the life of a country gentleman. As a landed bourgeois *rentier*, Sophie's father was offered a Prussian patent of nobility in 1840, which he refused, since 'he found it more appropriate for himself and his children to belong to the bourgeois estate'.[13] Clemens Theodor did accept an appointment to the upper house of the Prussian Diet in 1850 just before his death. Sophie was born on the family estate in 1841, but soon after her father's death moved with her mother to Kassel at the age of 10, where she later met her husband.

Sophie and Oskar Henschel were considered an improbable pair by some friends and observers. In her unpublished memoirs, Sophie recorded how a trusted older friend of the Henschel family advised Oskar against choosing Sophie has his bride: 'He told him [Oskar] he had heard that I'm a *Blaustrumpf* (bluestocking) and the daughter of an estate owner and was certainly not suited to be the wife of a factory owner.'[14] But the Henschel match produced not only a companionate marriage – Sophie was only four years younger than Oskar – but also a committed working relationship that furthered the interests of the business. Instead of a proper honeymoon, the young newlyweds visited an old friend of Sophie's family, the Cologne banker W. L. Deichmann, whose positive impressions of Oskar and of Henschel & Sohn inspired him to extend a generous line of credit, allowing a significant expansion of the firm and its production. Sophie Henschel played an even more direct role in the firm, informing herself of all aspects of the business. During his frequent travels to secure new contracts, Oskar Henschel sent long, detailed reports, which Sophie vetted and responded to on a daily basis. From his research in the 1970s, business historian Wilhelm Treue reported finding over 1,000 letters exchanged between husband and wife, all of which have been lost or destroyed.[15]

This early phase of their marriage witnessed dramatic growth for Henschel & Sohn. Following the Austro-Prussian War of 1866, Hesse-Kassel was incorporated into the Prussian state. When King Wilhelm I visited in 1867, Oskar made his acquaintance, and later that year hosted the monarch's visit to the factory. Soon after this Henschel received the title of Prussian *Kommerzienrat* (Commercial Counsel), an honorific that signalled his economic importance to the Prussian state. In 1875 Oskar Henschel was recognized again, this time as *Geheimer Kommerzienrat* (Privy Commercial Counsel). These titles facilitated access to the Berlin Court and served Henschel & Sohn very well after the Franco-Prussian War of 1870. Both French war reparations and German unification in 1871 fuelled an economic boom, which increased the construction of railroads and in turn the demand for locomotives.[16]

The development of Henschel & Sohn also placed new pressures on the family management of the firm. As Jürgen Kocka has noted, the 'process of industrial bureaucratization' that accompanied rapid growth in the last third of the nineteenth century compelled many family-owned businesses to professionalize their traditional management structures. Of course, trained outsiders were often more competent than spoiled family members who might enter the firm unwillingly or expect a leadership position as birthright. The obvious conflict between the interests of the firm and those of family members generated unbearable tensions that could lead to financial ruin. While Henschel & Sohn avoided these strains, expansion created pressures to develop a more formal management structure.[17]

Henschel & Sohn remained family owned and operated, but elements of this bureaucratization process are clear. In 1867 Oskar Henschel offered his sister's brother, Ferdinand Gerland, a generous employment contract that included 3 per cent of the firm's profits. Within six months Gerland also received signing privileges. By 1869 Henschel had introduced new management practices that included daily business conferences with Gerland and the other firm directors, among them half a dozen engineers and sales managers. The selection of Gerland – as a brother-in-law – set a significant precedent, however, by restricting the firm's ranking directors to family members. Up until the death of Oskar Henschel in 1894, management of Henschel & Sohn remained entirely within the family, a critical factor for explaining the later influence of Sophie Henschel.[18]

In the medium term, however, this development marginalized the participation of Sophie, who increasingly filled the traditional role of domestic helpmate and hostess. Analysis of the differentiation and gendering of spheres has always emphasized the physical separation of work and domestic spaces and the removal of women from the 'masculine' realm of production.[19] The stereotype corresponds well, at least superficially, to the evolving work and residential arrangements of the Henschel family. In 1871 Oskar, Sophie and their three daughters (born in 1863, 1865 and 1868) moved out of their quarters on the factory campus and into a new villa, some 25 minutes distant on foot. (This was also where the Henschel's fourth child and only son, Carl, was born in 1873.)[20]

This grand family home not only distanced Sophie from her husband's workplace. It also created a new set of responsibilities and preoccupations. With her involvement in a number of women's associations after 1867, Sophie Henschel found herself drawn into the circles of Kassel's local elite. Her social position transcended Kassel, moreover, and in October 1871 the Henschels hosted the Prussian Crown Prince and his family in their new villa. Through philanthropic work and social engagements, Henschel not only filled her days with a whirl of activities but also played an important role as the representative wife of one of Germany's leading young industrialists.[21]

Yet the good economic fortunes of the *Gründerzeit* (the period of German unification) soon gave way to the depression that followed the stock-market crash of 1873. The struggle to compete with other German locomotive manufacturers forced Henschel to lower prices and ultimately to lay off workers. From 1875 to 1880, the number of locomotives produced annually sank from 107 to just 61. In this same period Henschel's employment force dropped from 1700 to 718. The crisis forced Oskar Henschel to resume travelling himself to promote the company and secure contracts. In turn, Sophie re-established her role as her husband's representative, not only in his absence but also when resident and working in Kassel.[22]

Even though Henschel production and employment numbers recovered rapidly after 1880, Sophie Henschel remained firmly ensconced in her husband's business affairs. This also represented another period of tremendous expansion. After 1885, the firm averaged 200 locomotives per year and completed its 3,000th machine in 1890. Henschel & Sohn also emerged as the dominant German locomotive manufacturer and controlled 50 per cent of the domestic market in 1890.[23]

The strains of business took its toll, however, and by 1891 Oskar was suffering from a broad range of ailments. Increasingly incapacitated or away at health spas, Oskar relied that much more on Sophie, not only for sickbed comfort but also as his unofficial representative. A lung infection hastened Oskar's death in 1894, and Sophie became the sole heir of Henschel & Sohn. The testament which the couple had drawn up in 1887 stated: 'We mutually bequeath the other life-long use and the full unconditional administration along with the free disposition of the substance of our estate and we free the surviving member from any type of inventory, the placing of security, or accounting, so that he or she can immediately control and administer the estate of the one who died first.'[24] As a will drafted mutually by husband and wife with identical terms for both, this represented a truly remarkable document. Not only did Oskar disregard his son Carl – now already 21 years old – he entrusted the entire Henschel concern to his wife.[25] The absolute confidence that Oskar placed in Sophie reveals not only his profound respect for her judgement but also the manifest expertise with which she had earned it.

Sophie Henschel as Firm Manager

If faced with a daunting responsibility, Widow Henschel never wavered in asserting not only her control but also an unbending independence. Both the size and the complexity of Henschel & Sohn – employing a cadre of engineers and mechanics and thousands of highly skilled workers – threatened to undermine family control. The same forces that compelled Oskar Henschel to rationalize management in the 1860s now placed pressure on Widow Henschel to reorganize the firm as a joint-stock company. Large family firms often faced difficulties when one generation succeeded the next, even with a son or nephew at the helm. The expectation that Sophie would yield her authority to a board of stockholders was that much greater since few anticipated her abilities or willingness to use them.

Incorporating Henschel & Sohn would certainly have conformed to the broader trend among German industrial enterprises. According to Jürgen Kocka, by 1887 only fifteen of Germany's 100 largest enterprises – including Henschel & Sohn – remained 'partnerships' or privately held firms. Counting Henschel & Sohn, only seven of the largest 100 German businesses still held this status just ten years later.[26] This was clearly the result of Sophie's ability and resolve. Within months of Oskar's death, the Cologne banking house Sal. Oppenheim jr. & Cie, which had maintained close ties to Sophie's old family friend Deichmann, inquired discreetly to learn if Sophie were interested in transforming Henschel & Sohn into a joint-stock company. Her immediate response was 'no'.[27]

Widow Henschel was equally decisive if unobtrusive in her management style. According to business historian Wilhelm Treue, she avoided making appearances in the factory – unlike Oskar, who always observed his workers and engineers first hand – and 'ruled' instead from her villa offices 'through a *Kabinett*' of directors. Since it was inappropriate for her to travel or represent the firm formally, her villa also served as a place for business meetings and the reception of guests and business associates. Based on verbal and written reports, she made decisions and gave directions, but also delegated certain responsibilities, though always with clear restrictions and controls.[28]

She was also aggressive in expanding the firm so that it remained competitive. Begun just before Oskar's death, a new industrial foundry for locomotive boilers was completed and opened in 1896 in Rothenditmold (a neighbouring village later incorporated as a Kassel suburb). One of the Widow's greatest successes was modernizing the Kassel factory complex, a project begun in 1896 and completed in 1904. This allowed the firm to meet the competition of Germany's other locomotive manufacturers, including Borsig and Hanomag.[29] While production had stagnated in the 1890s, falling from 286 locomotives in 1891 to just 169 in 1894, the number increased again to 294 by 1899, reaching 374 by 1904.[30]

Perhaps the most telling evidence of Widow Henschel's authority was the power she wielded over her only son Carl. Although his birth in 1873 was celebrated as the arrival of a future firm executive, Carl was a sickly and unimpressive youth. In his will, Oskar Henschel had directed: 'If our son Carl has achieved the necessary perspective and diligence after completing his practical and theoretical studies to run the factory ... my wife can turn the operation of the factory over to him ... More specifically this remains the judgement of my wife alone, especially whether he should direct the firm entirely on his own or only in part.'[31] In effect, Carl's ability and aptitude caused serious concern for both of his parents, and Sophie was specifically charged with determining Carl's suitability for leadership of the firm.

To the end of preparing Carl for a position, Sophie sent him regular business reports. With the completion of his military service in 1895, Carl had planned to study at the University of Darmstadt. This was delayed and ultimately abandoned, however, due to a case of acute appendicitis, which required an operation. While recovering on a trip to London in the summer of 1896, Carl reported to his mother that he was considering an engagement with an English woman. Widow Henschel responded:

> when you write of engagement, I never know if this is meant in earnest or jest. Thanks to papa's tireless work, you, like your sisters, are able to follow your heart without

worrying about a dowry. That you choose to marry into a solid and honourable family is self-understood. ... It is also in your own interest that the girl is from a healthy family and both vibrant and capable.[32]

Carl returned to Kassel and took up a position in the factory in 1896. But he travelled back to London in the summer of 1898 and married his fiancée there before bringing her to Germany.

Widow Henschel made few concessions either to her son or her directors, and, despite suffering a mild stroke in 1900 and undergoing surgery for cataracts in 1905, she continued to guide the business as independently as before. After 1900 she also presided over a dramatic shift in the firm's top management. Her most trusted advisor – her husband's brother-in-law Ferdinand Gerland – had already retired in 1897, and another senior director, August Schäffer, retired after fifty-two years with the firm in 1904. Sophie now turned increasingly to trained engineers and merchants to fill top managerial positions.[33] The performance of Carl rather diminished than bolstered her confidence in him and likewise strengthened her resolve to preserve her own control. At Carl's initiative, the firm purchased an iron and steel works for 2.5 million marks. This proved a foolish investment, however, and required huge capital investments drawn from the Henschels' private family foundation.[34]

Despite these losses, the wise administration of Widow Henschel, especially the factory expansion completed in 1904, supported an impressive increase in production. By 1909, Henschel & Sohn controlled just under 30 per cent of the domestic market, nearly double the share of its closest competitor. At the end of the decade, the factory employed some 3,000 workers and delivered – within a twelve-month period – more than 1,000 locomotives. Half of these fulfilled German contracts, and roughly the same number was shipped to European, Asian and South American customers.[35] Carl Henschel was credited with much of this business, since his activity included drumming up foreign sales. In 1904 Carl had represented the firm at the World's Fair in St Louis, where he also accepted a prize awarded to Henschel & Sohn for the fastest locomotive.[36]

As Widow Henschel aged and Carl increasingly proved his merit, a changing of the guard became foreseeable. The fabulous success of Henschel & Sohn likely influenced Sophie, but so did the improved fortunes of Carl's personal life. In 1906, after eight difficult years of marriage, Carl's English wife finally left him. Following a speedy divorce, Carl was soon engaged, but this time to the daughter of a Prussian general and *Freiherr* (baron). Carl's fiancée Hildegard von Scheffer represented a far more appropriate match and even shared Sophie's philanthropic and associational interests. With Widow Henschel's blessing, the marriage took place in Kassel in 1909.[37]

In 1911 Sophie Henschel celebrated her 70th birthday, which was recognized not only by local dignitaries but also with a telegram from German Empress

Augusta Victoria. Now a very old woman and satisfied that both her husband's and her own life's work was secure, Widow Henschel agreed to relinquish her control to Carl. But before signing over her rights, she demanded that he submit a written agreement recognizing the terms of her retirement. She insisted on receiving the monthly management reports and on the right to request information about business matters from her son or employees. She also required that Carl discuss with her any larger decisions involving acquisitions or changes to the factory. Finally, she demanded that Carl never incorporate the factory as a joint-stock company or allow company shares to fall into the hands of outsiders. Following the advice of his financial director, Carl refused his mother's final demand and agreed only to provide her with unlimited information on business affairs. If unable to control Henschel & Sohn from the grave, the Widow would at least monitor her son's management until the very end of her life.[38]

Sophie Henschel as Philanthropist

Though Widow Henschel retreated from company governance after 1912, she maintained her philanthropic and civic engagement until her death in 1915. One of her chief commitments was to the *Vaterländischer Frauen-Verein* ('Patriotic Women's Association'). Founded by Prussian Queen Augusta on armistice day at the end of the Prussian – Austrian war in November 1866, the Berlin-based organization was a response to the nursing and hospice needs of the war wounded and later helped to co-ordinate the International Red Cross in Germany. At the outbreak of war in the summer of 1866, Sophie Henschel worked with other Kassel women to support wounded soldiers. This early initiative forged the associational core of Kassel's *Vaterländischer Frauen-Verein*, which Henschel helped to found in 1869. From its inception, Sophie served as a member of the board of directors and in 1879 she was elected chairwoman.[39]

Following Prussia's annexation of Hesse-Kassel, the new chapter demonstrated its loyalty to the Hohenzollern dynasty and embraced the Queen as patron and sponsor. According to Jean Quataert, these groups linked the associational culture of bourgeois women with aristocratic and dynastic patronage in a patriotic compact. The groups were loosely organized across the North German Confederation after 1866 but then consolidated within a national structure following German unification in 1871. Participants typically included bourgeois and civic elites as well as aristocratic women. Sophie's counterpart, wife of the 'locomotive king' Borsig (who represented Henschel's chief competition at this time), joined the Berlin chapter in 1867. Significantly, the first Prussian president of the society, Countess Charlotte von Itzenplitz, was also the daughter of the Prussian minister of commerce who presided over railroad concessions. Sophie's life-long participation secured her the friendship of the Prussian empresses, moreover, contributing to the profile of Henschel & Sohn. For her donations of time and money following the Franco-Prussian War in 1870, she received the Imperial Service Cross for Women and Girls.[40]

Under Sophie's leadership, the Kassel *Vaterländischer Frauen-Verein* raised funds for the construction of a Red Cross Hospital, which was opened in Kassel in 1882. In recognition of this and her other services, Henschel was elected to the national board of the *Vaterländischer Frauen-Verein* in Berlin and likewise given the medal of the Prussian Order of Luise, First Class, Second Division, which recognized the social engagement of women. Five years later, in 1887, Henschel was made a formal member of the Order of Luise, with the 'permission of Emperor Wilhelm I'.[41] Founded by Prussian King Frederick William in 1814 to commemorate his deceased wife Queen Luise (1776–1810), the Order of Luise initially recognized women's contributions during the Napoleonic wars and later acknowledged humanitarian and social service. Formal membership meant that Henschel might participate in the Order's social events held in Berlin.[42] Sophie's appointment in 1887 was especially gratifying since she filled the position that had just been opened by the death of Frau Borsig. The timing was conspicuous since Henschel & Sohn had recently displaced Borsig as Imperial Germany's top locomotive producer. In effect, Henschel's social recognition corresponded closely to the position of the family firm.[43]

The welfare of Henschel & Sohn employees was also an important object of Sophie's philanthropic activism. Like other large nineteenth-century German industrial concerns, Henschel & Sohn provided its workers with a range of institutions and services, a paternalistic tradition that can be traced back to the social housing built by the Fugger banking family in sixteenth-century Augsburg. The motivations behind the 'social policy' of German industrial firms were certainly humanistic, but they also reflected efforts to prevent unionization and stem the appeal of the German Social Democratic Party. The insurance programmes of Henschel & Sohn and other concerns also provided a model for the state welfare programmes introduced in 1881 by Bismarck, who was motivated similarly by a desire to marginalize the German Socialists.[44]

Already in 1854 the Henschels had begun providing health insurance for their employees, and they followed this with a special fund for invalids, widows and orphans in 1866. These programmes were augmented in 1887 with a 30,000 mark endowment, which commemorated the twenty-fifth wedding anniversary of Oskar and Sophie, who supplemented the fund with 100,000 marks following Oskar's death in 1894. A fund for the convalescence of sick or injured workers was created in 1898, but later folded into the broader health insurance offering. In 1899 a separate pension fund for white-collar employees, and their widows and orphans, was established. The firm constructed low-cost housing for blue-collar and later managerial employees. By 1890 more than 120 'Henschel families' were housed in economical company apartments, and by 1914 this figure exceeded 500. The firm also provided domestic skills training for workers' wives and daughters, a kindergarten, and in 1905 an industrial training center for 400 apprentices. Other company benefits included small cash bonuses to commemorate special occasions as well as sponsorship of choral and gymnastics associations. Most of these programmes and bonuses were introduced to mark special occasions, particularly production milestones and Henschel family birthdays and weddings but also national holidays.[45]

Conclusion

While recognized already in the 1870s for her work in the *Vaterländischer Frauen-Verein*, Widow Henschel was increasingly extolled as a model of social-welfare activism after Oskar's death in 1894. Her profile as a member of the Order of Luise (and her association with the Hohenzollern court in Berlin) brought her not only local but also national recognition. Public celebrations and firm commemorations singled her out for her philanthropic leadership. Like the 1910 *Denkschrift* marking Henschel & Sohn's centennial, an 1899 publication commemorating the 5,000th Henschel locomotive cited the Widow's philanthropic activities.

Yet these same volumes studiously ignored her role as an entrepreneur. Instead of identifying Sophie as the legitimate and highly effective successor to Oskar Henschel, the 1899 volume included the portraits of five Henschel generations, concluding with her son Carl. Sophie herself was nowhere to be seen.[46] But at this point she had still not given Carl formal partnership or signing privileges. Moreover, Widow Henschel never relinquished her covert management until 1912. A gesture of modesty, perhaps, her self-effacing manipulation of the firm's image reflected more than 'feminine' reticence. Sophie Henschel successfully managed not only the public representations of Henschel & Sohn. She also managed quite self-consciously the images of her own gender.

Acknowledgement

I would like to thank Dr Kerstin Wolff and Dr Ortrud Wörner-Heil from the Archiv der deutschen Frauenbewegung in Kassel for their help in clarifying the apparent loss of the family and firm archive of Sophie Henschel and Henschel & Sohn.

Notes

1. See the commemorative brochure *Zur Erinnerung an die Feiern am 14. und 15. August 1910 aus Anlass der Vollendung der Lokomotive Fabriknummer*

10,000 und des hundertjährigen Bestehens der Firma Henschel & Sohn (1910), Kassel: Henschel & Sohn.
2. *Denkschrift aus Anlass des hundertjährigen Bestehens der Maschinen- und Lokomotivfabrik Henschel & Sohn Cassel und der Vollendung der Lokomotive Fabriknummer 10000* (1910), Kassel: Henschel & Sohn.
3. Ibid., p. 21.
4. Ibid., p. 115.
5. Ibid., p. 115–45.
6. Davidoff and Hall, 1987; Smith, 1981
7. Augustine, 1994; Frevert, 1995.
8. *Denkschrift*, 1910, p. 18.
9. Vickery, 1993; Trepp, 1996; Habermas, 2000; Beachy, 2001.
10. Frevert, 1990 and 1995; Gall, 1989; Evans, 1991; and Augustine, 1991.
11. German business historian Wilhelm Treue published a short firm biography of Henschel & Sohn (1974–5), and more recently Heidemarie Ecker-Ertle published a dissertation on Sophie Henschel (1998). Tragically, the private family and firm archive that both historians relied on for their research has since been destroyed. Along with Henschel & Sohn company publications, these works provide an important basic context for this chapter.
12. *Denkschrift*, 1910, p. 16; Meinhold, 1942; Treue, 1974, pp. 4–5.
13. Ecker-Ertle, 1998, p. 53.
14. Treue, 1975, p. 4.
15. Ibid., p. 12.
16. Ecker-Ertle, 1998, pp. 79–81.
17. Kocka, 1999a, p. 39.
18. Treue, 1975, pp. 7–8; Ecker-Ertle, 1998, pp. 79–80.
19. Brunner, 1968; Hausen, 1981; Davidoff and Hall, 1987; Kocka, 1999b.
20. *Denkschrift*, 1910, p. 21.
21. Ecker-Ertle, 1998, pp. pp. 81–6.
22. Ibid., pp. 93–7.
23. Ibid., p. 99.
24. Treue, 1975, p. 9.
25. Although married women controlled their own property in Hesse-Kassel, the liberality of Oskar Henschel was still uncharacteristic of late nineteenth-century businessmen. See Holthöfer, 1997; Gerhard, 1978; Spree, 1994; and Vogel, 1993.
26. Kocka, 1999c, p. 166.
27. Treue, 1975, p. 11.
28. Ibid., p. 10.
29. Ibid., p. 14.
30. Ibid., Ecker-Ertle, 1998, pp. 138–40.

31. Ecker-Ertle, 1998, p. 125.
32. Ibid., p. 142.
33. Ibid., pp. 150–4.
34. Ibid., pp. 152–4.
35. Ibid., p. 153.
36. The firm published a large pamphlet in German, English, French and Spanish commemorating its prize-winning locomotive: *Weltaustellung – St. Louis 1904 – Henschel & Sohn Lokomotivfabrik*, 1904.
37. Ecker-Ertle, 1998, pp. 156–7.
38. Ibid., pp. 180–4.
39. Ibid., pp. 118–20.
40. Quataert, 2001, pp. 67–74.
41. Ecker-Ertle, 1998, pp. 121–3.
42. Quataert, 2001, pp. 170–4; Hagemann, 2002.
43. Ecker-Ertle, 1998, p. 123.
44. Fischer, 1978; Sachbe and Tennstedt, 1988; Schulz, 1991; Steinmetz, 1993; Hilger, 1996.
45. Ecker-Ertle, 1998, pp. 112–14, 184–8; Wörner-Heil, 2002, p. 37.
46. *Rückblick*, 1899.

–6–

Artisan Women and Management in Nineteenth-century Barcelona

Juanjo Romero-Marín

> The strength of a chain relies on its weakest link
> Spanish proverb

Introduction

For centuries Spanish trade guilds – the institutions that regulated craftsmen's lives and activities in the *ancien régime* – controlled urban manufacturing. The methods of work, the standards of production, labour relations and, above all, guild access were carefully prescribed and monitored. In the 1830s liberal politicians gained control of the Spanish state and then banned guilds and other labour associations. This also spurred the beginning of an industrial revolution in Barcelona, transforming the city's social structure and economy. While the rest of Spain's agricultural base remained unaffected, these changes stimulated the reorganization of the social and professional strategies of Barcelona's artisans, which ultimately strengthened family and kinship structures. In this new context the women of guild families participated increasingly as shop workers and managers and contributed to a new artisan strategy for coping with modernization.

This response by Barcelona's artisans was different from that of other middle-class groups. Unfortunately, there is no systematic study of Barcelona's or Spain's nineteenth-century trades. Apart from the pioneering book of Vicens, which focused on the first industrial manufacturers, or the more recent work of McDonogh and Solà,[1] small manufacturers have inspired little interest. In the Spanish case, manufacturing women have recently attracted more attention, though general analysis remains scarce, and the focus has been directed exclusively to lace-making.[2] In the field of labour history, work on artisan women – in this case 'journeywomen' – simply does not exist.[3] In general, most of these studies have adopted a 'separate spheres' paradigm, following the work of Davidoff and Hall, that assumes that middle-class women retreated into a cocoon of domesticity.[4] This model reflects the ideological distinctions between public and private spheres in nineteenth-century

Spain promoted – perhaps ironically – by both liberal culture and the Catholic Church. However, as Vickery has emphasized, the separate spheres paradigm provides a *prescriptive* ideology rather than an *analytical* approach.[5] While Spanish historiography has produced a number of different perspectives on relations of gender in nineteenth-century Spain, these works have been limited to the working class.[6]

This chapter will address this thematic void and offer a general approach to the artisan women who managed and *co-managed* craft businesses in nineteenth-century Barcelona. The analytical perspective taken here is based on family strategies and the life courses of women rather than on labour-market segmentation or business history. This approach also rejects older methodologies that adopted notions of gendered or separate spheres. On the contrary, as we will see, the intersection of traditionally gendered spaces was a prominent feature of the response of Barcelona's artisans to modernization. In order to analyse this process the chapter will be organized in four main sections. The first provides a short description of Barcelona's economic and political development in the nineteenth century, paying special attention to the last years of the guilds. The second section considers the new definition of the trades after the abolition of the guilds and explores the character of the workshop and of family relations. The third and fourth sections explain the role of craftswomen within family-run artisan businesses and women's management within the context of new trade and industrial policies.

Nineteenth-century Barcelona

The Spanish *ancien régime* collapsed in 1833 with the death of the last absolutist sovereign, and, after a three-year civil war, liberals assumed control of the national government.[7] The first liberal decrees on 'Freedom of Trade' affected the guilds, and two laws promulgated in 1834 and 1836 abolished all Spanish trade and craft corporations. These measures taken against the traditional trade guilds were not accompanied by any kind of compensation, however, and a new restrictive electoral system based on corporate suffrage excluded most craftsmen from the political arena until the end of the century.

The corporate guilds had been the foundation of the urban crafts in *ancien régime* Spain, and were particularly strong in Madrid, Valencia and Barcelona. To become an artisan or run a workshop was impossible outside of such a corporate structure. Guild ordinances regulated access to the trades, the number of shops run by a single master, and the number of workers employed in a single workshop – all efforts to create an egalitarian community. This organization of labour adapted urban manufacturing to the *ancien régime* economy, which was characterized by a geographically stable industrial development under a strict social hierarchy.

This guild regulation had an obvious effect on women, since Barcelona trade ordinances strictly prohibited women from working in city crafts or from managing workshops. These trade regulations – most of them reformed at the end of the eighteenth century to conform to the Bourbons' mercantilist policies – excluded women from controlling workshops, including even masters' widows.[8] The guilds forced the widows of their own deceased masters either to hire a master or to marry another guild member. For example, the locksmith's widow Teresa Bartomeu was obliged to place a master in the workshop she had run for years with her husband in 1836, even after the 1834 anti-guilds legislation.[9] Of course, the guilds' aims were again to limit competition and if possible open workshops to unemployed masters, in this case through marriage with a master's widow.

Barcelona's guilds were not completely closed, however, and the sons of non-crafts families often gained access (Table 6.1). This meant that every boy who successfully completed the apprenticeship, the journeyman period and the master's exams could achieve the category of independent artisan and establish his own shop with guild approval and support. This career remained closed to women, however, and especially to women from non-artisan families.

By the 1830s Barcelona was fast becoming Spain's first, largest and – until the late nineteenth century – only industrial city. During the second half of the eighteenth century Barcelona's calico print workshops mushroomed, producing for Spanish colonial markets, and the first large steam-powered factory was built in 1832. Modern cotton factories then propelled the urban economy, stimulating not only industrial but also commercial sectors. In the next half century, at least until the 1880s, Barcelona functioned as the 'Factory of Spain', producing consumer goods for the rest of the country.[10]

These economic changes affected traditional artisan manufacturing not so much through the competition of new industry but because Barcelona entered a matrix of national and international economic networks, which included migration flows. The city's population doubled from 80,000 inhabitants in 1818 to 160,000 by 1864. Some trades such as cloth making (tailors, lace-makers and embroiderers) had to deal with the pressure created by external and inexpensive imports. At the same time most independent artisans continued to dominate the local market, which increased due to the population growth and the affluence of emerging middle classes. The work methods and products of small craftsmen's workshops remained under the control of family businesses whose labour skills could satisfy a closed market. Following the paradigm of Sabel and Zeitlin, Barcelona's artisan manufacturers can be defined in economic terms by 'flexible specialization', in which they co-existed and thrived alongside the mass production of large cotton factories.[11]

Women's Role in the Reorganization of Urban Crafts

Production practices changed suddenly after 1834–6 with the abolition of guild monopolies and the 'Freedom of Trade' declaration. The reorganization of the craft guilds was based on the creation of personal links within workshops – primarily family ties – and the restructuring of labour organization around these private networks. In the end this meant the 'patrimonialization' of the trades: family structure and workshop organization became inextricably intertwined within the artisan household, which served as the new centre for production and replaced the guilds' old institutional framework and functions.

Table 6.1 Independent Masters without Consanguineous Relatives Running Shops in the Same Trade's Workshops, Barcelona, 1823–60 (%)

	Guild period (1823–36)	1838	1860
Chair-makers	91.2	60.7	67.4
Wax-makers	81.8	60.7	87.5
Tailors and hat-makers	81.5	52.3	54.4
Shipwrights	83.8	70.0	–
Rope-makers	80.6	56.1	63.6
Glaziers and tinsmiths	72.8	53.1	67.3
Comb-makers	84.0	60.0	50.0
Semolina-makers	62.9	43.4	61.9
Shoemakers	62.9	46.1	55.9
Metal crafts	69.5	45.4	50.9
Bakers	69.0	47.9	46.2
Leather crafts	91.8	41.3	38.3
Carpenters	72.8	42.7	52.6

Note: Family ascription is established based on the repetition of surnames. This is simplified for Spain, where both maternal and paternal surnames are used.
Sources: Tax records; 1823 and 1838 War Taxes and 1860 Industrial Subsidy, Municipal Archive of Barcelona.

The first fundamental change was the introduction of family groups into the trades. Table 6.1 shows the proportion of independent masters *without* consanguineous relatives working within the same trade. Before 1836 a vast majority of masters did not have close family members who shared their craft or guild affiliation. Already by 1838, however, just a few years after the new freedom of trade legislation, these numbers had dropped dramatically. In other words, most of the crafts were being reorganized around family and kinship; family trade groups were increasing their control on local handicraft manufacture. Though the strength of some trade families declined between 1838 and 1860, generally this was due to the arrival of newcomers rather than to family crises. In fact, the number of artisans' workshops grew steadily in this period from 1,469 in 1823 to 1,941 in 1860. From the figures in Table 6.1 we can conclude that while the guilds dominated artisan labour under the *ancien régime*, family groups rarely controlled more than one-third of the workshops. At the end of this period (after 1834–6), families controlled almost 40 and even 50 per cent of their craft's respective workshops. Such concentration of trade resources – workshops and trade members – into family groups implied the direct involvement of family members, and to a much greater extent than had previously been the case.

The increased importance of family structure for artisan and crafts organization is evident from other sources as well. As tanners were trying to organize themselves into a mutual aid society in 1860, they explained their conception of the fusion of family and craft: 'We, for the same reason, must guarantee that such goods [old guild patrimony] will be preserved and kept in the families by means of a brotherhood ... '. The significance of this became clear when the tanners defined the potential members of the new mutual aid society: 'the association will be perpetuated by the present masters and their sons ... the same will be applied to the masters' daughters ... '.[12] Indicated clearly was a role for female family members in the elaboration of a new artisan strategy. Women were now being identified as critical agents for transmitting the skills of the craft (the tanners used the term 'perpetuate' to describe the role of women). A similar strategy can also be identified among the *faquines* (dockers and porters), a vocation where marriage to the daughter of a master facilitated access to the trade. In the period 1830–42 there were seventy-one new masters in this trade, and thirty-five of them achieved their status by marrying a master's daughter.[13]

Another element must be considered in explaining the strengthening of family ties within the trade, namely the spatial organization of the production unit. In the working worlds of Barcelona artisans, there were no spatial differences between the household and the workshop; both shared the same room, usually at street level. The traditional production and residence unit consisted of the street-level shop floor, where working activities, including sales, were performed, and the second floor that provided the family home. The family's living space often intersected the shop as an inner balcony. Only in some cases – tanneries or metal workshops – were households established in a completely separate location. Additionally, the required workforce was small and partially joined with the family unit. Workshop labourers consisted of the master, one apprentice, and one or two hired journeymen. Apprentices generally lived in the artisan household as co-residents, responsible for performing certain domestic tasks.[14] It is likely that artisan families took on apprentices when spouses were pregnant, which implies that boys performed women's domestic labour and that apprenticeship was integrated into the artisan family-course and reproductive strategy.[15]

Links between household and workshop were profound, and one of the most telling characteristics is that the artisan production unit was rarely established outside of marriage. A young master did not wait for his father's death or retirement to establish his own workshop, which implied that he could not rely on significant economic support from parents at this stage.[16] Therefore, the general artisan strategy was to marry male sons with 'brides of the trade' in order to acquire material and non-material resources, including the young wife's contributions to production.[17]

The final point to consider about changes to artisan production after the abolition of the guilds is related to training and skill. Although this is not the place to debate the nature of artisan skill – whether it was a technical or a social achievement – it is quite clear that in the first third of the nineteenth century Barcelona guilds provided social recognition of skill.[18] Consequently, the disappearance of trade corporations produced a void in skill 'legitimization' mechanisms, which was filled instead by the trade families that now transmitted craft skills to their members and apprentices. Progressively, surnames became identified with skill and reputation. Thus the expertise once represented by the guilds was increasingly dominated by a closed system of specific families. In general terms, the artisan trades were subjected to a process of 'patrimonialization' and privatization, which favoured specific family groups and their members, including women.[19]

The Involvement of Craftswomen in Artisan Business

Within this new context, women's work and participation were increasingly integrated into artisan production and strategies of family reproduction. Of course, only those women belonging to artisan families could follow a path comparable to that of a formal apprentice. In this case, the Catalonian common law played a central role. Different from Castilian common law (the basis of the Spanish Civil Code passed in 1889), Catalonian legal tradition prevented the division of familial property (partible inheritance) by transmitting the entire family possession to the eldest child, either son or daughter (impartible inheritance but not primogeniture), also called the 'universal heir'.[20] At the same time, the remaining siblings received a dowry 'in life' (called *dote* for women or *legítima* for men) as compensation. This legal system favoured commercial and industrial business by averting the division of family patrimony between descendants, exactly the contrary of the Castilian law, which divided up a family's resources. Catalonian liberals, most of them cotton manufacturers and merchants, fought successfully in the national parliament for the preservation of Catalonian common law. Consequently the Spanish civil code was never introduced in Catalonia, which even now continues to enjoy its own family law. Thus the Catalonian common law promoted the household economy built on family patrimony and in this sense was crucial for the participation of women in the artisan economy.[21]

One of the most striking features of the old crafts' world was the near invisibility of women in guild documents. Based on old guild books, it appears that no women entered the crafts as apprentices. However, if we consider the papers of the Commerce Board (the institution that controlled all city guilds before 1834), we realize that many girls were working in workshops during the first third of the nineteenth century. In the textile sector, for example, there were women like the lacemaker Rosa Pujol who managed businesses with the support of their daughters and other female relatives.[22] Only after the abolition of the guilds does specific information about women apprentices appear in the written record.

Thanks to the work of Cerdà, we know that female apprenticeships became widespread in the textile sectors, as well as in basket weaving, chair production and the manufacture of gloves, shoes and buttons. Although Cerdà's most interesting observations are that girl apprentices were generally masters' daughters, as in other European cities, there remained significant differences between the apprenticeships of girls and boys.[23] While boys completed their training outside of the family household, even if learning the family craft, girls did their apprenticeship at home.[24] These practices must be explained by trade policies: boys were sent to other masters' workshops not only to learn new techniques but also to establish or strengthen ties with other families. This does not mean that girls did not play any role in the construction of trade networks, but they did so primarily through marriage. In addition, this different apprenticeship was part of the legitimization of skill developed after the guilds were abolished: boys' external training meant the recognition of expertise by outsiders, while girls' professional recognition was tied to the family.[25] As in the case of boys, the artisan training of girls included all those matters related to the management of the family business.[26] After all, the aim of apprenticeship was to train independent craft workers who could manage their own workshops or *perpetuate* – as the tanners said – their specific craft.

The next step in the career of a craftswoman was marriage with a man of the same trade. This moment was crucial not only because it represented the birth of a 'neo-local' household but because women became directly involved in the administration of business. This was possible, apart from women's previous training, thanks to the existence of the dowry, an old practice that found new meaning under changing economic conditions since it helped to prevent the rupture of lineage patrimony.[27] In the case of divorce, the dowry was returned to the woman's family or, if she died, preserved for her heirs. In addition, the dowry was a key element in the constitution of a new household-workshop.[28] In 1854 Cristina Ribas, whose spouse had 'disappeared' years before (it was believed that he had fled to America), recovered her dowry from her husband's family. With this money, she opened a carpentry shop with the carpenter José Rovira Viliella.[29] This was evidently an extreme example, but it provides a clear idea of the relative independence achieved by women through this old tradition. Generally, the dowry was directly linked with marriage and was used as initial capital by the new family unit. This was the pattern followed by the baker Ramón Bou, member of a wealthy bakers' lineage, who established his own bakery in 1843 with the money provided by his bride, the daughter of another baker.[30] However, the Ramón Bou case is interesting not only because of the origins of his capital but also because his mother, Mariana, managed the family bakery on her own. This also counters general assumptions about the retirement of widows from business following a son's legal commercial independence.

Despite the importance of the dowry, integrating this financial resource into mercantile networks created certain difficulties. In effect, the dowry was a financial reserve that families took from circulation.[31] It does not mean, however, that dowry funds did not circulate in the artisan economy; on the contrary, they circulated in discrete sums outside of the 'market'.[32] According to Catalonian law, it was impossible to seize dowry funds in case of debt or bankruptcy. Thanks to this feature, artisans could run their businesses as 'limited liability' firms.

A woman's managerial independence as secured by the dowry was limited, however, because it remained the patrimony of her heirs. In the end, the restriction placed on dowries represented the limitations of the artisan economy more generally, a pattern based not on the unlimited accumulation of capitalist production but on the society of small-scale producers.[33] Thus if women hoped to increase their control of familial business, they needed to find 'external' resources. A good example of the use of extra-dowry funds is offered by Dolores Artigas, spouse of Antonio Artigas Berenguer, a candle-maker, who established a soap factory in 1848. The initial business was not successful, so Berenguer's wife, Dolores, using her personal contacts and funds, opened a second soap factory. By 1859 her husband's soap workshop had collapsed, while her business was growing steadily – at that time her factory was exporting to foreign countries and she owned stocks in shipping companies. In the same year she decided to involve her son in the management of the factory by entering into an agreement with him and with her husband, which banned the latter from factory management.[34] Dolores Artigas could do that and maintain complete control of her firm because of the 'extra-dowry' origin of her capital, a fact that she emphasized in the contract.

With the establishment of an artisan household, a wife's work was considered 'natural' and taken completely for granted. For this reason, information on women's skilled labour is relatively easy to find but records of their managerial roles are more difficult to locate. Only when artisan families formalized 'external' agreements – usually with merchants – are written sources available, and, evidently, such practices were uncommon in a family-based economy. A fuller description of the artisan economy and a few examples provide a basic picture, however, of the shop management of married craftswomen. As suggested already, the training of artisans included managerial matters, so it was therefore not strange that masters' daughters and wives were prepared to carry out these tasks. When the tailor Juan Bertran established a tailor's shop in 1846, his wife, Rosa Bartomeu, became responsible for bookkeeping, accountancy and payments to suppliers.[35] Women's management was also common in the metal trades – considered a highly skilled sector – due in part to production practices and to the employment of many journeymen. A typical cutler's business around 1900 illustrates well the managerial role of wives: while the husband manufactured and repaired knives and other metal devices, the wife managed the business, making deliveries and attending to customers.[36] Here the wife clearly developed and regulated relations between the workshop and the public sphere. This is less striking if we consider that women in pre-industrial societies managed household consumption, bridging the family economy with local markets.[37] Another example of women's managerial skills is provided by those cases where wives managed a second family shop: in 1853 the comb-maker Juan Anglada opened a second shop, leaving the first one in the hands of his wife, Antonia Marimon.[38]

An artisan's decision to put family women in managerial positions, especially in larger workshops, was always well grounded. Though these women were generally 'daughters of the trade', journeymen viewed their interference in 'shop-floor' activities as an affront to their professional status.[39] To avoid such conflicts, master women more often managed employees in those workshops where workers were women or children (the number of workshops employing primarily women and/or children grew significantly in Barcelona throughout the century). The shoemaking shop of Antonio Mallart and his wife, Paula Codina Dimas, who was descended from shoemakers on both sides of her family, illustrates this very well. Since the 1840s the couple's workshop had grown steadily. But unlike the cutler family described above, Paula managed the work of the women and girls employed in the shop, while her husband was responsible for sales.[40] The case of Pelegrin Tuyet and his spouse was similar: together the two owned a large silk-weaving factory (in 1852), but it was the husband who sold products in the first floor of the workshop. Two years later the Tuyets hired a manager, but the wife continued to manage factory production and employees.[41] A few years later, in 1860, María Bonet and her husband, Pablo Canals, established a large silk factory with other partners. The agreement established Pablo as the firm director with his wife as the *administradora* (woman manager) and overseer of the working women employed in the factory.[42]

As these examples illustrate, the craftswomen of artisan families were trained not only in production techniques but also in those skills related to workshop management and labour control. The roles these women played was buttressed by the existence of the dowry and the survival of Catalonian family law, which favoured the establishment of family businesses as well as the direct involvement of women, not only in the household but also in the workshop. Thus when craftswomen married, they tended to share responsibilities for running the family workshop – where artisan production and family reproduction were combined – with their husbands and male family members. By participating in production and labour administration or even by running a second shop, women's *co-management* was ultimately crucial for the expansion strategies of many artisan businesses.

Women Running Workshops

Another critical stage in the life course of a craftswoman was widowhood, when an older woman often assumed complete, independent control of a workshop. Many scholars have argued that this was an incidental and provisional arrangement with little larger significance for either the firm or the family.[43] As we have seen, however, the establishment of sons as independent masters did not necessarily imply the withdrawal of widows from the business. In fact, many Barcelona crafts-widows continued in their shops after their sons had gained their master's qualification, sharing the business with them. Even in highly skilled trades like carpentry, widows often controlled the management despite a son's involvement; such was the case with Madrona Martí, who directed the family's carpentry and wood-importation shop in the mid-1840s while her son worked on the shopfloor.[44]

Statistical figures would provide a valuable tool for measuring the pervasiveness of widowed shop managers. Yet sources are notoriously unclear about who controlled a family workshop and whether widows managed independently. For instance, tax records often listed the sons of 'master-women' as owners of a business, even if they were still underage children. The figures in Table 6.2 must be considered approximate, therefore, and that is the reason for the use of ranges of percentages.

The average percentage of women managing shops in the period 1823–60 was between 2.8 and 5.8 per cent of the total number of workshops in Barcelona (Table 6.2). The names of just over 227 master-women have been identified from the sources (from a total of 1,682 open workshops during the period). Women were involved in the management of all crafts – wood, leather-making, as well as the production of foodstuffs – countering some assumptions about traditional 'women's crafts' or the 'gendered' character of certain trades.[45]

However, these figures say nothing about the extent or nature of the management of craftswomen. It can be observed that the administration of women was neither accidental (improvised) nor provisional – in the sense that it served as a stopgap until underage sons could assume their inheritance. In 1837 Miguela Palanca was a glove-maker, running a shop from which she also provided small loans to neighbours. In 1849 she was listed as a tanner and by 1862 she managed a tannery composed of two different workshops, which employed four workers. As the daughter of the former tanners' consul (guild representative), she enjoyed certain advantages. Clearly, her strategy was to move from retailing to the sector

Table 6.2 Women Running Artisan Workshops by Sector, Barcelona, 1823–60 (percentage range)

Sector	1823	1838[A]	1849	1860
Food	2.2–3.6	4.3–6.8	4.3–6.5	3.8–4.9
Cloth-making	1.8–2.6	3.1–10.6	2.3–5.4	0.9–1.5[B]
Wood	2.6–3.3	1.7–5.1	2.9–6.0	0.4–1.7
Metal/glass	2.9–3.2	3.3–4.4	2.8–3.8	0.9–2
Leather	1.1–4.6	3.1–5.4	3.0–4.4	4.8–5.6
Wax/tallow	0.4–4.5	6.2–12.5	0.0–11.0	10–20
Highest proportion crafts				
Comb/Shuttle-makers	16.6–	6.2–16.6	14.8–18.5	7.1–
Rope/espadrille makers	6.2–10.0	9.8–	3.5–8.3	3.5–7.1

Source: Tax records (1823, 1838 War Taxes and 1860 Industrial Subsidy) and 1849 *City Guide*. Municipal Archive of Barcelona, and Notary documents from the Protocols Archive of Barcelona
Notes: Percentage range: the first number (on the left) offers the percentage of women running workshops according to tax sources, and the second number includes those women who did not appear in tax records but in other sources including notary documents, contracts, loans and wills.
(A) Many artisans were members of the National Militia, particularly poorer ones (tailors and shoemakers), and therefore engaged in battle far from Barcelona from 1836 to 1839. This explains the higher percentage of female workshop management in the 1838 tax contribution.
(B) This figure includes only those women running tailor workshops (formerly a guild trade) and not the hundreds of women working as dressmakers.

that controlled the provision of raw materials, the tannery itself. In the same family Ramona and Jacinta Palanca managed two other glove shops in the city. While Jacinta ran her business for at least twenty-five years, Ramona opened her glove-making firm with another glove-maker in 1856.[46] In other crafts – like the manufacture of silk garments or glassmaking – widows sometimes controlled workshops for twenty years or longer. José Pujol's widow and Rosa Rius managed two different glassmaking businesses from no later than 1837 up until 1860. The former was also involved in the building sector, providing window glass, as did her husband.

Again, there was no direct correlation between the kind of trade and the management contributions of women. According to Table 6.2 the proportion of women running highly skilled businesses, like metal and leather works, was more or less the same as in other artisan trades. Many of these women managed relatively large businesses – large at least within the artisan context. One explanation for these practices can be found in the high proportion of capital invested in metal and leather shops, which made the businesses more resilient and therefore likelier to fall under the control of a widow. But this dynamic also makes it more difficult to consider how many widows ran the smallest – or the poorest – artisan shops.

It is unlikely that widows' management was conservative or served only to preserve family patrimony. On the contrary, widows expanded and modified the orientation of family businesses, maintaining at the same time the extra-productive activities of the family group as a money lender. The women bakers Mariana Bou, Maria Mangot and Isabel Puig helped to organize a bakers' consortium in 1848 – composed of thirty partners – in order to control the city's wheat supply. A decade later these women formed the economic elite of the trade.[47] Others, like the glass and pottery maker Maria Tarafa, completely transformed an inherited workshop by reorganizing it into a porcelain shop and then leaving her son a much larger business. The shift from glass and clay production to porcelain and glass selling was an astute strategy at a moment when cheaper glass and clay products imported from Valencia threatened the sector (this strategy was followed by other glass-makers' widows and helps to explain the decline of 'master-women' in the 1860 data). The widow Rosa Bofill Buch did something similar by transforming her husband's pottery into a mass tile factory.[48] The widows of semolina-makers implemented similar strategies. Thanks to the steady industrialization of cotton production, starch became an important commodity and demand for it grew spectacularly. Semolina-makers were well positioned to provide this material, and many, including some widows, transformed their shops into starch factories . The widow of one semolina producer named Prat managed a typical semolina shop in 1838, which by 1860 appeared in tax records as a starch factory. Catalina Pey Tintore did something similar in approximately the same period, and then invested the profits from her starch production in real estate. We can conclude that despite the invisibility of widows – and women in general – women's control of artisan businesses became entrenched in Barcelona's crafts culture following the guilds' abolition. But this was an active management that helped families adapt to the changing and threatening conditions of a new liberal economic age. In addition, women's management was not only limited to the smallest artisan business. Rather, the proportion of familial capital (patrimony) invested in large shops suggests an even greater involvement by women in the preservation and transmission of family businesses.

Conclusion

That women's management of and involvement in artisan business does not emerge clearly in the sources is not unique to Barcelona.[49] Nor does it mean that craftswomen did not play a significant role in family-based business. Artisan women – master's daughters and wives – were involved in Barcelona crafts as part of a broader strategic response to the challenges of free trade. Similar practices could be found in other European countries undergoing a similar economic transformation.[50] And women's involvement in family workshops, alongside their husbands, was not limited to handwork but also included managerial tasks, which reflected the specific trade, the size of the shop, the employment of journeymen, and the economic status of the household. Thus women's work was not circumscribed by a domestic sphere; in the milieu of nineteenth-century artisans in Barcelona the distinction between production and reproduction was far from clearly established. In addition, independent management by women, usually widows, was much more than a provisional arrangement; it was more often an integral strategy for the survival of the family trade. For the same reason, the widow's contribution cannot be considered a conservative measure, since one of its aims was to provide new solutions for unpredictable changes, which could ultimately secure the family's patrimony and status.

Women's involvement in the artisan economy must be analysed in the context of Barcelona's initial modernization, when the formerly corporatist crafts became a family patrimony. The privatization and 'patrimonialization' of trades redefined kin-group roles and realigned the position of family members in relation to patrimony – as spouse or heir – instead of by gender.[51] The aim of this artisan strategy was to guarantee a secure transmission of patrimony – in its broader sense, including material and non-material resources – rendering modern boundaries of private and public ultimately meaningless.

Notes

1. Vicens, 1958; McDonogh, 1986; Olivé, 1998; Cruz, 2000; and Marín, 2001.
2. Alvarez, 1995; Borrell, 1999; Sarasúa, 1995; Solà, 2002; and Romero, 1997.
3. Despite the increasing interest in nineteenth-century artisans there are no general studies on the role of women in workshop production and management. See Díez, 1990; Huget, 1990; Martínez, 1994; Nieto, 1996; Buisiné, 2001; and Peiró, 2002.
4. Davidoff and Hall, 1987.
5. Vickery, 1993, p. 393.
6. Borderías, Carrasco and Alemany, 1994; Borderías 2002.
7. There was a short-lived liberal experiment between 1820 and 1823 known as the *Trienio Liberal* [Liberal Triennium].
8. 1779 and 1784 Royal Laws 14 and 15, Title 23, Book num. 8; *Novísima Recopilación*.
9. Barcelona Archive of Protocols (hereafter APB). Notary Pich, J., 1838, p. 117.
10. Pascual, 1990, p. 219.
11. The 'flexible specialization' concept emphasizes small-scale and skilled production as the historical alternative to 'mass production', see Sabel and Zeitlin, 1985, p. 142. Spanish literature under the influence of Piero Sraffa has invoked this in order to explain the 'slow economic development' of Spain. See Lluch and Sevilla, 1978, pp. 178–201.
12. APB Notary Rodríguez: 1860, p. 2.

13. *Faquines'* masteries documents were compiled during the 1840s in the protocols by notary Benito Xammar and afterwards by notary Ramón Odena (APB).
14. In some private apprenticeship agreements there were specific references to the domestic work of children. APB, Notary Lafont, R., 1842, p. 221. Such practices provoked constant complaints from boys who considered domestic work a *servant's job*. Archive Municipal of Barcelona (hereafter AMB). *Fondo Junta de Comercio*, Box 15, file 1.
15. This information is difficult to confirm because there are no complete books on apprentices, or, if these books exist, there is no direct information about artisan family cycles (pregnancies, births, deaths). I have drawn this conclusion on the basis of a few cases where it has been possible to determine the birth dates of masters' sons and the entry of apprentices into the workshop.
16. Romero, 2001, pp. 211–12.
17. While recognizing the involvement of women in trades and occupations, Angelique Janssens, 1997, p. 5, argues that women's work was always linked to their husbands' or fathers' trades. Of course it is no less the case that boys (at least in Barcelona) also followed the vocations of their fathers, see Romero, 2001, pp. 211–12.
18. Arranz, 2001, p. 74.
19. John Rule, 1987, p. 111, has commented on how workers began to consider skill as a transmissible property, particularly in reaction to the first stage of industrialization. For a gender perspective on 'patrimonialization' see Liu, 1996, p. 67. The absence of clear divisions between family and labour favoured the 'holistic' training of girls in the sense that they be taught the whole productive process including administration; see Harden, 1996, p. 91.
20. Harty, 2002, p. 19.
21. Harty, 2002, pp. 4–6.
22. AMB *Fondo Junta de Comercio*. Box 41, file 8.
23. In 1859 Ildefons Cerdà, the designer of the Barcelona town extension, published a vast study of the working class of Barcelona. See Cerdà, 1859, vol. 2, p. 616; Davis, 1986, p. 169.
24. Romero, 2001, p. 216.
25. Howell, 1986, p. 200. From a feminist perspective one might argue that the unequal apprenticeships of girls and boys reflected the direct misogynist control of the master-patriarch. However, in Barcelona one must consider that at least since the eighteenth century virtually all gender theorists had agreed that women's 'natural' skills and capabilities were far inferior to those of men. For this reason it became very difficult in the nineteenth century to counter the progressive dilution of expertise within some crafts – an inevitable effect of the abolition of the guilds – and argue simultaneously for women's apprenticeships.

Artisan Women and Management in Barcelona • 95

26. Since the end of the eighteenth century, some of the humbler guilds – like the porters – had created schools to provide 'academic' training – reading, writing and maths – to masters' sons and daughters; see Colldeforns, 1951, p. 69.
27. Chacón, 1995, p. 80; Harty, 2002, p. 22.
28. Crossick and Haupt, 1995, p. 69.
29. APB Notary Torras, M.: 1854, p. 72.
30. APB Notary Maymo, F.: 1843, p. 113.
31. Busto, 1994, p. 34; Harty, 2002, p. 19.
32. Meillassoux, 1975, p. 96.
33. Hobsbawm, 1968, p. 29; Roemer, 1982, pp. 14–15.
34. APB Notary Benito, R.: 1848, p. 74, and Notary Anglora, C.: 1859, p. 65.
35. APB Notary Torras, R.: 1846, p. 262.
36. Casas, 1989, p. 64.
37. Berg, 1988, pp. 90–91.
38. APB Notary Palaudaries, M.: 1853, p. 367, vol. 1.
39. Davis, 1986, p. 174.
40. APB Notary Andreu, J.: 1851, p. 392, and Notary Gibert, C.: 1865, p. 94.
41. APB Notary Torras, M.: 1852, p. 202, and Notary Marzola, J.M.: 1854, p. 64.
42. APB Notary Soler, M.: 1860, p. 139, vol. 2.
43. Honeyman, 2000, p. 20; Horrell and Humphries, 1997, p. 27.
44. APB Notary Corominas, M.: 1847, p. 515.
45. Honeyman, 2000, p. 19.
46. *Diario de Barcelona*, 27 January 1854, p. 17; APB Notary Cebria, E: 1856, p. 251.
47. APB Notary Lafont, B.: 1848, p. 18, and Odena, J.: 1849, p. 72.
48. APB Notary Pallós, L.: 1852, p. 231, vol. 2.
49. Reyerson, 1986, p. 119.
50. Pellegrin, 1994, p. 34.
51. Comas, 1995, pp. 49–50.

–7–

Women and Publishing in Nineteenth-century Spain

Gloria Espigado

By the end of the eighteenth century, Western European women had begun to assert themselves as authors, periodical editors and even publishers. This located them firmly in the public sphere, both as shapers of public opinion and as economic agents. Spanish women were no exception, and their experiences are important on several counts. First, they offer a valuable counterpoint to French and Anglo-Saxon works on the subject by shifting focus away from the political, economic and socio-cultural features that characterized northwestern Europe, including early industrialization and the development of representative political systems. In contrast, southern Europe represents a region of late industrialization, the slow development of liberal political institutions, and the influence of the Catholic Church – differences that profoundly affected Latin feminism. While Anglo-Saxon countries witnessed women's formal protest and participation in political debate, especially over the right to vote, Spanish women were absent from the political sphere for most of the nineteenth century and instead sought to enter the workforce and gain access to education.[1]

The history of women's involvement in Spanish publishing also challenges many nineteenth-century stereotypes that depict Spanish women as exclusively domestic or incapable of initiative. The presence of women in the publishing industry disrupted the gendered dichotomy of private and public in two ways. Together with other productive activities, publishing was a new employment opportunity for women. Although modest in scope, it allowed Spanish middle-class women to become self-supporting. Contributing to a periodical was also a way for female authors, marginalized by the book industry, to reach a broad audience and establish a literary reputation. Both editing and writing made it possible for women to achieve the professional status they were seeking: it gave them public recognition as writers and, in turn, a platform from which they could express political and social views. Through their writings, Spanish middle and working-class women, as well as members of radical groups, entered the Habermasian 'public sphere'. Against the backdrop of dramatic political and economic change – the establishment of the first constitutional government with the 1812 Cortez, the reactionary backlash of 1814, the civil wars, the loss of Spain's colonial empire, the short-lived republic of 1873–4, and the beginnings of industrialization – they helped shape public opinion, including bourgeois representations of womanhood.[2]

Women could not easily realize their aspirations, however, in a traditional and even reactionary social climate. Limited access to education, work and political participation facilitated the subordination of women, which was taken for granted in nineteenth-century Spain.[3] Coming slowly to terms with economic and political modernization, Spanish society embraced the notions that men and women were meant to play different roles in distinct or 'separate spheres'. Gender identities were marked by differences, complementarities and exclusions.[4] These cultural strictures compelled women to articulate their wishes and opinions individually, as well as collectively, and newspapers became a valuable medium for this purpose.

The first Spanish-language newspaper was published in the seventeenth century, beginning the gradual growth and diversification of mass communications and culminating in the constitution of a consumer market, which also included women. By the early nineteenth century Spanish newspapers and magazines pursued the goal of educating the public and influencing issues of collective interest. During the Romantic period, however, this objective changed, and newspapers sought to articulate more radical and creative opinions characteristic of the movement. Over time, the markets for newspapers that provided political opinion and cultural commentary were consolidated.

It was also during the Romantic period that the first generation of female publishers emerged. They asserted their status as authors, collaborators and editors, but only rarely challenged prevailing notions about women's nature and roles. More often these female print pioneers advocated conventional female role models. Only the subsequent generation of women publishers, who came of age in the wake of the turmoil of the mid-nineteenth century after the demise of the first republic, was more likely to use print media as a tool for challenging the social positions of women, if not political and economic systems more generally.

The Origins of Women's Publishing in Spain

One milestone of female publishing dates to the seventeenth century, when Francisca de Aculodi from San Sebastián, 'printer of this noble and loyal province of Guipozcoa', issued a paper entitled 'Main and True News' between 1687 and 1689. Written in Spanish, the periodical was published in Brussels, which then belonged to Spain, and reported on general events as well as local news. A second important development in Spanish female journalism was *La Pensadora Gaditana*, published from 1763 to 1764 under the signature of Beatriz Cienfuegos (though her authorship remains debated by specialists). The journal responded to the misogynist attacks found in the work *El Pensador* and belonged to a type of Enlightenment didactic literature which criticized traditions and customs. In its fifty-four 'thoughts', *La Pensadora Gaditana* referred to the necessity of defending the weaker sex.

The first publications written by and for women, however, appeared in the context of the upheavals of the nineteenth century, which witnessed a veritable publishing explosion in response to the War of Independence (against France) and the first attempt to found a Spanish constitutional government. These projects received an additional boost with the freedom of press proclamation in the 1812 constitution. Women were also centrally involved at this stage and included María del Carmen Silva, who took charge of the radical newspaper *El Robespierre Español* while her husband was held prisoner on censorship charges. In 1809 Eulalia Ferrer founded the newspaper *Diario de Palma* in Mallorca, which she directed until her return to the peninsula in 1811.[5]

Women were thus present at the birth of Spanish journalism, no matter when one dates it to. Not until the middle of the nineteenth century, however, were Spanish women able to consolidate their positions in this field. At this time a new type of publication, the *Salon y Modas* ('Salon and Fashions'), had begun to appear, targeting a potential female market. These journals were very similar to their French and British counterparts, and their pages were dominated by discussion of the latest fashions, as well as beauty and hygiene tips. They also contained some entertainment and literary features, including poems and puzzles. Although they were initially edited almost exclusively by men (female contributors were rare), this changed gradually.[6] Included among these publications were *El Correo de las Damas*, published in Cuba in 1811 (a Spanish colony at the time), and *El Amigo de las Damas* founded in Cádiz around 1813. There was also *El Periódico de las Damas*, published in 1822, which was especially keen to attract women to the liberal cause. In the same category was *El Correo de las Damas*, founded in Madrid around 1833, which could boast 250 subscriptions, including 65 noblemen and 96 women.[7] Among other male-edited periodicals targeting women were *El Defensor del Bello Sexo* (1845–6), *La Educanda* (1861–5), presented as 'the newspaper for ladies and dedicated to mothers of families, teachers and college headmasters', *La Guirnalda* (1867–83), and the most important Spanish women's publication, *La Moda*, which was founded in Cádiz in 1842 and then published in Madrid from 1870 to 1927. All of these publications were edited by men but eventually included contributions from the most influential female writers of the time. Some of these male publishers and authors even passed themselves off as women with the objective of gaining more readers. This was true of a businessman from Madrid, for example, who, in 1845, founded the *Gaceta de las Mujeres, redactada por ellas mismas*.[8]

This small-scale publishing existed alongside other published material of a more political nature. But both political and popular-literary genres faced enormous difficulties in expanding their markets and developing distribution networks.[9] Indeed, the Spanish press operated for most of the nineteenth century under adverse conditions. First, freedom of expression was curtailed by restrictive laws and censorship. Second, most publishing enterprises were family businesses that experienced frequent and severe financial problems. Publishers were unable to modernize equipment and many could not purchase new machinery until the end of the century. Finally, the print market was weak due to widespread illiteracy and poverty, which precluded the luxury of a daily paper for most. Thus Spanish publishing had difficulties expanding and did not become a genuinely lucrative business until the twentieth century. The professional Spanish journalist, a person who earned a living writing for a newspaper, simply did not exist. Publishing could only survive with the collaboration of a famous writer, lawyer or politician, who would use the newspaper as a mouthpiece and public platform but not as a source of income.

The situation was even worse for periodicals aimed at women, since women tended to have less purchasing power and lower education levels. For their part, female publishers had fewer business opportunities and more limited technical means for carrying out their plans.[10] The greatest obstacle, however, was the illiteracy of Spanish women, which remained very high throughout the nineteenth century. Compulsory schooling for boys and girls aged 6 to 9, was not introduced until 1857. Even then the curriculum for girls was curtailed and limited to topics related to housework and domesticity. At the beginning of the twentieth century, 70 per cent of Spanish women were still illiterate. Access to secondary education was even more difficult and rarely led to a profession. Legal impediments to women's access to universities were not removed until 1910, and as late as 1930 only 4.2 per cent of university graduates were women.[11]

Female Publishing at Mid-century

Despite the constraints placed on nineteenth-century Spanish publishing, fundamental changes occurred from the decade after 1840, which included the arrival of female writers on the Spanish literary scene. Spain was then entering an important transition: the political system was becoming increasingly liberal and stable, and an incipient capitalism stimulated economic growth. These broader trends, coupled with the success of the new concept of authorship prompted by Romantic individualism, eased the challenge of joining the literary world. Periodicals provided women with an efficient means of publishing their creative work, which usually included smaller pieces such as poems and commentaries. This evaded the difficulties involved in book publishing, which Spanish women were only rarely able to do. The serialization of novels in newspapers was another way of overcoming this obstacle. Despite their limitations, periodicals gave female authors valuable support as well as the opportunity to establish a reputation. Women often began writing poetry, then moved on to short prose pieces, and finally to fiction. Married women used their husbands' surnames for extra protection, and those who had already published work anonymously or under a pseudonym began to sign their full names. By mid-century the first newspapers directed and written by women began to appear in the main Spanish cities of Barcelona, Cádiz and Seville. Of course, the capital Madrid asserted itself as the centre of Spanish journalism for both men and women.[12] This publishing activity reached significant proportions by the end of the nineteenth century, and catalogues list nearly a hundred female-oriented titles for the nineteenth century.[13]

The legal impediments to periodical publication remained significant, however, and affected female proprietors and directors more harshly than their male counterparts. The most restrictive nineteenth-century press law, the Nocedal law of 1857, required (among other things) that all articles be signed by their authors. Strict political and religious censorship also imposed costly security deposits. This compelled publishers with fewer resources, and consequently most female publishers, to produce cultural periodicals, since these were exempt from the payment of deposits. Newspapers were usually owned by male publishers, who frequently appointed a professional editor responsible for the content. Women who took over the work of directing, editing and distributing a paper were typically financed by a member of their own family, usually a father, brother or husband who provided the capital to set up the paper. Keeping the paper going was a difficult matter, because direct sales were insignificant, and one had to secure a sufficient number of subscriptions. Censorship was responsible for the demise of some of these female newspapers, but more often than not they were simply short-lived affairs and closed due to the lack of necessary subscriptions.[14]

All the successful Romantic Spanish female authors, including Cecilia Bohl de Faber [known as Fernán Caballero], Carolina Coronado and Cuban-born author Gertrudis Gómez de Avellaneda, contributed to periodicals from the 1840s. With this activity they sought not only an income but also an organ for their work and the opportunity to establish themselves in the republic of letters. Gómez de Avellaneda, who denounced slavery in *Sab* in 1841, sponsored publishing ventures of some importance, both in Spain and in her native Cuba. She produced magazines such as *La Ilustración, Album de Damas* (1845) or *El Album Cubano de lo Bueno y de lo Bello* (1860–4), while pursuing her own extensive literary activities. None of this helped her get elected to the Royal Academy of the Spanish Language, however; her candidacy was vetoed by the male academicians in 1853. These female authors also acted as sponsors for less fortunate female authors and contributed to the emergence of what Susan Kirkpatrick has described as a 'literary sisterhood'. Female authors created solidarity networks and worked together to try to solve the problems involved in the distribution of their work.[15] The typical nineteenth-century female writer came from the middle classes, the daughter of a skilled worker or civil servant, sometimes with liberal ideas. Some had been politically exiled, most had received a domestic education and many were self-educated. Frequently they had to overcome family resistance to their desire to pursue writing and sometimes married an author or another prominent literary person in order to gain access to the realm of publishing.[16]

These women produced didactic pieces extolling Victorian bourgeois and domestic values. In their work, the woman was depicted as the epitome of goodness, the true 'angel in the house'.[17] It is debatable, however, whether this literature reflected a newfound bourgeois individualism, since it also bears the mark of traditional Catholic doctrine and deep-seated anti-liberalism. Indeed, Catholic doctrines underpinned many of the discourses aimed at Spanish women, and this influence is a primary reason why reading the Spanish experience through the prism of Anglo-Saxon evangelical domesticity is misleading. In Catholic Spanish traditions female withdrawal into the house had been a religious prescription stretching back to the work of Fray Luis de Leon in *La Perfecta Casada* (1583), a book that was published in new editions and widely distributed into the modern period.[18]

Despite the rebellious character of the Romantic era, the women writers of this period were not really subversive. Most were indifferent to expressing their artistic subjectivities and committed instead to giving literary form to the concept of the 'angel in the house'. Their work was prescriptive and upheld Catholicism. The best and most successful representatives of this domestic genre, Angela Grassi, Faustina Sáez de Melgar and Pilar Sinués de Marco, achieved fame through their novels and didactic texts, as well as publishing enterprises. They were respectively editors of *El Correo de la Moda* (1851–93), *La Violeta* (1862–6) and *El Angel del Hogar* (1864–9).[19]

These women fell into disfavour with the following generation, however, which preferred realism if not naturalism. Authors like the renowned Emilia Pardo Bazán reacted against the domesticity genre, which she deemed silly and moralizing. Under the influence of Bazán and other critics, mid-century female authors have been lumped together with the outmoded Romantics, whose successes consequently have been widely overlooked. Other scholars, however, have warned against accepting these facile judgements, which misleadingly blur the literary chronology. They note that this literary period was dominated by recognized female authors, and they suggest that this may have been the reason why its literature has been dismissed as secondary.[20] At the very least, we should recognize the contribution these women made to the world of Spanish arts through their activities as publishers.

Apart from the authors considered above, we should also mention Joaquina García Balmaseda, who, after the death of her predecessor Grassi in 1883, continued directing *El Correo de la Moda*. The journal *Flores y Perlas* (1883–4) was also edited by illustrious writers such as Eulalia González Barbarroja, who was in addition the proprietor together with Pilar de Sinués and Josefa Pujol. Another important title, *El Vergel de Andalucia* (1845), was published in Cordoba and edited entirely by women and for women – men were not allowed to subscribe. *La Mujer* (1851–2) claimed to be written by 'a society of ladies', and *La Mariposa* (1866–7), directed by Fernanda Gómez, was aimed especially at 'the school mistresses of primary education'. *Los Ecos de Auseva* (1864–9), founded and directed by Robustiana de Armiño, had among its honorary subscribers Pope Pius IX, the Queen of Spain, Mª Cristina and the emperors of Mexico. *La Voz de la Caridad* (1870), directed for fourteen years by the well-known feminist Concepción Arenal, campaigned for prison reform. It was written and administered free of charge and the benefits were given entirely to the poor. *La Ilustración de la Mujer* was a very common title shared by several periodical publications. One of them was directed by Concepción Jimeno de Flaquer (1872–4), another by Sofia Tartilán (1873–7), and a third by Gertrudis Gómez de Avellaneda, Josefa Pujol and Dolores Monserdá (1887).[21]

Only in a few cases did newspapers or periodicals manage to last for a significant number of years. Their principal challenge was securing a subscriber base large enough to establish adequate support. But in spite of the short-lived nature of many of these businesses, some female directors repeatedly entered new publishing adventures, of which few were likely to succeed. For example, Faustina Sáez de Melgar took advantage of the political change brought about by the revolution of 1868 to bring out a magazine called *La Mujer* in 1871. After its failure, she started two more periodicals: *Paris Charmant et Artistique* and *La Canastilla Infantil*. Subscriptions were sold through bookshops in the readers' home town. The published letters to the editor provide some insight into the geographic distribution of the readers. In many cases, subscribers' loyalties were secured with the promise of a free sewing pattern or a novel. These rudimentary sales strategies accompanied the development of a female market, which, although still weak, was continuously growing. But it was not until the twentieth century that advertising began to provide much needed revenue to support publications.

However, these women did not share the same political and social views. While most were conservative, a significant fraction was not. Many female authors upheld stereotypical images of womanhood, espoused Catholic moral principles, and defended the notion that female influence was key to the preservation of the family. Paradoxically, this defence of the excellence of the female sex and the affirmation of its superior ability to defend faith and family laid the groundwork for important social changes, and opened new avenues for women. Female magazine editors all agreed on one point: women should be properly educated and equipped to carry out their domestic duties. This demand for better education was the basis of a lukewarm feminist solidarity shared by all female publishers. On the other hand, these women saw little reason to ask for more radical changes in women's status. While moderation protected their reputations and prestige, radicalism would have undermined them.[22] The example of *Ellas* (1851-3), directed and written solely by Alicia Pérez de Gascuña, illustrates this dynamic well. In its first issue, *Ellas* (subtitled 'Official Organ of the Female Sex') published articles demanding an end to 'cruel male domination'. However, Pérez de Gascuña quickly changed the rhetoric of the journal to avoid losing public support or being discredited. After the third issue, the provocative subtitle was changed to 'Gazette of the Beautiful Sex'.[23] In this fashion, female publishers and editors remained self-sufficient as authors and print entrepreneurs, yet this independence relied on their relative commercial success, which required in turn that they promote submissiveness and modesty for their female peers. This feminism was pragmatic and perhaps opportunistic but also rooted in a Catholic discourse on female excellence and the role of women as natural social benefactors.

Those who championed the cult of domesticity, however, always co-existed with a small group of women who did not share this ideology. Among the first generation were disciples of Fourier, the French Utopian Socialist. They founded various newspapers in Cádiz and were very active in the region between 1856 and 1866. Successively they published *El Pensil Gaditano*, *El Pensil de Iberia*, *El Nuevo Pensil de Iberia*, *El Pensil de Iberia* y *La Buena Nueva*. The 'Pensiles' were truly tremendous achievements for these women, who did not enjoy the success of their more conservative colleagues. Since the journals covered topics of universal interest, they became much more than just women's publications intended to support women's domestic interests. Their main promoters, who were in some cases also the newspapers' directors, like Josefa Zapata and Margarita Pérez de Celis, did not limit themselves to what was found in typical female publications. Their agenda faithfully reflected the emancipating doctrines of Fourier, including the social redemption of women and the poor. They opened their pages to the leaders of the democratic movement, which became the Republican Party, the most radical party on the Spanish political scene. These newspapers were one of the few available platforms for feminist social and literary rebellion. They barely survived, however, plagued by limited subscriptions and the frenzied attacks of political and religious authorities, who succeeded in silencing at least two editions.

These radical and republican writers espoused doctrines that clearly subverted the domestic order assigned to women. They earned modest livings as schoolteachers or seamstresses, and their lack of literary success mirrored the conditions of the Saint Simonians more generally, who carried out similar publishing ventures in neighbouring France.[24] These women criticized the institution of marriage for denying female autonomy. Although they stopped short of calling for the abolition of marriage, as Fourier would have done, they demanded its thorough reform to ensure female freedom. Their sensitivity towards the social question also led them to denounce the exploitation of female workers, and to demand fair salaries and better working conditions. They also insisted on access to formal education. And they framed their demands with a redeeming form of social Christianity, which the Church hierarchy rejected as socially subversive and heretical.[25]

The Turn of the Century and the Road to Professionalization

The literary scene in the last third of the century witnessed the arrival of a new generation of writers committed to realism. The tenets of Spanish realism never approached the extremes of Emile Zola's French naturalism. But like the French realists and naturalists, the Spanish authors Clarin and Galdos, two of the most representative members of this school, rejected the prescriptive agenda of the previous generation in favour of realism. The working class also began to be featured in fictional writing.[26] Women followed this trend, including Galician Emilia Pardo Bazán, who took her place alongside other famous contemporary male authors. Her achievements earned her a professorship in 1916, the first to be granted to a Spanish woman.[27]

By this time, feminism had taken root in Spanish society and women writers and publishers joined the most progressive political movements, firmly committed to improving women's conditions. Many, such as Belén Sarraga, became Freemasons, a movement linked in the public eye with free-thinking and vehemently condemned by the Church. In 1895, at the age of 20, Sarraga took over *La Conciencia Libre*, publishing first from Valencia and later from Málaga. She also participated in the International Conference on free-thinking in Brussels in 1902.[28] Adherence to rationalism led many of these women, including Emilia Pardo Bazán, to support the Republican Party, either locally or at the federal level.

Spiritualism, a religious belief at odds with Catholicism, provided another common bond among these writers. Thus the magazine *La Luz del Porvenir*, published in Barcelona by Amalia Domínguez Soler (1879–94) with the collaboration of other free-thinkers, defined itself as a spiritualist publication. *El Progreso*, also published in Barcelona in 1896, was sponsored by Ángeles López de Ayala as a republican periodical and contained many anticlerical writings. This magazine was joined at the beginning of the twentieth century by a similar periodical, *El Gladiador*, advertised as the organ of the 'Progressive Feminine Society'. The sisters Carvia, Amalia and Ana, known members of the Cádiz Masonic lodge called 'daughters of the regeneration', established around 1895, founded periodicals in Valencia such as *El Pueblo*. They fought the obscurantism in which they claimed the Catholic Church had immersed women.[29] Women also ran publications resembling those directed by men with similar beliefs, such as *Las Dominicales del Libre Pensamiento* (Madrid) for which Rosario de Acuña wrote. At the turn of the century, the loss of the last colonies strengthened anti-clerical and republican activism. Contrary to their foremothers, women from that generation joined the democratic and liberal movements. They denounced the backwardness of the Catholic Church, and the submissiveness it demanded from Spanish women. They believed it would be impossible for women to achieve full citizenship unless this damaging influence was removed, and they called on women to become aware of their own ability to fight for and obtain political rights.

The two powerful Spanish workers' movements, the Socialists and the Anarchists, also fostered important feminist writers and activists. Although high female illiteracy rates had restricted female readership to bourgeois circles throughout the nineteenth century, by the 1890s progress in women's education had begun to create a larger and more diverse group of potential readers. Working-class women joined the ranks of those who consumed female publications. The workers' movement also invited women to contribute to their organization, and join their male comrades in denouncing the situation of female workers. This could be disadvantageous, however, if it imposed the Marxist priority of subordinating women's demands to the struggle for proletarian revolution, whose success was alone deemed capable of introducing lasting social change. One effect of this doctrine was that women were rarely in charge of socialist and anarchist newspapers. One exception, *La Humanidad Libre*, founded in Valencia in 1902, listed Teresa Claramunt, Soledad Gustavo, María Caro, Angelina Vidal, Louise Michel, Emma Goldman and Rosa Lidon among its contributors. The paper was edited by Teresa Mañé (also known under the pseudonym of Soledad Gustavo), a rationalist teacher and wife of the anarchist Juan Montseny (Federico Urales). (Mañé's daughter, Federica Montseny, was the first Spanish female minister and member of the Republican government during the Spanish Civil War.) According to Montseny, the most important anarchist publishing company at the beginning of the century was run by her mother. It issued *La Revista Blanca* in Madrid (1898–1905) and in Barcelona (1923–36).

Anarchism, the movement most sensitive to the subordination of women, promoted women's improvement in education and working conditions. However, and in sharp contrast to the Catholic Women's Movement which the Anarchists opposed, it ignored the issue of suffrage (the Catholics had come to support it). Instead, the Anarchists called for the elimination of the old sexual morality, like the Utopian Socialists had done before them. They denounced the oppressive nature of marriage and supported 'free love'. The Anarchists lent support to the contemporary eugenic and neo-Malthusian movements, which called for sexual reform and defended the concept of 'conscious motherhood'. They were in favour of family planning, contraception and abortion as a last resort. The defence of this programme intensified during the Second Republic (1931–6)

But like the Catholics, bourgeois feminism also rallied behind the cause of suffrage and in the process mobilized a new generation of women. Some of these women were also involved in successful publishing ventures that found receptive publics at the beginning of the twentieth century. One, Carmen de Burgos, who wrote under the pen name Colombine – she is also considered the first female war correspondent – declared herself in favour of the vote for women, though only after some initial doubts.[30] She articulated demands for female suffrage after the First World War with the founding of the first suffrage associations: the Asociacion Nacional de Mujeres Españolas (ANME) and the Union de Mujeres Españolas (UME). Other women followed a more nationalist agenda, such as the Catalonians Dolores Monserdá and Carmen Kar, whose *Or y Grana* (1906–7) appeared in just twenty-one issues, but was later continued by *L'ilustració Catalana*. Carmen Kar also published the more successful *Feminal* (1910–17), which was suspended after 228 issues, a victim of the First World War (it did manage to resume publication in 1925). Benita Asas Manterola (*El Pensamiento Femenino*, 1913) and Celsia Regis tried unsuccessfully to develop a female school of journalism from the pages of the long-established *La Voz de la Mujer* (1917–31). The ANME itself published *Mundo Feminino* (1921–36), which supported a feminism respectful of Catholic beliefs but still actively fought for systematic improvements for women. These efforts led to the right of women to vote at the end of the 1920s.

Conclusion

The topic of women in Spanish journalism deserves more than the few pages devoted to it here. We can highlight the main features of these women's achievements, however, which were reflected in the work of women throughout Western Europe. Although feminism had a slow and difficult birth in Spain, female writers and publishers, and their determination to see their work in print, established a greater awareness in the twentieth century of the inequalities faced by women. Despite the struggle for survival, the crude presses and the marginal circulation, periodicals helped to support women authors whose talents otherwise went unrecognized. Journals and papers provided the print venues for poetry and prose, and even the opportunity to serialize entire books.

Catholicism and its ideology of domesticity weighed heavily on these women, or at least on those publications and their authors who managed to gain a reputation and survive. However, we cannot reduce the written production of nineteenth-century Spanish women to this single model. The mid-century Utopian Socialists and the Fourierists rejected portrayals of women as the 'angel in the house'. Towards the end of the century, female Masons, spiritualists, free-thinkers and republicans devoted their full attention to the damaging impact of the Catholic Church; they focused their efforts on emancipating women from oppressive religious influence.

In contrast, neither the Socialists nor the Anarchists believed in the possibility of improving women's conditions within the framework of a liberal government or a bourgeois society. They rejected calls for women's suffrage; harking back to the Fourierists of the previous generation, they promoted free love, 'conscious' motherhood, female unions and the rights of workers. If economic backwardness, political difficulties and the persisting influence of the Church delayed the emergence of a more vigorous feminist movement, these forces could not prevent women from establishing a position in the Spanish republic of letters.

Publishing offered an alternative path that nineteenth-century women could follow to escape their own constricted 'separate sphere'. They could use it to earn a living, gain a literary reputation and promote reforms favourable to women. Although they faced greater obstacles than women in northwestern Europe, they did not give up. Publishing provided a space where they could express themselves, and a platform from which they could influence public opinion. They used the written word to forge a path that future generations of women could follow, to articulate demands for social reform, and to help the women's movement achieve maturity. Contemporary women are indeed indebted to these nineteenth-century pioneers who led the way towards Spanish women's emancipation.

Notes

1. Caine and Sluga, 1999; Bock, 1993; Nash, 1994.
2. Habermas, 1989. For a feminist critique of the public sphere see Ryan, 1992.
3. Cabrera, 2000.
4. A synthesis of the history of women in Spain which covers these themes is Garrido, 1997.
5. Roig, 1977, pp. 9–15.
6. The examples of female authorship in Spain during the first decade of the nineteenth century are admittedly very modest. By comparison, Carla Hesse has counted 329 works written by French women between 1789 and 1800 (Hesse, 2001). To date, there are no studies of female participation in the world of Spanish literature during the French Revolution. Carmen Simón Palmer suggests a total of 1,200 female writers in Spain between 1832 and 1900, with 120 publishing before the 1868 Revolution (Simóne Palmer, 1990, p. 10).
7. The number of copies was modest throughout the century, normally equalling the number of subscriptions (Jiménez, 1992, pp. 27, 34).
8. Kirkpatrick, 1989 and 1990, p. 82.

9. For a study of journalistic activities in Spain see Botrel, 1993; Seoane, 1996; Fernández, 1997.
10. Apart from their professional activity as writers and editors of women's newspapers, women were only marginally active in the printing trade itself. Around 1866 a Madrid woman, Javiera Morales Barona, directed a printing press whose entire staff was female. It was in fact a typographic academy, maintained through the patronage of 500 'protectors', 100 of whom were wealthy, philanthropic women. Their pupils published a short-lived paper called *Album de las Familias* (1865–6), which questioned the continuity of the business itself (Jiménez, 1992, p. 127). In other cases it was common for the widows of printers to continue directing the family business. In this connection consider chapter 6 by Juanjo Romero-Marín.
11. Ballarín, 2001; Flecha, 1996; Capel, 1982.
12. Specifically, eighteen women were identified as press directors and editors in Madrid during the century (Matilla, 1995, pp. 100–1).
13. Estimates of the number of periodicals including those associated with specific towns such as Barcelona and Madrid can be found in Perinats and Marrades, 1980, pp. 403–6. Other sources give higher figures: ninety-eight women's magazines during the nineteenth century (Simón Palmer, 1991).
14. American studies of the relationship between female writers and the publishing business include Coultrap-McQuin, 1990; Cyganowski, 1988. For Great Britain see Zlotnick, 1998.
15. Kirkpatrick, 1990, pp. 25–42.
16. Simón Palmer, 1991; Ruiz, 1997; Carmona, 1999.
17. A classic historical study of separate spheres in England is Davidoff and Hall, 1987. In a literary context see Armstrong, 1987. For Spain, see Charnon-Deutsch, 2000.
18. Aldaraca, 1982, pp. 62–87, and more recently Aresti, 2000, p. 369.
19. Blanco, 1998, pp. 9–38, and 2001.
20. Sánchez, 2000.
21. Blanco, 1998; Ruiz, 1997; Simón Palmer, 1991.
22. Sánchez, 2001.
23. Jiménez, 1992, p. 82.
24. Adler, 1979; Riot-Sarcey, 1994.
25. Espigado, 1998, pp. 171–5.
26. Studies in the evolution of the fiction of the 'angel in the house' can be found in Aldaraca, 1992, and Jagoe, 1994.
27. This famous feminist writer contributed to many contemporary newspapers and she started several businesses herself. She also published the literary magazine *Nuevo Teatro Crítico* (1890–3), financed by the inheritance she received from her father, and in 1892 she set up the 'La Biblioteca de la

Mujer' (the Women's Library), where the most important feminist works were translated, including those of John Stuart Mill and August Bebel. On the feminist dimensions of Pardo Bazán's journalism see Bieder, 1998, pp. 25–54.
28. Ramos, 2002.
29. Aguado, 1999.
30. Tavera, 1999.

–8–

Businesswomen in Austria
Irene Bandhauer-Schöffmann

Introduction

More than one million women lived in Vienna in 1910, and more than one-third of them worked outside the household: 9 per cent were white-collar workers, 39 per cent were blue-collar workers, 26 per cent were domestic servants, and 3 per cent worked with spouses or relatives in family firms.[1] Some of these working women were self-employed or members of the free professions, but others worked in industry or in the crafts and trades. Of course, many contributed their labour and management skills to family firms. Among these working women, 42,000 or over 11 per cent were self-employed businesswomen in industry, trades and commerce.[2]

The history of these businesswomen has never been a significant topic of Austrian historical research.[3] Marxist scholars have worked to develop adequate theories of housework that might also shed light on the living and working conditions of wage labourers but they largely ignore self-employed women.[4] Business history has likewise failed to take account of women entrepreneurs, and this deficit is generally not even recognized.[5] Early research on the Austrian bourgeoisie, first published in the second half of the 1980s, focused on men, but continued to ignore the self-employed bourgeoise even as attention turned to women. Women's history – together with research on the middle classes – has investigated the construction of dichotomous and separate gender spheres and various forms of gender inequality. But the bourgeois women who broke through the prescribed roles of housework and childrearing and entered the public world of economic competition have been largely overlooked. Additionally, this neglect of female entrepreneurs has an impressive political tradition. Although many middle-class leaders of the Austrian women's movement came from prominent business families, businesswomen were never a subject of interest for the incipient women's movement.[6] The term 'entrepreneur' has had such masculine overtones that even feminist activists, despite their entrepreneurial undertakings in the founding of schools and in managing women-only hotels, restaurants and residential homes, have avoided using the word or describing themselves as such.[7]

This chapter seeks to redress these shortcomings in Austrian history and more specifically in women's history. I will first consider the legal framework for self-employed women. Three sets of laws were significant for a woman who wanted to enter the business world: the Austrian Civil Code of 1812 (*Das Allgemeine Bürgerliche Gesetzbuch, ABGB*), the Trades Regulations of 1859 (*Gewerbeordnung*), and the Commercial Code of 1862 (*Handelsgesetz*).[8] I will then analyse Vienna's self-employed women using census data. A final section develops a profile of Vienna's wealthiest businesswomen based on a sample of fifty-two firm managers – registered at the Viennese Commercial Court – who died between 1896 and 1910. Throughout the chapter, I will stress the ways in which law and the economic development of women in industry, trade and commerce were interconnected, and how Austria's comparatively liberal legal system permitted women to enter the marketplace but ultimately contributed to an economic gender gap.

The Legal Framework for Austrian Businesswomen

The Austrian Civil Code of 1812 was the most progressive of its time, securing women a high degree of economic independence, which they had enjoyed in many territories of the Austrian monarchy since the late Middle Ages. Unlike most of the German states, in Austria there was no fundamental guardianship of men over women. An unmarried woman was an independent legal actor who could manage her possessions by herself and was capable of suing or being sued. As in other countries, a married woman was subject to her husband, who functioned as head of the family. But in Austria a wife was clearly in a better position with regard to her economic opportunities. In contrast to the French Civil Code and most of the German legal systems, the Austrian Civil Code conferred married women full legal rights, apart from those of their husbands. In addition, Austrian women retained rights to their property when they married. Despite personal legal subjection to her husband (with regard to herself and matters of mutual concern), a wife did not hand over her property to her husband when she married.[9]

Due to this protection of female property (the so-called *Gütertrennung* or 'separation of goods', which allowed both marriage partners to control their respective property), married Austrian women had a much better starting point when they wanted to become active in business. This had been commonplace among the Austrian urban and upper classes since the Middle Ages, and was written explicitly into law with the 1812 Civil Code. When a bride and groom wanted to establish joint property possession in their marriage (the so-called *Gütergemeinschaft* or 'community of property'), they had to set up a legal marriage contract, which was also necessary when the bride wanted to give her future husband a dowry. In Austria it was never the case that the husband could automatically lay claim to his wife's property, since any form of dowry for the husband always required a contract. Usually the bride's dowry was reciprocated with a gift to the bride, generally of the same amount, which was not placed at the wife's disposal but passed into her possession upon the husband's death.[10]

While the Austrian Civil Code did a reasonable job of protecting the property of married women, the 1812 law also subordinated wives to the judgement and control of their husbands. First, the Civil Code presumed that any property gains made during marriage represented the husband's effort.[11] The Civil Code also assumed that the husband would manage his wife's property, although the wife or her parents could easily protest this arrangement. Another article of the Civil Code entitled the husband of a woman who managed her own property to put a stop to her 'un-orderly business' and declare her to be a 'squanderer'.[12] A wife was also denied the right to work outside her own household if her husband so insisted.

In contrast, the wives of farmers and small businessmen in trades, crafts and food services were actually obliged to assist in their husbands' businesses without payment, as far as it was customary for that kind of business and compatible with the duties of housekeeping and childrearing.[13] But if the wife of a farmer or a businessman was not formally a co-owner of the business, she could not ask for compensation for her contribution in the event of divorce. This law pertained to women who ran a business outright while their husbands were absent, due, for example, to military service.[14] Thus a wife's contributions to the business were as little compensated as housework.[15]

Clearly the Austrian Civil Code protected the material goods of the upper classes, including those of married women. But it also disadvantaged working-class wives; women from the lower social orders who entered marriage with little property often had legal obligations to assist their husbands but without compensation. Thus the working-class and petit-bourgeois women of those countries that established joint property after marriage had a clear advantage over their Austrian counterparts. According to the French Civil Code, for example, a widow or divorced woman had a legitimate claim to the property acquired during marriage. In the event of divorce, a French woman could demand the capital that had accrued through her own work contribution.[16]

But Austrian women gained additional comparative advantages under the Austrian Trades Regulations of 1859, enacted 1 May 1860 and effective until 1973.[17] Influenced by a widespread liberalism, the 1859 Trades Regulations set the basis for the free exercise of self-employed trades, regardless of gender. As a general rule, before 1859 a majority of the guilds had not been accessible to women.[18] But section four of the new trade law addressed this explicitly, stating: 'Gender does not constitute a difference in regard to access to trades.' With satisfaction of all legal prerequisites, including the attainment of majority status (i.e. the age of 25), every man *and* woman could run his or her own business.[19] In theory, at least, the new law realized freedom of trade for women. With the exception of a few branches – fourteen trades were subject to obligatory regulation because of their pronounced public interest – it was only necessary to register in order to carry on a trade. What was important here was not the protection of those who already practised a trade but the idea of promoting entrepreneurial spirit.

These progressive principles were soon undercut, however, by amendments in 1883 and 1907, which reflected the new anti-liberal political pressures of Vienna's petit bourgeoisie. With the worsening economic situation after the 1873 stock-market crash the government abandoned liberal economic policies. Influenced by the rising Christian Social Party, the 1883 Trades Regulation amendment made it more difficult to gain entry to a trade and attempted to limit competition. While not containing any passages that explicitly discriminated against women, the amendment was still biased in the way that it complicated women's access to trade. To limit competition from newcomers, proof of qualification now had to be produced for certain trades, which required formal training in one of the newly founded trade schools or practice with a master.[20] Women could not easily find a master with whom to train, however, nor were they accepted into the trade schools, which were placed under the direction of the guilds after 1883. With the exception of those trades specifically practised by women – including dressmakers and seamstresses, hat-makers, manufacturers of artificial flowers, or plumage makers – women were effectively excluded from most crafts.[21]

The 1907 amendment continued this illiberal tendency by establishing new requirements for many fields of the retail industry (including trade in assorted dry goods, colonial wares, delicacies, drugs and spices). Aspiring shopkeepers now had to undergo vocational training for a minimum of five years before they could obtain proof of qualification, and only then could they become independent. The apprentice's diploma could be substituted with a certificate from a trade school or *Handelsakademie*, but very few of these admitted women. Since access to wholesale trades was not limited, the large number of small female shopkeepers were affected disproportionately.[22] Here we can see how the reduction and decline of entrepreneurship among women resulted from the increased division of labour and a form of restrictive professionalization.[23]

The number of women practising a trade nevertheless increased. This growth was concentrated, however, within the very few professions that were regarded as typically female. The trade law promoted this development by introducing special provisions for those trades traditionally run by women, and thus access to the typical 'female' trades was made easier. While the 'male' crafts were increasingly protected from outside competition (including that posed by women), women competed freely with other women in the 'female' trades. With easy access to certain 'female' trades, Austrian legislation acknowledged a woman's right to gainful employment, but at the same time refused to make fundamental changes that would promote equal opportunities for women, namely by opening the educational system. Destitute women who wanted to work as dressmakers did not have to show proof of school attendance or of a successfully completed apprenticeship (which was paid for by the apprentice). They could start their own business without having to meet these formal requirements as long as they opened a store in which neither apprentices nor journeymen were employed. From 1883 to 1907 it was left to the local trade authorities to define which trades they considered to be 'female'.[24]

A final and critical legal context for considering the economic agency of women was the law of inheritance and a widow's right to run the business of her deceased husband. According to the inheritance law of the 1812 Civil Code, a spouse could not lay claim to the property of a deceased partner, unless the partners had established joint property in a marriage contract. Aside from her children, the widow was left only with lifelong usufruct to a share from the inheritance. And since the Civil Code established the wife's obligation to assist in her husband's business, the inheritance law tended to discriminate against women.[25] Husbands could legally deny inheritances for their future widows even if they had helped to increase the family's property during the marriage. Only with the partial amendment of the Civil Code in 1914 were spousal inheritance rights extended; at that point the spouse inherited a quarter and – if the marriage had remained childless – half of the inheritance, if not indicated otherwise by a will.

The widow's right to continue to run the business of her deceased husband (in order to support herself and her children) had been established by the late Middle Ages.[26] This had been considered a necessary measure since a widow was not a blood relation of her husband and therefore not eligible to inherit his property.[27] But the widow's right had differed from guild to guild and was generally limited: widows were allowed to fill in until their sons could take over, or else a deadline was set by which time they had to remarry. In the Trade Regulations of 1859, widow's rights were consistently regulated and they were allowed to continue to run the business of deceased husbands. The amendment of 1883 limited this right to the 'duration of widowhood', and this prohibition on remarriage remained in effect until 1973.[28]

Many businessmen also stipulated in their wills that the widow's inheritance be contingent on her not remarrying. This can be viewed in part as an effort to secure the children's material interest over and against that of the widowed mother. This meant of course that many who chose not to remain single not only lost their right to continue directing a family business but also sacrificed substantial family assets. In effect, a married woman might be required by law to contribute to her husband's business but denied the right to assume control after his death or even claim the portion she contributed.

Even more vulnerable to disinheritance than widows were daughters. In order to ease the transmission of a firm, the family property was often given to an oldest son. The exclusion of younger children affected primarily daughters, who were rarely considered worthy firm directors and tended to receive smaller inheritances anyway. One strategy for unmarried daughters was to confer a share in the firm, though generally without signing privileges (or rights of active participation). Towards the end of the nineteenth century, women began to wage legal battles to secure their shares of a family patrimony or to gain access to a particular profession.

One prominent case was that of Mathilde Tischler, the first independent female house painter in the Habsburg monarchy. Until Tischler pursued her right to be a self-employed master painter, the trade had no women other than widows.[29] After her father's death in 1891, Mathilde's mother, Widow Tischler, managed the firm as a 'widow's business' with a required male proxy-manager. At the same time, Mathilde learned the painting craft but was rejected three years later when she applied to the guild of painters to be accepted for a master's exam. After she had already become a successful businesswoman, Mathilde wrote in an autobiographical sketch: 'Of course I was rejected by the great majority for the reason that there had never been women painters, and only men had the right to exercise this craft. ... After that, I looked into the Civil Code and couldn't find one passage that pointed out that females were not allowed to practise the painting trade, and from this I understood the contradiction in the guild's position.'[30] Mathilde then turned to the governor of Lower Austria, the next higher court of appeal, who required that she be examined by outside experts. In November 1894 she finally gained the title of 'Master'. For Austria's liberal public, a woman master painter (*Fräulein Meisterin*) who supervised forty workers was a clear mark of progress.[31] At least in this case, Austria's liberal Civil Code – when finally observed – proved a progressive force for women's economic and market participation.

Self-employed Women in Vienna

Austrian liberalism self-consciously promoted economic growth, which, together with immigration, led to a rapid expansion of Viennese industry and commerce. The city's 1869 population of 842,951 (including the suburbs, which were only incorporated in 1890) had reached 1.6 million by 1900 and exceeded 2 million by 1910. Destruction of the medieval city walls in 1858 and the city's geographic extension had provided a powerful impulse for the economy, which only subsided with the great stock-market crash of 1873.[32] By the 1880s the impact of industrialization had led to a broad economic restructuring. The traditional domains of the small trades (furniture manufacturing or shoemaking, for example) lost out to industry. A period of strong economic growth beginning in 1896 ended the stagnation that followed the 1873 crash and created a powerful impetus for a new economic boom, sometimes described as a 'second age of industrial expansion'.[33] This dynamism promoted the growth of ever larger enterprises, above all in iron and metalworking, the burgeoning electrical industry, the graphic trades and transportation, which were dominated by men as company owners, managers and wage employees.

The impact of this rapid growth both promoted the entry of women into the worlds of business and commerce and increased the relative number of women among Vienna's self-employed crafts and business people. In 1837 only 6.5 per cent of Vienna's self-employed were women, but in 1869 (counting city suburbs) that figure had reached 18 per cent.[34] By 1890 women constituted just under 34 per cent of those self-employed in Vienna's industry, trades, and commerce, and this percentage rose slightly to just over to 35 per cent by 1910.[35] Over the same period, the proportion of women among salaried and wage labourers fell rapidly: from just under 31 per cent in 1867 to just over 21 per cent in 1900.[36] The absolute and relative increase in self-employed women reflected the increasing divergence between male and female trades, or what some scholars have described as a gendered market segmentation.[37] Although some women were active in practically all business sectors, the vast majority were engaged in traditional women's branches or in fields that had emerged from the impact of rapid and disruptive industrialization.[38] One of these sectors was the clothing industry, which traditionally employed a large number of women. Vienna's textile industry embraced nationwide market production from the 1830s but then moved out of the city altogether by 1860. What remained of Vienna's clothing industry experienced a significant expansion, however, during the depression (after 1873) but on the basis of a radical change in the organization of labour. Unlike the male-dominated industries, Vienna's self-employed tailors and seamstresses were often married, petit-bourgeois women who worked as small subcontractors from home. Sometimes they employed helpers and extra seamstresses, but the size of their operations declined significantly in the last decades of the nineteenth century.[39] In 1869 each independent garment worker still employed, on average, 5.4 paid workers, but by 1900 this number had dropped to just 2.7.

Table 8.1 Self-employed Women and Men in Industry, Trades and Commerce in Vienna

	All	Male	Female	Female %
1869	61,110	50,031	11,079	18.12
1890	96,108	63,506	32,602	33.92
1910	120,771	78,405	42,366	35.08

Note: These figures exclude those who advertised for domestic service and were formally self-employed with their own places of residence as well as the minor category of 'miscellaneous trades', which included grave diggers. The census counted these as belonging to the self-employed in industry, trades and commerce. If included here – especially those self-employed in domestic services – the percentage of women among the self-employed would be much higher, namely 40.2 per cent in 1890 and 45.78 per cent in 1910.
Source: Census data of 1869, 1890, 1910.

The small self-employed women in Vienna's garment industry characterized the majority of Vienna's female business owners at the beginning of the twentieth century. Drawn from the 1910 census data, the main professions for self-employed women were tailoring and dressmaking (6,697 women or 15.80 per cent of all self-employed workers), sewing and shirt-making (6,345 women or 14.97 per cent), followed by the retailing of food and beverages (5,754 or 13.43 per cent), and laundry and clothing repair services (5,446 women or 12.85 per cent). In aggregate, of 42,366 self-employed women, 20,972 or nearly half owned tailoring, needlework and laundry businesses, 13,441 or nearly one-third were in retailing, and 1,731 women ran pubs and restaurants. Over 80 per cent of all self-employed women appeared in only two vocational categories, and more than 92 per cent appeared in only four. The rest were distributed among nineteen other categories of profession.

Table 8.2 Viennese Trades with the Greatest Number of Self-employed Women in 1910, and the Average Number of Employees, Collaborating Family Members and Domestic Servants

	Males	Females	Female %	Employees per self-employed person	Collaborating family members	Domestic servants
Tailoring	8,800	6,697	43.21	2.93	0.03	0.10
Sewing and shirt-making	480	6,345	92.97	2.05	0.03	0.08
Retailing of food and beverages	3,467	5,754	62.4	0.95	0.16	0.26
Cleaning and repair of laundry and clothing	812	5,446	87.02	1.32	0.05	0.07
Grocery	4,812	2,701	35.95	0.27	0.26	0.28
Restaurants and inns	3,639	1,731	32.23	4.44	0.30	0.48
Millinery, plumage and artificial flower production	300	1,461	82.96	4.93	0.06	0.20
Production of embroidery, crochet and lace work	146	1,023	87.51	2.85	0.04	0.15
Trade with materials and products of textile industry	2,223	1,108	33.36	4.70	0.09	0.96
Door-to-door sale, hawking	1,438	941	39.55	0.04	0.01	0.03

Source: 'Berufsstatistik nach den Ergebnissen der Volkszählung vom 31. Dezember 1910', 1916. 1910 population census (including leaseholds). Employees included white- and blue-collar workers, apprentices and day-labourers. Comparison with the first census in 1869 is limited given the changes in occupation categories. Milliners and hatters were counted together with furriers and no longer formed an extra category.

The small size of women's enterprises was certainly not anomalous among self-employed crafts and businesspeople. In the Viennese business census of 1902, 80 per cent of all companies had five or fewer employees, and 31 per cent of all companies were one-person businesses.[40] Though gender was not considered in the 1902 company census, it is clear that women were strongly represented, since 52 per cent of all small businesses were in the garment and laundry industry. More generally, businesses in the so-called women's professions had far fewer employees, reflecting the fact that businesswomen were not prominent in those branches that supported large-scale enterprises.

Table 8.3 Marital Status of Self-employed Women in Industry, Trades and Commerce in Austria, 1890–1910

	Unmarried		Married		Widowed/Divorced	
	Number	%	Number	%	Number	%
1890	92,708	41.65	48,298	21.70	81,572	36.65
1900	107,846	41.41	71,664	27.51	80,944	31.08
1910	164,762	40.76	124,676	30.85	114,749	28.39

Source: 'Berufsstatistik nach den Ergebnissen der Volkszählung vom 31. Dezember 1910', 1916. Census data of 1890, 1900 and 1910. This includes the leaseholds and the persons who carried out domestic services as self-employed.

An additional factor for explaining the small size of most companies operated by women was the marital status of the female self-employed. From 1890 to 1910 the ratio of married to single self-employed women rose steadily from 21 to over 30 per cent. This increase reflected a general trend in the increase in the percentage of married women within Vienna as a whole. Yet it also reveals the growing acceptance that women might combine a business or occupation with the obligations of childrearing and housework.[41] At least among the lower middle and working classes, the cultural ideal of separate spheres appears to have lost rather than gained influence in this period. Of course, accepting the additional burden of running a small shop or laundry often reflected a family's difficult financial situation.

Table 8.4 Wives as Business Partners in Vienna and its Suburbs, 1869

	Vienna	Suburbs of Vienna
Dairy owners	92.4	83.3
Victuallers	82.8	81.1
Artificial-flower makers	81.3	71.4
Innkeepers	80.6	79.6
Seamstresses	78.7	23.6
Coffee-house owners	76.6	79.1
Second-hand-goods dealers	75.4	74.9
Umbrella makers	73.6	68.4

Source: Census data of 1869. Schimmer, 1974, pp. 52–3.

The statistics on self-employed women offer at best an incomplete picture of working women, however, since many were active as managers or partners in their husbands' companies and firms. Among the 113 types of business and industry listed in the 1869 census, 23 in Vienna and 32 in the suburbs included firms in which wives made significant contributions. In dairies, grocers' shops, artificial-flower shops, inns and restaurants, sewing shops, cafés and second-hand shops women were important assets to their husbands. Although the evidence is not complete, married men with workshops and businesses almost certainly relied on their wives for labour and managerial assistance. Of course, married women were legally obliged in many cases to contribute to the family business. It becomes clear that very few artisan, shopkeeping or small manufacturing families ever achieved the division of domestic labour and business suggested by the prescriptive model of separate spheres.

Vienna's Affluent Businesswomen

If any group could have realized the rigid ideal of female domesticity, then certainly Vienna's elite bourgeoisie had both means and motivation. But even the city's wealthiest commercial classes included a significant number of successful businesswomen. Of course, these businesswomen differed significantly from their more modest peers, not only for their commercial success, but also because of their religious affiliations and business interests.[42] Since self-employed women were heavily concentrated in just a few occupations – small laundry, seamstress and retail businesses – that did not usually sustain larger enterprises, there were virtually no rich businesswomen in these fields.

Vienna's elite businesswomen were thus active in a broader range of commercial branches than their more modest counterparts: some 35 per cent were merchants, 20 per cent produced fancy goods, and 13 per cent owned businesses in the woodworking or metal industry. The typical women's trades were far less lucrative – not surprisingly – and only one of the eight richest businesswomen was active in such a field, namely Hermine Laufer, who started as a dressmaker in 1883 and built up one of the most exclusive ladies' fashion salons on the Karlsplatz.[43]

The high percentage of religious minorities is perhaps the most striking characteristic of elite Viennese businesswomen. Generally, the proportion of Jews and Protestants among self-employed business owners was substantially greater than that of the general population, with Jews particularly overrepresented in commerce. Of course, this reflected centuries of discrimination, including the guilds' exclusion of all non-Catholics. Fundamental milestones for the emancipation of Jews were the lifting of the obligation to join a guild with the 1859 Trades Regulations, the right to own land (finally extended to Jews in 1860), and the establishment of civil equality for all religious faiths with the Fundamental Law of the 1867 Constitution. As a consequence, Vienna's Jewish population rose rapidly to around 9 per cent in 1890. In 1910 just under 9 per cent of Vienna's population was Jewish, 87 per cent was Catholic, and about 4 per cent was Protestant.[44] Like their male co-religionists, Jewish and Protestant women were disproportionately represented among wealthy businesswomen. The proportion of Jewish entrepreneurs among the wealthier businessmen was 40 per cent – much higher than their proportion of the total number of self-employed, which came to only 14 per cent. Jewish women constituted 7–8 per cent of Vienna's self-employed women, while more than 21 per cent of the wealthiest businesswomen were Jewish. Protestants made up some 3 per cent of the total number of businesswomen but 7.69 per cent of the wealthiest businesswomen. For Catholic women we find the opposite relationship: while 90 per cent of businesswomen were Catholic, among the group of wealthiest women entrepreneurs only 71 per cent were Catholic.

Table 8.5 The Religious Affiliation of Self-employed Viennese in Industry and Trades in 1910

	All Number	%	Women Number	%	Men Number	%	In Vienna %
Catholic	64,068	84.73	22,699	87.07	41,369	83.51	87.00
Protestant	3,095	4.09	764	2.93	2,331	4.71	3.78
Jewish	7,919	10.48	2,474	9.49	5,445	10.99	8.63
Others	523	0.69	133	0.51	390	0.79	0.59
Total	75,605	100.00	26,070	100.00	49,535	100.00	100.00

Source: 'Berufsstatistik nach den Ergebnissen der Volkszählung vom 31. Dezember 1910', 1916. Census data of 1910.

Wealth distinguished elite businesswomen more than anything, and over half of this group left behind net assets exceeding 40,000 crowns (a cook with an average wage would work 74 years to earn this sum, while a nurse would work 133 years).[45] Exceptional was the fortune of 1,484,680 crowns left by Maria Schreiber, mother of five who ran her husband's haulage business and sand pit.[46] Still, some 20 per cent of Vienna's elite businesswomen died with estates exceeding 100,000 crowns. This does not compare unfavourably with the wealthiest businessmen, some 30 per cent of whom left 100,000 crowns or more.[47]

The wealthiest businesswomen also had the largest families: on average married or widowed businesswomen from this elite group left behind 2.4 children, while the very richest 20 per cent among them had an average 4.5 children.[48] These women also tended to combine residence with workplace. Drawing from Commercial Court records and published business directories, it is possible to determine that over 70 per cent of elite businesswomen had their homes and their businesses in the same district, usually with both located in the same house or building. Here one sees a definite advantage in combining family responsibilities with the business, a feature common to small seamstresses and laundresses as well as affluent businesswomen.

Commercial Court records make clear that 61 per cent of the elite businesswomen inherited their firms or companies, and more than half from husbands. But women themselves founded 31 per cent of these elite firms, and 8 per cent of the firms were bought by women. Those who took over family firms from their deceased husbands assumed responsibility on their own account for quite some time, and frequently refused signing privileges to their sons who were also working in the business, indicating the extent of their independent management. In short, they were not mere stopgaps in a male business genealogy but rather self-confident and capable businesswomen. The life stories of these extraordinary women help to correct the stereotype of the elite indolent bourgeoise, a woman who retreated – willingly or not – into a sequestered domesticity and limited her public engagement to high culture or philanthropy.

Conclusion

This historical revisionism is even more critical when considering non-elite women: again, census data for 1910 indicate that 35 per cent of all Viennese women worked outside the household![49] This remarkable figure raises a number of questions. Did the legal situation for Austrian businesswomen have a positive influence on the participation of women in economic activities? Indeed, nothing stood in the way of an unmarried woman who wanted to become an independent businesswoman. And compared to the situation of women under the Anglo-American model of coverture or the continental doctrine of Community of Property, Austrian law appears to have been more conducive to the independent action of married women. Of course, a more mundane explanation for the high percentage of women in the Austrian workforce with respect to other countries might be found in the different and more exact statistical methods of registration. Perhaps the Austrian anomaly is really only a question of record-keeping?

But the interconnection of women's economic status with the Austrian legal framework remains a significant and complex dynamic for understanding the activities and relative success of Austrian businesswomen. While Austrian law guaranteed women's property rights and secured their economic independence from men, lack of access to vocational training and apprenticeships greatly disadvantaged women. Additionally, the inconsistent application of the law together with the 1883 and 1907 amendments actually increased gender segregation. Ultimately, the policies promoted by the guilds and the Christian Social Party prevented female access to certain professions. As a result, in 1910 almost 50 per cent of all Viennese businesswomen were active in only seven out of 175 possible professions.[50] Since most occupations in which women were active had lower earning potentials, it is little wonder that the wealthiest Viennese businesswomen managed firms in sectors that were not considered traditional women's branches. These negative external circumstances limiting and obstructing women's entrepreneurial activities meant that the exceptional cases of women who succeeded as businesswomen, sometimes over decades, were that much more remarkable.

Notes

1. For an overview of women's work in Austria see Rigler, 1976; Bolognese-Leuchtenmüller and Mitterauer, 1993; Ehmer, 1981. For statistical data see also Bolognese-Leuchtenmüller, 1978; and Banik-Schweitzer, 1979.
2. Ehmer, 1981, p. 472, table 6.
3. Initial research has investigated Salzburg women traders and Viennese craftswomen of the eighteenth century, and women participating in the 1873 Great Exhibition of Vienna: Barth-Scalmani, 1996; Barth-Scalmani and Friedrich, 1995; and Kretschmer, 2000.
4. An overview of the literature on Austrian women's history is provided by Saurer, 1993.
5. See Friedrich and Urbanitsch, 1996; and Brix and Fischer, 1997.
6. Marianne Hainisch, matriarch of the Austrian women's movement and wife of an industrialist in the metal sector, was not the only woman from an entrepreneurial family to become involved in the women's movement. The first president of the *Frauenerwerbsverein* (Commercial Women's Association), the most important bourgeois women's association founded in 1866, was Helene von Hornbostel, daughter-in-law of one of the first silk manufacturers in Austria. Priska von Hohenbruck, founder, member and later president of the *Frauenerwerbsverein*, was also a member of the Hornbostel family. Other functionaries of the organization had husbands who were bank directors. See Friedrich, 1992 (and for biographical details, *Österreichisches Biographisches Lexikon* 1815–1950) and Wurzbach 1856–91.
7. For a feminist critique of the construct entrepreneur, see Bandhauer-Schöffmann, 2003.
8. On the discrimination against women through the application of the trade regulations see Herda, 1997 and 2000.
9. Holthöfer, 1997; Beachy, 2004.
10. Ibid.
11. The so-called *praesumptio muciana* in § 1237 *ABGB*, see Floßmann, 1992.
12. § 1241 of the Austrian Civil Code.
13. Ent, 1979. The reform of the Austrian Civil Code in 1975 gave these regulations a gender-neutral formulation; before 1975 the obligation to assist in a

spouse's business affected only wives, but now husbands are similarly obliged. However, women still bear the brunt since wives were (and still are) more likely to assist in their husband's businesses than vice versa.

14. In a far-reaching decision, the Supreme Court of Austria ruled in 1924 that a wife who managed the business of a husband who had been engaged in military service during the First World War did not have a right to payment. The case of the woman who took her ex-husband to court because she wanted compensation for this work was dismissed. 'The plaintiff', according to the Court, 'has only managed the business of the defendant in the interest of the family during his temporary absence due to military service ... '. See Obergerichtshof 29.4.1924, SZ 6/164. In Austria, the right to compensation for assistance in the spouse's business was only set down in law in 1978. However, because this law contains a number of ambiguities, divorced women still cannot count on receiving adequate compensation for the work performed in their husbands' businesses during the marriage.
15. Vogel, 1992, p. 276.
16. Ibid, p. 287.
17. Gewerbeordnung, RGBl 1859/227.
18. Kretschmer, 2000; Barth-Scalmani, 2000.
19. In 1919 the age of majority was reduced to 22. See Lehner, 1987, pp. 128f.
20. RGBl 1883/39.
21. Herda, 1997, p. 117.
22. RGBl 1907/26. See Chaloupek, Eigner and Wagner, 1991, 1: p. 377. For the politics of the Christian Social Movement see Boyer, 1981, pp. 42–59.
23. Hlawatschek, 1985; and Frevert, 1995.
24. Herda, 2000.
25. Section 92 of the Civil Code.
26. Koch, 1997, p. 83.
27. Floßmann, 1992.
28. In the same year, the discrimination against widowers was eliminated. Until that time, widowers were not allowed to continue to run the business of their deceased wives.
29. Files from the estate of the painters' guild are in Wiener Stadt- und Landesarchiv (hereinafter WrStLA).
30. Schwarzmann-Tischler, 1906.
31. *Neues Wiener Tagblatt*, 17 November 1894.
32. For an overview of the economic characteristics of Vienna see Chaloupek, Eigner and Wagner 1991; and the articles 'Gewerbe', 'Handel' and 'Industrie' by Meißl, 1992–7. See also Good, 1966; Komlos 1983a and 1983b; and Banik-Schweitzer and Meißl, 1983.
33. Banik-Schweitzer and Meißl, 1983.

34. Schimmer, 1874; and Ehmer, 1980.
35. Hofmann, 1874; Prazák, 1898; and Bartsch, 1908.
36. Ehmer, 1981.
37. Ehmer, 1980, p. 448.
38. Widow Countess Anna von Fries (1737–1807) offers one example of an influential woman banker who played an important, long-term role in the Fries banking house, which systematically underwrote the industrialization of the Habsburg Empire. See Barth-Scalmani, 1996.
39. Ehmer, 1980; and Rigler, 1976.
40. 'Ergebnisse der gewerblichen Betriebszählung vom 3. Juni 1902 in den im Reichsrate vertretenen Königreichen und Ländern', 1902; Banik-Schweitzer and Meißl, 1983, pp. 34, 36; and Ehmer, 1980, p. 81.
41. Ehmer, 1981.
42. This analysis is based on the probate records in WrStLA of fifty-two affluent businesswomen who died between 1898 and 1910 and were registered at the Viennese Civil Court for Commercial Affairs. My sample includes about one-third of all of the extant probate inventories for businesswomen. The number of women's estates registered in the Vienna Commercial Court is very small, only 3 per cent of the total. Since every businessperson above a certain tax limit was required to register at the Commercial Court, these probate records are generally representative of well-to-do entrepreneurs and constitute some 3–5 per cent of all Viennese self-employed people in industry, trades and commerce. These probate inventories provide assets and liabilities of individual business owners at the time of death and include information on the business venue, the machinery, the workshops, the office equipment and the warehouse stock. See Pammer, 1996.
43. WrStLA, probate record A 127/1899.
44. See the statistical data provided by Oxaal and Weizmann, 1985; Oxaal, Pollak and Botz, 1987; Beller, 1989; and Rozenblit, 1983.
45. The taxable net wealth was calculated on the balance of private assets (cash, savings, securities, real estate, life insurance, claims, furnishings, clothing and bed linen, jewellery, horses and coaches) and private liabilities (private debts, unsettled bills, tax liabilities, hospital and funeral costs) and the company assets which were taken from a balance drawn up on the day of death. In 1910 the average monthly income of a female cook was 45 Crowns; of a nurse 25 Crowns. See Pammer, 1996.
46. WrStLA, probate record A 79/1898.
47. Of the total number of estates at the Vienna Commercial Court in 1872, 36.84 per cent left more than 50,000 Guilder (100,000 Crowns). In 1890 this figure was 17.10 per cent, in 1906 33.11 per cent and in 1913, 36.26 per cent, averaging 30.82 per cent over a forty-year period. See Streller, 1989.

48. The average number of children left behind by all entrepreneurs listed by the Commercial Court in Vienna was 2.5. See Streller, 1989.
49. Bandhauer-Schöffmann, 1997.
50. Ibid.

–9–

Belgium's Tradeswomen

Valérie Piette

Belgian tradeswomen have not attracted much scholarly attention, despite significant research on women's work.[1] Until now, most studies have focused either on women workers in large-scale industries whose labour force was highly visible, such as coal mining and manufacturing, or on those in declining sectors, such as lace making, linen production and other cottage industries. Historians have paid scant attention to the place of females in traditional sectors including agriculture, domestic service, crafts industries or retailing. In the past twenty years scholars have begun to explore Belgian retailing, often in combination with crafts production, in order to understand better the wealth and fortunes of the so-called 'middling sort'.[2] Indeed, retailing and small-scale production were prosperous sectors in nineteenth-century Belgium, thriving in the context of industrialization and urbanization and not yet adversely affected by the competition of department stores. Most of these studies have focused on the activities of men or on male groups and associations; only very recently have some scholars begun to examine the place of women in retailing and small-scale production. This scholarship reflects a newer historiographical trend that considers women's contributions to the economic transformations of nineteenth-century Belgium.[3]

Recent research has also highlighted the significance of the petit-bourgeois family as a labour unit. The importance of this unit as well as the social and gender relations it produced are now much better understood.[4] Historians have demonstrated that the family functioned as an economic unit, which relied on specific roles played by the husband, wife and children, who all shared a single space that combined both work and family living quarters. This research also suggests that older assumptions about women's commercial activities had largely underestimated the reality. Often a man's name and vocation obscured the activities and contributions of his wife, who thus rarely appeared in official documents and workforce statistics. This situation was not unique to Belgium and, as Crossick and Haupt note, 'many more [shops] were recorded under the husband's name while [being] in reality the responsibility of the wife'.[5]

Identifying and analysing the place of women in trade and retail means first confronting a body of preconceived ideas, caricatures and stereotypes. One is inevitably faced with the idealized image of the homemaker which took shape over the course of the nineteenth century. In addition, one is also faced with traditional images of small-scale retailing, depicted either as a supplementary source of family income, as a temporary activity relied on in time of crisis, or as one of the few occupations open to widows. In Belgium the term 'tradeswoman' usually conjured up visions of shopkeepers, street peddlers or milk merchants. Female shopkeepers were part and parcel of the collective imagination, and some, like the milk women who did the delivery rounds with a dog-drawn cart, even belong to folklore! Novels frequently depicted these energetic women, witnesses to the daily life and social activities of their neighbourhood. In all cases, these images were of women in small-scale retailing.

These depictions are not entirely inaccurate. In the nineteenth century, neighbourhood shops were usually female spaces, and tradeswomen were frequently involved in buying and selling.[6] While women were numerous in the retail sector, there were also occasional female wholesalers and merchant-traders and even, if we use the legal definition of 'trader', female manufacturers. A few such women have emerged from the shadows and escaped anonymity. One thinks of Chantal Coché, who manufactured and sold China; Joséphina Dessauer, who headed the Brépol Company which manufactured playing cards; or Ida Ceuppens who ran the Wilemans-Ceuppens brewery. The existence of these women is seldom mentioned and even less frequently explained. The result is that, only a few years ago, one historian could claim that the fact that 'members of the weaker sex may have had access to managerial functions in the economic sphere was generally perceived as odd, if not unseemly'.[7]

When we look systematically for these women, however, we soon discover that the 'exceptions' to the rule were not so exceptional. Quickly we can establish long lists of overlooked women heading their own firms or running their own shops. Recent research has brought some of the less famous to light and allows us to understand and explain their behaviour. Famous and not so famous women took an active role in the process of industrialization and in the intensification of commercial exchanges in Western societies. Married women, single women and more frequently widows left their mark on the history of private and corporate firms. Sometimes they came to head a business as a consequence of the sudden death of a spouse or as the result of inheritance. They frequently ignored a seemingly hegemonic moral code that prescribed a domestic role for all women and elevated domesticity to a social ideal.

Visibility Problems

The problem of terminology is an old one and can be traced back to the first occupational census taken in 1846. A trial census carried out in 1842 had listed an occupation for every male or female. But in 1846 the census authorities introduced the new occupational category of 'assistant' without giving any justification. The number of female shopkeepers fell immediately from 1,960 in Brussels in 1842 (35 per cent of Brussels' total retailers) to 1,093 in 1846. Almost 900 women were thus purged from the occupational statistics solely because of the new terminology.

Other sources besides the census displayed the same confusion between owner/assistant and housekeeper. A comparison of the data from the *patente* register (the *patente* was a form of business licensing tax), with the data from the population registers and the trade directories highlights practices that all artificially enhanced the position of men in trade at the expense of women.[8] Marie Mathys, who lived in St Pierre Street in Brussels in 1846, was listed as a shopkeeper in the tax register – as far as the tax collector was concerned, she ran the business and paid the taxes on it. But the population register lists her as a 'housekeeper' and therefore outside of the labour force. Similarly, Antoine Van Bever, who paid the *patente* for several activities (barbering, storekeeping and retailing drinks by the glass), was listed in the population register only as a barber. His wife, on the other hand, was listed as a grocer. The occupation of women varied from source to source, and shopkeepers turned into housekeepers and vice versa. This was not unique to the nineteenth century; the practice persisted into the twentieth century.

Women, and especially those who married, were also consistently underrepresented in the trade statistics. A detailed analysis of *patentes* records for Brussels in the nineteenth century reveals the marital status of tradeswomen. Again, married women often remained hidden; husbands sometimes paid the tax for an activity which was not theirs, but their wives'. If the couple worked together, only the husband was listed in the tax rolls, and consequently the wife's contribution to the family economy was hidden. Nonetheless, even married women could play a significant economic role. One finds wives engaged in activities completely unconnected to their husband's professions. Such was the case of a tailoress married to a cabinet maker, or the 'wife of Corneille Vanhaelen', listed in the 1846 census as a lace maker and merchant employing six workers, with a husband, a mercantile broker, who paid considerably less tax than her.

In contrast to marriage, widowhood made trading women more visible and strengthened their economic position. A quarter of the retailers in the 1846 census were widows, though they constituted only 13 per cent of the total female population aged 18 and above. This sudden visibility was a legal construct, however. Since 1804 the Civil Code had reduced married women to the status of minor children.[9] A woman who married lost control of the right to dispose freely of her property. Article 215 of the Code declared her incapable of 'giving testimony in front of a court; [or to] give, alienate, mortgage, acquire, through purchase or gift, goods without her husband's consent, or by default, the permission of the court'. Married women's legal incapacity was not eliminated until the twentieth century, and only in successive steps. Married women were therefore made invisible by the Code's restrictions. However, the prescriptions of the Code may be misleading. The female trader (femme *marchande*), a label encompassing female retailers as well as women in production trades, had always constituted a separate legal category.[10] The 1807 Commercial Code treated married tradeswomen differently from the Civil Code, and at times even contradicted it. The Commercial Code did not eliminate the wife's need to gain her husband's permission, as required by the Civil Code, but it did limit the application of this rule. Among other things, the Commercial Code allowed tradeswomen to mortgage or alienate the real estate they held in their own name or offer it as security. Those provisions in favour of married tradeswomen echoed *ancien régime* customary laws, which also treated tradeswomen differently from the rest of the female population.

Electoral law has also been blamed for concealing the activities of tradeswomen. Universal male suffrage did not exist in nineteenth-century Belgium. The *patente* was one of the taxes that could qualify a man for the franchise. The political implications of the *patente* were thus significant, especially at municipal level; some men actually maximized their taxes in order to gain voting privileges. Men could thus be tempted to pay their wives' *patentes*, in order to raise their taxes and be able to vote. But even this trick was not needed. The law stated that upon marriage a man could add his wife's taxes to his own for electoral purposes.[11]

Record keeping policies, the Civil Code, tax legislation and electoral laws thus conspired to disregard a large proportion of the women who were active in trade. This marginalization, both within the sources and by the historians who subsequently studied them, does not mean women were hapless or economically inconsequential. Indeed, norms did not necessarily coincide with practices. One must discard the frequently stated notion that women began working only when widowed. This claim does not stand scrutiny. Some shopkeepers took over the activity of a deceased husband, but without giving up their own. They increased their commercial activities and their sources of income – something widowers rarely did. Others, far from acting as bridges between generations of males, dominated the direction of the family business even when they had adult sons to assist them. Some ceiling plasterers, house painters, coffee-shop owners or breweresses (the feminine form was then common) did not step down despite having adult sons.

Many women became socially and economically visible when they became widows. It is obvious they could easily take over the direction of the business because they knew how it was run – at least in general terms – before their husbands died.[12] One could suggest that widowhood provided a form of economic emancipation for some women. Freed from the limitations of coverture, widows also became visible in the sources. When her husband died, a wife became the mistress of the stores or shops that she had run with her husband or on her own with his permission. She then commonly brought an assistant into the business, either by entering a partnership with children or other relatives, or by remarrying. The latter option was very common in the case of a craft shop or when production and retailing were linked, as in the case of bakers', butchers' and even fishmongers' shops. For example, in Brussels Anne Elizabeth De Jongh was listed as without occupation in the Brussels census. Her husband, Jean Bellis, a baker, died on 27 April 1847. Anne was 43 and had four children aged 15, 13, 3 and 1. She took over the bakery in her own name as required by law, and thus suddenly appeared in the trade statistics. She soon hired a servant to help her. Three years later, she married Jean Christophe Eghels, her journeyman. She was 46, and he was 30. The union did not cause scandal; on the contrary, the two witnesses to the marriage were her first husband's brothers.[13]

In some cases, the widow quickly announced the 'change' of ownership by advertising in her own name. Some trades were even characterized by the presence of many widows, like the hospitality industry or printing. Some widows quickly gained a reputation in these areas and made a name for themselves. This was the case of the widow Contempre, who owned the Grand Hôtel du Boulevard du Régent in Brussels. She was a well-known and respected figure in the city. She had a keen nose for publicity and regularly advertised in various periodicals.

Retailing: A Female Realm

According to the Belgian census of 1856, 32 per cent of people in retailing in the country (almost one-third) were women. In 1890 and 1900, women made up slightly over one-third of retailers, and their proportion was increasing (see Table 9.1).[14] This figure remained stable until 1910 (33 per cent), and then grew significantly between the wars (37 per cent in 1920 and 42 per cent in 1930). This partly reflects the fact that between 1910 and 1930 retail trade expanded considerably. The female advance in this sector was, however, particularly noticeable (Table 9.2). This was a consequence of the depression: during economic downturns, the opening of a small shop by a wife was often necessary for the survival of working-class families. The above figures are nonetheless lower estimates and should be treated with caution.[15]

Small shops, like neighbourhood taverns, were female domains – and most tradeswomen were retailers. But women could also be found in a surprisingly broad range of trades outside retailing. They sometimes worked in professions commonly defined as masculine. The 1865 census for Brussels, for instance, listed

Table 9.1 Men and Women in Retailing in Belgium, 1890 and 1900

	1890		1900	
	Number	%	Number	%
Men	215,559	65.9	248,336	64.5
Women	111,532	34.1	136,900	35.5
Total	327,091	100.0	385,236	100.0

Source: *Recensement général de la population au 31 décembre 1890*, t. 2, Brussels, 1893, pp. 330–1; *Recensement général de la population au 31 déc. 1900*, t. 1, p. LXXIII.

Table 9.2 Men and Women in Retailing in Belgium, 1910–1930

	1910		1920		1930	
	Number	%	Number	%	Number	%
Men	407,148	66.9	214,623	62.4	315,299	57.9
Women	200,793	33.1	129,492	37.6	228,458	42.1
Total	607,941	100.0	344,115	100.0	543,757	100.0

Note: Figures include assistants. The 1920 figures must be handled with caution; the census was taken in haste after the war, at a time when the economy had not yet fully recovered.
Source: *Recensement général de la population au 31 décembre 1910*, Brussels, t. V, 1916, pp. 661–6; *Recensement général de la population au 31 décembre 1920*, t. I; *Recensement général de la population au 31 décembre 1930*, Brussels, 1937, t.V, pp. 10–57.

women who were printers, travelling saleswomen, commission agents, sales directors, and even chimney sweepers. The same was true of the 1880 census; one woman headed a house-painting business, another worked as a mercantile agent, and there were also antique dealers, barbers, repairers, paper manufacturers, tinsmiths, corporate managers, lamp makers, cabinet makers and watchmakers. In the 1910 census two women sold industrial scales, two were gun powder merchants, seven traded in tanning bark, four rented cars and bikes, twenty-eight were shippers, two worked as real estate brokers and five as auctioneers. Women could therefore be found in most sectors and sometimes they completely dominated. As might be expected, food and textiles were sectors where women formed a majority, but they were also prominent in the sale of tobacco and paper products, which were not necessarily perceived as 'feminine' trades (Table 9.3).

One discovers the same situation in the city of Brussels.[16] Women dominated the trade in bread, pastry and confectionery (155 women/105 men), in lace (188/88), in haberdashery and trimmings (214/118), in fashion, undergarments and hats (483/428), in newsprint (169/153) and in religious objects (8/6). Women constituted the majority of rag-and-bone merchants (46/31) and small retailers (616/451). But they also held their own in other less stereotypically feminine

Table 9.3 Sectors with a Majority of Women in Belgium, 1910

Sector	Number	%
Bakery	3,336	66
Grocery	24,809	58
Eggs and dairy products	4,718	56
Haberdashery	4,634	54
Lace	929	65
Woollen hosiery	646	59
Notions	3,518	70
Fashion	3,740	61
Shoes and gloves	1,494	54
Cigars and tobacco	2,147	52
Wallpaper	159	56
Stationery	805	51
Reading cabinets	3	60
Devotional objects	61	56
Small retailers	11,012	65

Source: See Table 9.2.

sectors: rubber items (15/34), soap and perfume (59/75), seeds and grain (33/82), fish (76/129), canes and umbrellas (43/49), second-hand clothing and household items (153/157), and jewellery (83/165). Most peddlers were also women (610 out of 660).

At the same time, the presence of women in other trade-related activities such as transportation, banking or insurance was relatively rare. This had not always been the case. During the *ancien régime* the widow Nettine (1706–75) had been a key player on Brussels' financial stage as a banker for the Austrian Low Countries, and was a well-known social figure. She was intimately involved with the government's secret activities, and her bank enjoyed a dominant position for many years. At her death, the bank was taken over by her sons (and gradually lost its status as a state bank), despite the fact that the widow had wanted to bring her eldest daughter into the business, Dieudonnée Louise Nettine, wife of Adrien-Ange de Walckiers, who became court treasurer in 1775.[17] This famous example is not an isolated one. It was not unusual at that time to see women, often widows, at the head of important industrial, commercial or financial concerns. Other women had been bankers to the state even before the widow Nettine, including Aldegond Pauli and widow Proli (1685–1761), who held this position from 1733 to 1744.[18] Such prominent women were very rare by the nineteenth century; in 1856 the census lists 174 bankers and mercantile brokers in Belgium, and only five of them were women.

Beyond Retailing: Women as Producers

Most women in trade were retailers – but there were some noticeable exceptions, especially in areas that combined production and sales, a commonplace in the nineteenth century. It is even harder to estimate the number of women in those sectors, as they were more likely to work alongside a husband than were retailers. Censuses, *patentes* registers and city directories give the impression that producer-retailers were mostly men: the number of independent women in this sector appears much smaller than the number of men. As one climbs higher in the business hierarchy, it is even rarer to find women. One then has to rely on qualitative sources to get an idea of the extent to which females engaged in these activities.

As expected, many of the female producer-retailers could be found in traditional female sectors, such as textiles and clothing. In Brussels, one could find many stay makers, bonnet makers, tailors, milliners, dressmakers and lace makers. In most cases, these women opened a shop in order to sell their own products. As their businesses grew, these women entrepreneurs hired female workers and shop assistants. But they were no more limited to this 'female sector' than retailers, and they too could be found in a wide range of commodity production activities and services. There were female locksmiths, cabinet makers, painters and mechanics, with feminized occupational titles (*serrurières, ébenistes, peintres, mécaniciennes*). These women set up or took over small businesses that required only a few workers.

One such woman received a visit from investigators who were part of the famous 1843 enquiry into the condition of the working class, and their report provides us with a rare description of this type of enterprise. Marie Bertrand was single and listed in the census as a manufacturer of straw hats, milliner and shopkeeper. Her premises, on the Marché aux herbes in Brussels, were described by the investigators:

[they] include manufacturing premises and several workshops; the latter are part of the dwelling house; we have not visited them. The business occupies 14 to 18 workers, and comprises three shops, including one used to dry the hats and wash the straw. Only two workers are in charge of this task and they must spend most of their time in this room, whose temperature is quite high. The workers who flatten the straw are in the other shops which are well lit and ventilated. All the workers, including the 15 or 16 in the workshops within the house are not from the city; they come from the Province of Liège. The owner provides them with room and board at her own expense, and pays them in addition one to two francs a day depending on their abilities. The shops open at 8 in the morning in winter and close at 10 at night. In summer, the workers begin at 6 and finish at 8. These workers are in good health and do not seem predisposed to any disease.[19]

This long description shows the extensive activities of a small business where production and sales were combined. It is also worth noting that the investigators paid no attention whatsoever to the sex of the owner-manager.

The evidence of women's involvement in larger scale business is more anecdotal and one must often rely on examples of 'exceptional' women – that is, women who until recently would have been deemed female exceptions in masculine enterprises. But researchers are finding more and more women who succeeded husbands or fathers as heads of prosperous businesses. Some even started their own businesses. Examples include china making, publishing and the dry goods trade. After the death of her husband in 1869, Chantal Coche (1826–1911) took over the direction of the family china manufacturing business on the chaussée de Wavre in Ixelles. She turned porcelain into an affordable product and this completely transformed the business. In 1871 the factory employed sixty people, while ten years later the number exceeded 200. Coche China sold well, enjoyed an international reputation and won many prizes abroad. In 1900 Chantal Coche, who was childless, handed the business over to her niece Marthe Coche.[20] In Brussels, the manufacture and sale of porcelain remained largely a female trade.

In Bruges, Caroline Popp emerged as the first female newspaper publisher in the country. Born into a middle-class family, Caroline married the map maker E. Popp at the age of 18. The couple settled in Bruges in a large house on the marketplace. The family spent the rest of their lives there. In 1837 Caroline Popp founded the liberal *Journal de Bruges*. She immediately assumed the direction of this political paper (the only liberal one in Bruges, a very Catholic town) and remained at the helm for fifty-four years, making the journal one of the leading Belgian papers outside of Brussels. In the meantime, her husband devoted himself to his beloved map making. Caroline really had three careers: newspaper editor, literary figure and mother of a large family. She wrote novels, tales and short stories. Most of them were translated into English or German. She also collaborated on several Belgian periodicals: *La Belgique Illustrée, L'Illustration européenne*, the *Globe* and the *Express européen*. She was a character of considerable repute and was publicly recognized in her lifetime, earning various distinctions in Belgium and even in France. She was also made an honorary member of the Belgian press association. Between 1827 and 1843 she gave birth to eight children, all of whom survived. Although the couple had three sons, the *Journal de Bruges* remained a female affair. After her death, it was taken over by her two youngest daughters, and remained in their hands until the death of the youngest in 1920.[21]

Opened in Brussels in 1828 by the Bierbeck family, the Jacqmotte coffee house was initially a shop that traded in colonial goods. It remained in business for a long time thanks to a succession of women, including Louise-Marie Jacqmotte (born in 1848), her daughter-in-law, Marguerite Hollickx, and finally a nièce, Simone

Jacqmotte.[22] The house experienced a spectacular growth (at one point employing 275 persons).[23] It capitalized on an expanding market for colonial goods at the turn of the century, and on the first 'industrial' coffee roasting.

Widows sometimes refused to relinquish control of their firms even when adult sons were prepared to step in. The W. C. brewery in Brussels was started and managed by Ida C. Wielemans after the death of her husband Lambert Wielemans, even though she had adult sons.[24] Anne Derauw, a Brussels breweress, continued managing her business for at least ten years after the death of her husband in 1835; her 31- and 35-year-old sons were listed as 'helpers' in the 1835 population registers.[25] Childless widows often relied on the help of family members, including sisters, cousins and nieces. Widow Knap ran a small distillery with her sister in 1846.[26]

Novels often reflected this reality and sometimes featured women taking over a family business after the death of the owner. This was the case in Emile Leclercq's novel, *The Story of Two Gunsmiths*, which focused on a family business. The sons of the house died during the Belgian revolution of 1830 'leaving J. and C. sole owners of an inventory of guns of all types and about 100 000 F'. The two sisters were determined to run the business together, 'working for those respectable people was as necessary as drinking and eating, therefore although trading in weapons was usually not a female activity, the Hendricks sisters never thought of giving it up. It was part of their lives – if not their very life.' But a trade carried out by women was not by definition a 'female trade' adds the novelist, who further noted that 'the house was not interested in friendliness and sociability; its occupants were not women but merchants'.[27]

Why Open a Shop?

Women who headed large businesses were usually heiresses; this was not necessarily the case for retailers. But why would a woman run a shop, if she had not inherited it? Economic reasons immediately spring to mind, but this was not the case for all. Motivations ranged from absolute necessity to hopes of social mobility.

Sometimes a woman opened a shop when she stopped working for wages. Louis Varlez's well-known investigation of industrial wages in Ghent shows that, among factory workers, one in ten had a wife who ran a shop.[28] These self-employed wives were usually former workers themselves, who had left the factory when they married and were attempting 'the natural transition from the working to the middle class'.[29] Most of these shopkeepers kept neighbourhood pubs (70 per cent), but a few poorer ones operated confectionery shops. Profits were tiny (one or two francs a week), but the initial outlay and the overheads were minuscule, and thus the risks were very low. Other wives sold food door to door, often fish, allowing them to get out of the hallowed domestic sphere for a few days a week (usually on Thursdays and Fridays).[30]

But besides those women who ran small stores to increase the family income, there were others for whom shopkeeping offered a means of social advancement. This happened, for example, among servants who saved their wages to 'establish' themselves and to become their own mistresses. A study of Brussels servants has shown the extent to which opening one's own shop was an economic goal of many servants. A good example is that of the famous Liberal minister Frère-Orban's servant. At his death, Frère-Orban left 4,000 francs to each of his servants, including the cook Justine Grooven and his cleaner Théophile Carpreau. Justine and Théophile decided to use this significant sum of money to open a pub;[31] 'they gave up domestic service and became their own masters'.[32] One also discovers an impressive number of former servants having a go at retailing, and opening various kinds of small shops or selling vegetables.[33] They did not always succeed – retailing was not a foolproof venture, but the attempts themselves reveal a mindset, the desire to be one's own mistress and thus join the lowest ranks of the middle class. They also reveal the symbolic importance attached to independence.

Some of the tradeswomen were thus keepers of small shops. These shops symbolized their owners' longed for upward mobility – but more often than not, they merely allowed them to survive. The majority of tradeswomen operated on a small scale – but some managed to head impressive concerns. The Voss sisters (Lambertine and Angelique) were typical of this group. They were originally from Prussia, and in the second half of the nineteenth century kept a 'store' in rue de la Montagne, Brussels. The 1846 census refers to their establishment as a fashion store. Its annual turnover was 275,000 francs and it paid the highest *patente* in the entire city. The staff were numerous: seven shop girls, a female head seller, a female office clerk, a cook, a female as well as two male servants. Later the sisters opened a second shop in the prestigious Galerie de la Reine (Queen's Mall). Angelique Voss then retired and ended her days as a rentière in the rue Royale.[34] Although such cases were not common, they show that women could become economic heavy weights.

Conclusion

Tradeswomen were first and foremost small-scale, independent operators who kept retail stores. The image of the female homemaker referred to in the introduction did reflect an economic and social reality. Women shopkeepers, retailers or peddlers sold everything, and were absent from no branch of trade. But they were especially visible in certain sectors where they formed a majority: food and textiles, tavern keeping, and street vending.

Retailing was dominated by married women, precisely the group least likely to be represented in the sources. Coverture was written in law and accepted in practice. It is therefore often very difficult to determine whether it was the husband or the wife who kept a family shop. Well into the twentieth century, census takers and tax collectors still systematically attributed a shop to the husband, thus swelling male labour statistics at the expense of women. Consequently, it becomes impossible to know exactly how many women derived an income from trade. Indeed, it would be very difficult to establish that a single individual kept and managed a store, as many trades were truly family businesses and employed – in addition to wives – daughters, sometimes sons, as well as other relatives like sisters and cousins.

In the manufacturing, merchant and wholesale trades, women could run businesses as heiresses, widows or founders. But whereas historians have tended to view female managers as bridges between two male generations, evidence clearly shows that some women clung to their power, even at the expense of adult sons. The alleged absence of middle-class women from the economic sphere does not reflect the reality as revealed by careful investigation. Historians must step outside traditional frames of reference and critically re-read contemporary discourses on the 'feminine private sphere' and the 'masculine public' one. The lower middle class could not always afford to keep its women outside of gainful employment. Most tradeswomen were small-scale retailers – but so were most tradesmen. What is surprising is the range of products these women sold and the range of trades in which they were active. Some were stereotypically 'masculine'. Even women belonging to the elite that produced the discourses of sharply segregated social and economic roles for men and women did not necessarily abide by them. Deliberately or not, many crossed over the boundary into the public sphere, and, like Angelique Voss in Brussels in 1846, might even count as the highest taxed urban retailer!

Notes

1. In Belgium, as in France, the term 'commerce' has two overlapping meanings. The common one refers to buying and selling. A *commerçant/commerçante* is a shopkeeper. Legally speaking, however, everyone covered by the *Code de Commerce* (Commercial Code) is a '*commerçant*' – a category that includes, besides storekeepers, wholesalers and merchant traders, some craftspeople and most manufacturers. Thus, the owner of a spinning mill is a '*commerçant*' – a 'trader'.
2. Hannes, 1973; Kurgan-Van Hentenryk, 1979; Kurgan-Van Hentenryk and Jaumain, 1992; Jaumain, 1995.
3. Piette, 2000a and 1996; Lemmens, 1987; Van Molle, L. and Heyrman, 2001.
4. Haupt, 1979; Jaumain, 1993; Crossick and Haupt, 1995.
5. Crossick and Haupt, 1995, p. 93.

6. Jaumain, 1993.
7. Richard, 1996.
8. The *patente* was a tax levied on everyone engaged in a profession, craft, retail business or trade. It was introduced during the French regime and expanded during the Dutch period (1815–30). See, for instance, Hannes, 1975 and 1965; Kurgan-Van Hentenryk, 1979; Van Neste, 1989; Piette, 1996 and 2000a.
9. Belgium was annexed to France between 1794 and 1815. The Napoleonic Civil Code has been in force ever since. For the first gendered analysis of the Belgian Civil Code, see Beauthier and Piette, 2003.
10. Nandrin, 2002 and 2001.
11. See note 8.
12. Richard, 1996, p. 54.
13. Piette, 1996, p. 23.
14. This steady progression has also been noted by Yernaux, 1964.
15. Yernaux, 1964.
16. *Ville de Bruxelles. Recensement de 1910*, Brussels, 1910, pp. 120–39.
17. Galand, 2000.
18. Ibid.
19. *Enquête sur la condition des classes ouvrières*, 1846, pp. 655–56.
20. Kurgan, Jaumain and Montens, 1996.
21. On the *Journal de Bruges* see Mathelart, 1994. On Caroline Popp see Biette, 1987; *Biographie nationale* (notice de A. Piters), t. XVIII, col. 33–8.
22. *Biographie nationale* (notice de L. Biot), t. XXXIII, col. 695–704.
23. Massange, 1987.
24. Vaes, 1990; Kurgan, Jaumain and Montens, 1996.
25. Archives de la ville de Bruxelles (AVB), Registre de population, 1835, n°8933 et 6N f°190.
26. AVB, Registre de population, 1846, N2 f°50.
27. Leclercq, 1864.
28. Varlez, 1901.
29. Ibid.
30. Ibid.
31. Piette, 2000a.
32. Bar, 1903.
33. Piette, 2000a.
34. Piette, 1996.

–10–

Limited Opportunities?
Female Retailing in Nineteenth-century Sweden
Tom Ericsson

> Look how very limited the Swedish woman's right to earn her own living is. She is allowed to sell small wares, trinkets, pieces of glass and bake pastries. This is no satire, it is reality. But a man is allowed to perform many occupations which are suitable for women. He can be a teacher for girls. He can be in charge of midwives. Men are also doctors for women. They also engage in many other occupations that could be as easily carried out by women, such as bookbinder, bookseller, greengrocer, furniture dealer, baker, painter, tailor, etc.[1]

When Carl Adolf Agardh, a professor at Lund University, made this statement in 1857, Swedish women's ability to be self-supporting was becoming a subject of concern. Female celibacy was on the rise, because the number of women aged over 15 years exceeded the number of men by growing margins. Agardh concluded that 'nearly half of all women who are allowed to marry will be unmarried, because there are not enough men'.[2] His contemporaries shared his concerns, especially as many believed increased female celibacy rates would translate into an increased number of illegitimate children.[3] Women who could not support themselves would instead lead an immoral life.

Demographic changes led the state to try to open trades to women that had until then been closed to them, and to facilitate their entry into new occupations. The opening to women of public sector lower middle-class occupations, including positions as clerks, telegraph and telephone operators and teachers, generated considerable public debate (until the middle of the century, the only white collar occupations opened to women were midwives and nurses).[4] But the state also wanted women to enter more traditional occupations such as crafts and retailing, which were also deemed suitable for unmarried women of that class, and between 1846 and 1864 it broadened women's rights to engage in trade.[5] This fitted into the context of removing, for both men and women, all restrictions on entry into trades, beginning with the abolition of guilds in 1846 and culminating in the establishment of freedom of trade in 1864. The legal status of unmarried women also changed: Sweden did away with the legal incapacity of adult unmarried women in several steps beginning in 1858. By 1884 unmarried women over the age of 21 could run their own lives without the permission of a male guardian, like men. By making it possible for unmarried women to engage in 'respectable occupations', the state believed it could counteract the consequences of female celibacy. In Sweden, then, the state took the initiative in bringing down some of the barriers that stood between women and employment, especially self-employment, and deliberately brought them into the 'public sphere'.

Despite this unusual attitude of the Swedish state, little research has investigated women's roles in small business in Sweden. There are several reasons for this. The first is that crafts and retailing, generally speaking, have not interested many historians. Traditional, as well as recent, Swedish historiography has focused on the emergence of larger-scale capitalism.[6] Historians have devoted their attention to the beginnings of the factory system, the introduction of new technologies in the production process, and the development of large-scale industries, as those are generally considered key to industrialization and modernization. By contrast, craftsmen and shopkeepers who were associated with pre-industrial and 'traditional' societies have attracted limited attention. In addition, the male historians who have studied this socio-economic group have focused on the most visible of those activities – which were the ones carried out by men. More than twenty years ago, Stadin Kekke pointed out that women were hardly mentioned in the history of Swedish small industries, and although the history of women in small business has not been totally neglected, it remains limited.[7]

The pioneering work was Gunnar Qvist's *Kvinnofrågan i Sverige 1809–1846*, published in 1960.[8] Qvist analysed labour legislation relating to women, the contemporary debate concerning women's work, and the social and demographic changes in Swedish society that formed the background to this debate. In subsequent studies, published in 1977, he also considered women's work in the late nineteenth century, but from a more general perspective.[9] Women in small business were also the focus of Kekke Stadin's study of early urban industry in Sweden and Ann-Marie Lennander-Fällström's research on women's work in the town of Örebro.[10] A majority of Örebro female ratepayers were widows engaged in retail trade, crafts or innkeeping. However, these studies are primarily concerned with the seventeenth and eighteenth centuries. Christine Lindqvist has studied, on the other hand, the retail trade in nineteenth-century Stockholm, and analysed the place of women in traditional trades such as innkeeping and costermongering. Lindqvist shows that those occupations were important for females, especially married ones. The women obtained rights to engage in such activities because of their sex, and because of men's inability to support their families.[11] Lunander, who also studied Örebro, but in a later period, found that in 1860 one out of every five shopkeepers was a woman, while female artisans were almost non-existent. Official statistics in the 1890s show almost identical proportions. However, Lunander found that women, particularly unmarried women, often went around the town visiting households to help with sewing, laundry and baking.[12]

This chapter looks at those women who took advantage of new opportunities to earn their living in the retail trades. Who were they? What was their social background? What was their family situation? Was the decision to open a shop the result of an individual or a family strategy? It focuses on three towns in northern Sweden: Sundsvall, Härnösand and Umeå. These places were rather small compared to many urban centres on the European continent, but they were typical of late nineteenth-century Swedish towns. In 1880 Sundsvall had a population of 9,116 inhabitants, Härnösand 5,370 and Umeå 2,818. Sundsvall, one of Västernorrland county's saw-milling centres, was part of the county's expanding lumber industry. The county itself was one of the fastest growing industrial areas of northern Europe. Most of the lumber activities, however, took place beyond the town limits, while Sundsvall itself was dominated by small trades, such as handicrafts and retailing, as well as by port activities. Härnösand was an administrative centre, the seat of the episcopal see of northern Sweden and of Västernorrland county government. Most of the townspeople engaged in small trades or worked for the government, the bishopric or the school system. Further north, Umeå was the seat of Västerbotten county government and had a relatively homogeneous social structure. There were hardly any industries, except for a few small sawmills located just outside the town. Retailing and handicrafts occupied most of the residents there.[13]

The Swedish state's desire to open trades to women had the potential to create a situation that contrasted sharply with the one that had existed in the eighteenth and early nineteenth centuries. It was, however, not completely without precedents. Adolf Agardh's remarks clearly indicate that at mid-century Swedish women were excluded from many occupations and trades, which made it difficult for them to earn their own living. More specifically, ownership of workshops and retail shops had been strictly regulated by laws and ordinances dating back to the eighteenth century. Coupled with the guild system, which was not abolished until 1846, such restrictions left a legacy of the exclusion of women from a wide range of trades. Both the 1720 ordinance regulating crafts and the 1734 ordinance regulating retail trade stipulated that only men enjoying burgher rights could become master craftsmen or retailers. The regulations were applied in the breach, however, and burghers' widows could continue their husbands' activities. Other ordinances regulated women's work in specific trades. In sectors like the fancy goods trade, for instance, female participants were drawn from specific sections of the population, and could work only if they met certain conditions.[14] Married women were almost totally excluded.[15] However, the situation was, different in Stockholm, the capital. At the beginning of the nineteenth century, married women in the city were allowed to work as innkeepers and hawkers, trades which were not regulated by the guilds. In 1747 the Stockholm municipal authorities had introduced regulations reserving innkeeping to poor widows and disabled women who could not support themselves, or be supported by a husband. A decade later, additional regulations stipulated that hawkers' licences would be issued only to unmarried men and women. Though these regulations were clear, actual practice was quite a different thing. It was unusual for a licence to be given to a poor single woman. Instead, many married women were granted a licence because their husbands could not support them.[16] It is also obvious from a close look at the way the regulations were implemented that the authorities did this purposefully.

One group of women, however, played an important, albeit passive, role in the transmission of craft shops. Under 'änkekonservering' (preservation of the widow), the widow of a master artisan remarried a journeyman, who became the new owner of the workshop. Until the guild system was abolished in 1846, this was often the only way for a journeyman to get a workshop of his own. As a consequence, the practice became common. In a range of different studies, historians have shown that at least 10 to 20 per cent of all Swedish journeymen obtained their workshop by marrying the widow of a master artisan. As was carefully noted in an entry in the marriage register for the town of Eskilstuna: 'He produced Major Nordwall's certificate of the 20th January that he, although until now merely a journeyman, possesses the full right to become a master as soon as he through marriage with this widow becomes the owner of a workshop and tools.'[17] In the city of Malmö, the percentage of widows marrying journeymen was lower. Lars Edgren found that about 10 per cent of master artisans' widows remarried. However, those who did remarry were usually the youngest ones. Those who became widows after the age of 44 seldom entered into wedlock again. The average age of widows of master artisans remarrying was 39, and the average age difference between bride and groom was eight years. Remarriage was also more frequent in those branches of the handicrafts that required large economic investments in capital and tools.[18] This suggests that many of these widows in the handicrafts sector were in a strong financial position. As a consequence, they were able to keep their place in the local social structure. The importance of the economic position of the widow, who owned property and a small workshop, has also been noted in other European societies. Additional female business activities were also often the result of inheritance. Women were regarded as an occasional workforce, but were also expected to act as a bridge between two generations of men. Widows or even other female relatives had the responsibility to run the business until a male heir was able to take over.[19] Although strictly regulated, women's involvement in trade was therefore not unknown under the guild system. Estimating the number of female shopkeepers in the Swedish retail trade before 1846 is almost impossible. More reliable figures appear in the mid-1850s, which suggest that there were around 1,600 female shop owners in Sweden in 1855.[20]

What was new in nineteenth-century Sweden was the rate of permanent female celibacy. From the middle of the century onwards, those women who never married constituted around 40 per cent of the Swedish population; married women accounted for around 47 per cent, and widows for around 12 per cent. During the nineteenth century the proportion of unmarried women increased in the adult age groups. For example, 13.7 per cent of the women born between 1801 and 1810 were still unmarried between 1841 and 1849 (age 40 to 49), and 24.3 per cent of the women born between 1871 and 1880, who reached 40, did not marry. There were 22,160 unmarried women in the age group 40–49 in 1840, and 46,828 in the same age group in 1880. This trend was largely caused by a general decrease in the frequency of marriages. Between 1751 and 1800 nuptiality stood at 8.47 per thousand; between 1801 and 1850 it fell to 7.88 per thousand, further declining to 6.59 per thousand in the second half of the century.[21] A large proportion of adult women thus stood the risk of having to support themselves, and this proportion increased with years.

Table 10.1 Civil Status of Women Aged 15 Years and over in Sweden, 1830–1900

Year	Unmarried	Married	Widows
1830	34.7	50.8	14.5
1840	39.1	47.2	13.7
1850	40.4	46.5	13.1
1860	39.6	47.8	12.6
1870	40.3	47.2	12.5
1880	41.1	47.1	11.8
1890	40.1	47.9	12.0
1900	41.3	46.8	11.9

(Percentage of all women)

Source: Historisk statistik för Sverige, Del 1. Befolkning, Stockholm 1967, p. 79, table 20.

Female Retailing in Sweden after 1865

In 1888, 55-year-old Emma Johanna Brandt applied to the municipal authorities of Härnösand in northern Sweden to be included in the town's trade register as a milliner.[22] At that time, all who wanted to carry on a trade had to be registered as the local authorities and the state wanted to keep track of the population and its business activities. Emma Brandt had been registered before. She began selling fancy goods in the 1860s. At that time it was very unusual for shops in small

Swedish towns to be so specialized. Emma Brandt's shop seems to have been successful for many years. She could even afford to have two employees in 1875.[23] But at the beginning of the 1880s, the economy took a turn for the worse and Emma Brandt ran into problems. In 1882 she went bankrupt.[24] Bankruptcy was common in the retail trade in Sweden, as elsewhere in Europe, so she was not unusual and, like many in her situation, she soon reopened her business.[25]

Emma Brandt had been born in Härnösand in 1833. Her father was the owner of a dye-works.[26] When he died in 1840, her mother became the owner of the dye-works. A year later, Emma's mother remarried a baker, who took over the business.[27] Emma Brandt thus came from a comfortable, although not especially rich, home. Her parents probably expected that she would marry a man with a similar social background and raise a family, but she never married. Emma Brandt was typical of the kind of women the Swedish state had in mind when it decided retailing should be opened to females: she was unmarried, from the lower-middle class and, if not able to work, would have to be supported by her parents, or by the state.

Women like Emma Brandt took advantage of the freedom of trade. After its introduction, the number of women in urban retailing increased from 2,359 in 1870 to 3,384 in 1895 (Table 10.2). Their share of the total number of retailers remained almost the same during the last decades of the nineteenth century, and national statistics give a picture of a rather stable proportion of female shopkeepers. During the last three decades of the nineteenth century about 25 per cent of all retailers were women. However, it is likely that there were more women than the official statistics imply. Very small shops were probably omitted from surveys, because the authorities did not regard them as important enough to appear in official commercial statistics. Women's business activities often took place in back yards and on temporary premises and were, consequently, never registered.[28]

Table 10.2 Women in Urban Retailing in Sweden, 1870–95

Year	Total women retailers	As % of all retailers
1870	2,359	29.0
1875	2,168	25.2
1880	2,462	24.9
1885	3,013	26.2
1890	2,912	25.0
1895	3,384	26.6

Source: Bidrag till Sveriges officiella statistik (BiSOS), *Inrikes handel och sjöfart*. Stockholm 1870–95; BiSOS, *Fabriker och manufakturer*, Stockholm 1870–95.

The sex ratio of retailers differed considerably between the three towns under investigation and in relation to the figures for Sweden as a whole (Table 10.3). The initial introduction of freedom to trade in these northern towns seems to have had very little effect on women in retail. Both the proportion and the number of female retailers were very low, and the figures reached the national level only during the last decades of the century. In each town, the changes were abrupt. As a consequence of the great fire of 1888, the whole of Sundsvall was rebuilt in the following years, and the town became more of a centre for trade and commerce. In 1885, 7.4 per cent of Sundsvall's retailers were women; after the fire, the proportion almost doubled. In 1890, 13.5 per cent of retailers were women.[29] The figures for Härnösand and Umeå were much higher earlier (see Table 10.3). Until 1890, there were more female retailers in those two towns than in Sundvall, despite the latter having a larger population. The proportion of female shopkeepers was in line with the national average in Umeå after 1880 and in Härnösand after 1885. And although the proportion of female shopkeepers was on the increase in Umeå, in Härnösand it declined before regaining lost ground.[30] It is difficult to draw strong conclusions from these figures, because the numbers are small. However, it seems that in the two towns where crafts and retail were economically significant, women asserted their presence earlier than in the more industrial centre of Sundsvall. Additionally, in Sundsvall and Härnösand, the sharp increase in the proportion of female retailers follows very soon after the final emancipation of unmarried women (1884).

Table 10.3 Women in Retailing 1865–1890: Sundsvall, Härnösand, Umeå

Year	Sundsvall Number	%	Härnösand Number	%	Umeå Number	%
1865	2	2.2	10	22.2	4	10.5
1870	2	2.5	7	13.7	4	10.3
1875	1	0.8	8	11.6	8	19.5
1880	5	4.4	9	13.6	11	26.2
1885	10	7.4	19	29.2	14	31.8
1890	30	13.5	27	36.5	10	23.8

Source: Bidrag till Sveriges officiella statistik (BiSOS), *Inrikes handel och sjöfart*, Stockholm 1870–95; BiSOS, *Fabriker och manufakturer*, Stockholm 1870–95.

In all three towns, the majority of female retailers were unmarried: 63 per cent of those registered in 1885 were unmarried, 30 per cent were married and 7 per cent were widows. The marital status of the retailers thus differed considerably from that of the whole Swedish female population, and single women were overrepresented in this occupation (see Table 10.1). But the state policy of liberalizing women's access to trade also created work opportunities for married women. The majority of the retailers were middle-aged: 28 per cent of the women in retailing and handicrafts were aged 20–34, 47 per cent were aged 35–49, and 25 per cent were above 50. The mean age was 41.9 in 1885. Married retailers were, however, significantly younger: unmarried women had a mean age of 43.4, widows 49.7 and married women 32.7. This suggests that retailing fitted differently in the life course of the different categories of women.

According to Sten Carlsson, women from different social and occupational backgrounds experienced distinct marriage patterns between 1805 and 1860. Daughters of farmers and the working population married more often, while daughters of the middle and upper classes were more likely to remain unmarried.[31] Retailing provided a way for single petit-bourgeois women to keep their social status. A shop served the purpose of avoiding downward social mobility, as argued by George Alter in his study of the Belgian town of Verviers. The majority of female retailers in Sundsvall, Härnösand and Umeå had a father who was middle class or upper bourgeois. Most fathers were master artisans, shopkeepers or lower middle-class workers. These women were often born in urban areas, either the town in which they carried on their business or in another town. About 20 per cent came from the countryside around the three towns (Table 10.4). Retailing was thus the preserve of lower middle-class urban women.

Table 10.4 Geographic Origin of Female Retailers, 1885

Geographic origin	Number
Born in same town	11
Born in the same region	
Urban	2
Rural	8
Born in other region	
Urban	13
Rural	9
Total	43

Source: *Indiko*, Demografiska Databasen, Umeåuniversitet, *Församlingsböcker*, Microfiche, Forskningsarkivet vid Umeå universitet.

Female Strategies

As was noted above, not all female retailers were single or widowed. A significant proportion was married. Retailing offered females of different economic statuses a variety of strategies for making a living.

Women were often responsible for someone else, an older mother or father, a younger sibling, or occasionally an illegitimate child. Being a spinster or widow did not necessarily entail living alone. It was common for both unmarried women and widows in small business to live together with someone else, either children of their own, foster children or relatives (for example, an old father or mother or both, and sometimes a younger brother or sister). More than 50 per cent of the unmarried or widowed retailers in the three towns lived in a household with a kin person or a foster child. In 1885, 16 lived alone, 3 lived in a household together with small children (under the age of 15), 5 had foster children, 4 lived together with parents, a father, a mother or both, and 6 lived in a household with siblings.[32]

Unmarried women sometimes tried to build a family without a husband by taking a foster child. Fostering was relatively common in nineteenth-century Sweden. In Stockholm, especially, it was prevalent among poor, working-class people, but less so among the middle class. The reason was economic: local authorities paid the foster parents a stipend to take care of the child. The same situation prevailed in Örebro, where Lunander found that low-income families often had foster children.[33] In Örebro it was unusual for foster parents to be unmarried. However, in the three towns under consideration here, self-employed women who had foster children were all single. The reason could have been economic too, as in Stockholm. But other explanations are plausible. Firstly, many of the women had reached an age when they would never marry, and taking a foster child was one way to create a family without a husband. It was a way for them to attempt to meet social expectations about women: marry and raise a family. Secondly, a foster child could also be economically useful. Children provided cheap labour. Even a small child could work in a shop, run errands and take orders. The sources available do not allow us to distinguish foster children from employees, as the latter are not listed by name. There is, however, indirect evidence that foster children worked in retail shops. For instance, in Umeå Sofia Stenman took two foster children in the middle of the 1880s. Until then, she had been registered as having no employees. Afterwards, she was listed as having two. Thirdly, foster children were a form of old age insurance – they could take care of the foster parent when she could no longer work, in the same way as a biological child would.

Single and widowed women had been able to become independent shopkeepers in the nineteenth century because the state emancipated them and removed other obstacles to their trading activities. Married women continued to face constraints. Even after freedom of trade was established in 1864, the authorities retained certain restrictive regulations concerning married women. They could not be financially responsible for a shop. A male, who did not have to be the husband, had to assume liability for the business.[34] But while the law restricted married women's autonomy, it did not prevent them from trading. Female married retailers may not have had to be self-supporting, but the shop nonetheless played an important role in their family's economy. For example, Brita Carlström and Christina Eriksson, who opened grocery stores in Härnösand at the beginning of the 1880s, were married to unskilled workers. The revenue from the small shop, even if it was minimal, was probably a necessary supplement to the total family income. These two women belonged to the lower strata of society and this made them unusual. The majority of married retailers had husbands who were better positioned on the town's socio-economic ladder. In Härnösand, for instance, five women were married to shopkeepers, two to wholesalers, seven to lower middle-class men, and only two belonged to the working class. These women were unlikely to open a shop because they were really poor – on the other hand, several had large families, and this may have enticed them to seek a supplementary income. When Sara Högberg opened her shop in 1885, she was married to a shipmaster, and they had eight children to support. Another woman – Anna Brita Hedin – had six children together with her husband, who was a shopkeeper.

The priorities of different phases of the female life course may have been behind the activities of women married to men in trade. While their children were young, they may not have been able to engage in autonomous activity; once the children could take care of themselves, or of each other, the women may have begun to assume greater economic power. Alternatively, they may have branched out into related economic activities: when husband and wife were both in trade, the man tended to run a general store and his wife to cater for a specifically female clientele. If one looks at the life course of these married women – in spite of the number being small – it seems as if their business activities followed a rather similar pattern. Before marriage they had no experience of working in a shop. There is no indication in the sources that they had had an occupation that could be linked to such employment. As long as they gave birth to new children, they did not work outside the house. When the children became older, they either started to work part-time or opened a shop of their own. In a very few cases these women gave birth to children after they had opened a shop.

Remarriage by artisans' or shopkeepers' widows seems to have become less common. The social and economic position of the widow was not as strong as it was under the old guild system. After 1864 there were fewer restrictions in the handicrafts or the retail trade that limited the possibilities for a journeyman or shop assistant to open a workshop or retail business. If a person had the necessary capital, handicrafts and retailing were open to anyone. Moreover, to open a small workshop or retail business required relatively little capital, which meant that almost anyone could do it.

The fact that the opening of a small business did not require a large amount of capital made it easier for women. In many shops, some of the stock could be obtained for next to nothing. Shops selling food were especially inexpensive to open, and thus attracted women. Many branches of the retail trade had much in common with traditional female household tasks. Trades that required knowledge about and skills in sewing, cooking or baking often attracted widows and spinsters. As has been pointed out in the case of Britain, 'many women turned their culinary skill to profitable use'.[35] In the handicrafts, women drew on the skills they had acquired while assisting their husbands. The selling of the products had often been the wives' responsibility, but they were also frequently involved in the production process. For example, the wife of a coppersmith burnished the vessels, while the wife of a shoemaker blackened the shoes and sometimes tanned and prepared the leather. Most of the women in trade in the three towns under consideration here were engaged in the traditional branches of retailing which had much in common with former household tasks. Businesses run by women had something else in common: they were very small. The majority of women, at least in the retail trade, worked alone, or they had only one employee, at least according to official statistics. This fitted the national pattern. Data from the late nineteenth century indicates that the majority of retail shops were small. In 1880 there were about 11,500 urban retail shops, with an average number of 1.2 employees. The average number of employees was slightly higher in the two largest cities of Stockholm and Göteborg: 2.0. The real difference between retail shops run by men and women is to be found when their incomes are compared. The majority of women had very small incomes, and almost all can be found among the least-taxed retailers in the northern towns. In Sundsvall in 1880, for instance, male shopkeepers paid an average of 49 Swedish Crowns a year in taxes, while females paid 10 Swedish Crowns. Swedish retailers fall into the category which in Britain is called 'penny capitalism'. One of its characteristics was the fact that it raised very little money for the person selling the goods. However, the Swedish situation appears to have differed from the British variety in one respect. In Britain, penny capitalism was frequent among working-class women. The British historian John Benson argues that almost all women of the working class had at some time tried to sell something to make a profit.[36] In northern Sweden at least, penny capitalism was more a characteristic of the lower-middle class. Swedish female retailing also broadly fitted into the trends identified by other chapters in this book: women tended to concentrate on activities which were extensions of their household activities and on very small businesses.

Conclusion

Swedish single women had historically been involved in the retail trade, but had been hemmed in by legal and ideological restrictions. Married women had been almost entirely excluded from this activity. Widows had been expected to act as generational bridges between two men, and poor women could be licensed as hawkers or innkeepers to ensure they supported themselves and did not become a charge on the public purse. When permanent female celibacy became an object of concern in the middle of the nineteenth century, the state authorities facilitated women's access to specific trades. Women took advantage of those opportunities. As in the rest of Europe, however, most female retailers opened shops that required little initial capital and the majority of these self-employed women had very low incomes. Their strategies also varied according to their marital status, and the phase of their life course.

Widows, especially those who had young children, had to find ways to support their families. Taking over their husband's trade would have seemed normal, a continuation of past practices when widows acted as bridges between two generations of men. Single women similarly had to support themselves and often other relatives as well. One should not, however, overlook other factors that may have encouraged those women to go into trade. One was a sense of emancipation gained from being their own mistress. Another was the preservation of their social status. Self-employment gave women a recognized social status and also prevented downward social mobility, as in the case of Emma Brandt. George Alter believed this motivated women in Verviers in Belgium and described shopkeeping as 'an opportunity for unmarried women and widowed women with sufficient capital to remain in the petty bourgeoisie'.[37] Married women's motives were probably more complex as they had husbands who were meant in theory to support them. Economics certainly played a role: shopkeeping supplemented the family income. But not all shopkeepers came from the poorest families, and in Sweden, as in France or Belgium for instance, they belonged to the lower-middle class. They may have sought to escape, at least for part of the day, the monotony of housekeeping; after 1874, when married women were allowed to control their own earnings, they may have sought a degree of financial autonomy and aspired to social mobility.

Notes

1. Agardh, 1857, p. 284.
2. Ibid.
3. af Forsell, 1844, p 122.
4. Ericsson, 1983, ch. 4. On wider legal changes affecting women see Ighe, 2004.
5. Qvist, 1980; Göransson, 1990; Ågren, 1999.
6. Torstendahl, 1984.
7. Stadin, 1980, p. 304; Söderberg, 1965; Lunander, 1988; Ericsson, 1988; Bladh, 1992; Artaeus, 1992; Svanberg, 1999; Petersson, 2001.
8. Qvist, 1960.
9. Qvist, 1977.
10. Stadin, 1980; Lennander-Fällström, 1987.
11. Lindqvist, 1987.
12. Lunander, 1988, pp. 30–2; Ericsson, 1988.
13. Steckzén, 1921; Historisk statistik för Sverige, 1967, pp. 61–62; Ericsson, 1997.

14. Qvist, 1960, pp. 44–5.
15. Qvist, 1960.
16. Lindqvist, 1987; pp. 136–41; Bladh, 1992.
17. Hörsell, 1982, p. 34; Hörsell, 1983, pp. 95 and 139.
18. Edgren, 1983.
19. Qvist, 1977, pp. 145–80.
20. Bidrag till Sveriges officiella statistik, 1864.
21. Carlsson, 1977, pp. 11–14.
22. Anmälningar till handelsregistret, 1888.
23. Årsberättelser över handlare och hantverkare. Städer, 1875.
24. Konkursdiarier, 1864–85.
25. Lunander, 1988, p. 101; Haupt, 1982, pp. 95–130; Martin, 1980, pp. 1251–68.
26. Födelse- och dopbok, 1833.
27. Husförhörslängd, 1840.
28. Ericsson, 1988; Alter, 1988.
29. Ericsson, 1988.
30. Årsberättelser över handlare och hantverkare 1885, 1890; Lunander, 1988, pp. 90–1.
31. Carlsson, 1977.
32. Husförhörslängder, 1885.
33. Öberg, 1989, pp. 161–88; Lunander, 1988, p. 150.
34. Alter, 1988, p. 110.
35. Benson, 1983, p. 116.
36. Benson, 1983.
37. Alter, 1988.

–11–

Retailing, Respectability and the Independent Woman in Nineteenth-century London

Alison C. Kay

Introduction

As in many British cities, the number of adult females outnumbered males in nineteenth-century London. This was particularly true among the middle class where the excess of women meant that, by necessity, many had to seek an independent living. There were simply too many women to be comfortably married off and harnessed in the gilded cage of private domesticity. These independent females turned to a variety of money-making activities, including teaching, self-employment and small business. It is estimated that about one-fifth of all businesses in Britain at this time, including self-employment, were owned and operated by women.[1] Despite this, women have been notoriously difficult to identify in conventional historical sources. This chapter will focus on the trade cards of London businesswomen, a dominant form of advertising in this period, and investigate the role they played in harnessing the ideology of 'separate spheres' to women's own advantage.

This premise differs from the traditional interpretation of women's withdrawal from business activity in Britain over the course of the nineteenth century. As an analytical framework, the separate spheres paradigm largely originates from the work of two pioneering female economic historians: Alice Clark's *Working Life of Women in the Seventeenth Century* (1919) and Ivy Pinchbeck's *Women Workers and the Industrial Revolution, 1750–1850* (1930).[2] The separation of home and workplace that supposedly accompanied the growth of factories and workshops over the period 1600 to 1850 was key to both Clark and Pinchbeck's analyses of the transition in women's labour-market participation. This separation constrained women's employment opportunities and reoriented their lives around the domestic sphere. Vickery has argued that it is likely that Clark and Pinchbeck's models of 'separation' were at least loosely informed by contemporary theories on the subjection of women, particularly that of Friedrich Engels. His book *The Origin of the Family, Private Property and the State* argued that the transition to individualistic commercial society drove a wedge between the public world of work and the private household, consigning the sexes to different arenas.[3]

One explanation for the enduring nature of this paradigm is the place it has been given in explanations regarding the formation of middle-class identity. Davidoff and Hall argue that between 1780 and 1850 the rise of the British middle class brought an increased emphasis on gender differences and the division of arenas into public and private, work and domesticity, men and women.[4] In short, the notion of separate spheres became an ideological motor of middle class formation. However, as Alexander has cautioned, we have to pick our way through the 'labyrinth of middle-class moralism and mystification'.[5] The middle class was a very broad group, stretching far up and down the income scale and encompassing professionals and trades-persons alike. Not all its inhabitants could afford to 'keep' a non-working wife or daughter and not all daughters married. Secondly, 'ideas of womanhood' need to be translated into evidence of legal, economic and financial tools of this female subordination, if the prescribed withdrawal of women from business is to be seen as reality. True, the Reform Act excluded women from the vote. However, not all barriers to public participation were so enduring. Vickery's study of genteel women's lives in Georgian England has illustrated that the public/private dichotomy had multiple applications, which only sometimes mirrored a male/female distinction, and then not always perfectly.[6] Similarly, in a study of several generations of women in the Paget family, Peterson uncovered a great variety of experiences. She concluded that we need to transcend the stereotype of the middle-class woman restricted to the private sphere:

> Even as an ideal, the angel in the house did not belong to these families. She was the dream of the lower middle class ... To her the angel was an ideal, a model of the gentlewoman that she aspired to become, little knowing that the angel she admired did not exist.[7]

The idea of separate spheres was, therefore, more an ideal than a reality. However, any study of women's business activities still faces the hurdle of finding evidence of these women and must necessarily be innovative in its use of sources. No clear measure of the number of women in business or the variety or value of their efforts exists for London or any other nineteenth-century British town. Consequently, historians have to look for reflections of female economic endeavours in other sources, including records of advertising, general government statistics relating to employment trends, trade directories and the census. All have their benefits and provide valuable snapshots of women that operated in the public sphere. However, the evidence also has its drawbacks. It was, for example, prohibitively expensive, for a large portion of the business population – both male and female – to place a newspaper advertisement until late in the nineteenth century. Similarly, trade directories were biased in their compilation and consequently coverage. The census suffers from a number of well-documented flaws.[8] Much of the explanation for women's invisibility in many of these sources stems from the fact that the government and other public bodies upheld and promoted the dominant ideology of separate spheres. Consequently there is a need to look beyond representations of the past created by masculine-controlled organizational bodies.

London Businesswomen

An alternative source of information on local business communities is fire insurance records. The broad patterns of the economic activities of metropolitan women can be gleaned from an analysis of the head office compilations of fire insurance policies taken out with one of London's largest insurance companies. Fire insurance was consumed vociferously in the nineteenth century and the hand-scribed Sun Fire Office series running from 1793 to 1863 contains over 1.3 million policies. Examining complete sample years (1761, 1851, 1861) reveals that policies taken out by women consistently constituted a 10 per cent share of all the Sun Fire policies in each year. Around 20 per cent of these policies held by women related to self-employment and small business ventures, covering stock, utensils, fixtures and goods in trust. Based on a 5 per cent sample, this compares to around 45 per cent of men's policies.[9] In raw numbers, London women's business policies increased fivefold from the mid-eighteenth to the mid-nineteenth century (1747 to 1861). Clearly metropolitan women were active in business in the nineteenth century. And yet, these women represent only the tip of the iceberg. This survey does not account for those women who turned to other insurance companies such as the Royal or the Phoenix, whose records no longer exist, or those that chose simply not to insure, perhaps because their capital commitments were small.[10]

Whatever their trade, in nineteenth-century London women in business were heavily, if not predominantly, involved in retailing. Around half of all women's business policies could be grouped into just ten trades in the two nineteenth-century sample dates and six of these trades were also in the ten most common trades a century earlier in 1761: milliners and dressmakers, chandlers, haberdashers and hosiers, victuallers, coffee-house keepers and linen drapers. By 1851 and 1861, stationers and tobacconists were also among the ten most common trades.[11] The presence of women in these trades no doubt reflects the fewer barriers to entering retailing activities compared with other economic endeavours. 'Selling' also offered other benefits to women. It could be dove-tailed with other responsibilities such as child care and was often carried on from within the home in a converted front room or outhouse. Therefore, the proprietor did not need to leave the sanctity of her home to sustain herself.

These considerations were important. As the Victorian period progressed, the ideology of separate spheres took hold: social rhetoric dictated that a woman's proper role was marriage and her proper place was in the home. Although it was increasingly recognized that this could not be a reality for many females, particularly in London, as those aged 20 to 40 exceeded men by 119 to every 100, women who needed to earn an income had to grapple with the competing forces of gentility, respectability and need.[12] As J. D. Milne wrote:

> a woman in the middle ranks, when cast on her own exertions, has two courses before her. Either she may endeavour to gain the means of subsistence in a way in some measure fitting her previous station in life; or, unable to do this, she may leave that status to join the ranks below.[13]

Many forms of employment detracted from women's standing in middle-class metropolitan society, and jobs deemed suitable to meet standards of feminine behaviour, that could 'be pursued without endangering their virtue, or corrupting their manners', were not plentiful.[14] However, in the forum of consumption women exercised a considerable degree of free choice. Hence, in creating their own retailing ventures targeted primarily at a female audience, women were harnessing this ideology to their own advantage, creating their own feminized marketplace of ritualized retail and consumption.

In several ways, women involved in retail trades shaped and were drawn into a variety of public networks of business activity. This was especially the case in relation to credit relations. Until the early nineteenth century, selling to customers for cash alone was nearly impossible and most transactions were based on credit. This had a number of advantages: it not only facilitated sales, it also helped to create a bond between buyer and seller, tying the one to the other. At a more mundane level, it enabled the trader to hold a smaller reserve of cash in the shop.[15] The dangers of extended or indiscriminate credit were widely recognized but most trade manuals and journals nonetheless openly recommended its adoption. Credit had obvious advantages for the customer. Indeed the possession of a 'book' among the middle classes, the amount of credit allowed and the ease with which it was obtained became status symbols in their own right. To be denied credit was one of the worst blows that could be inflicted upon a respectable, and by implication thrifty and independent, successful middle-class customer. To be refused was viewed as a slur on their character. Creditworthiness implied financial soundness and moral probity.[16] Female retailers whose activities depended on the effective circulation of credit thus played a key role in validating the proprietorial and public respectability of middle-class consumers. At the same time, like many businessmen they were exposed to the volatility of a credit-based economy through the danger of unmet bills. This was one aspect of the public, commercial world that independent women in business could not avoid.

The remainder of this chapter explores other aspects of the public and commercial world of women retailers in nineteenth-century London using evidence from trade cards. Trade cards were a very popular method of business promotion until a reduction in taxes on paper and newspaper advertising in the second half of the nineteenth century rendered the latter a more cost-effective advertising strategy.[17] Printed from plates engraved by local craftsmen, the trade card served as an *aide-mémoire* for customers, an invoice, a receipt form and often a price list.[18] The chapter uses evidence from these cards to establish the different sectors of retailing activity where women were prevalent. It also analyses the cards to consider the nature and organization of retailing activity and the customer base of metropolitan female businesses. Finally, it considers the ways in which cards and other advertising strategies were used to construct public reputation, status and trust – key ingredients to retailing business strategy. The emergent picture challenges the portrayal of nineteenth-century middle-class women as somehow separated from the activity of wealth creation in the public sphere, revealing the breadth of their activities and the range of skill and expertise implicit to this female economy.

Retailing and Respectability: Evidence from Trade Cards

The earliest trade cards were type printed by letterpress, but the introduction of commercial engraving, and later lithography, allowed almost unlimited pictorial and decorative treatments. Hogarth, Bartolozzi and Bewick were among the great names that accepted commissions to work on trade cards. However, the decorative conventions adopted by trade engravers became more or less standardized. As with the stock block of the letterpress printer, stock images soon appeared, often copied from one to another.[19] With advances in printing and literacy, single sheet posters replicating the trade cards, referred to as broadsides, also became an extremely common form of advertising.[20]

Trade cards were given away carefully. They were expensive to produce. They were more common in some trades than others and less likely to be needed by proprietors that could rely on a fast turnover and footfall custom. They operated on many levels, providing 'memories' of shopping experiences and communicating the marketing position of the shop as well as its topographical location. The impetus for their commission and use came from the women themselves. Women used trade cards to create a consumer desire for their products that went beyond the utility value of the goods on display. Social and cultural meaning was given to the process of shopping and consumption in this period and women used their trade cards as a targeted means of tapping directly into this early form of branding. In the words of Loeb:

> Ultimately the Victorian advertisement emerges as a graphic depiction of the deepest materialistic desires of the Victorian middle class. While it illuminates the material

reality of Victorian middle-class existence, it reveals Victorian hopes, fears and aspirations. It helps to dictate the Victorian paraphernalia of gentility.[21]

The great variety in content and style of the trade cards and billheads reveals not only differences in the taste of the proprietors but also in the messages they chose to convey to the marketplace. The level of illustration and detail varied enormously depending on the nature of the proprietor's trade, their coffers and the target clientele. In addition, they frequently utilized lengthy textual descriptions to communicate the proprietor's good standing and connections, the quality of their stock, the extent of their skill, the breadth of their experience, and crucially, the respectability of their existing clientele. Sometimes this was in the form of poetry:

Female
Reform Bill
Ladies
If you wish to *buy*,
Cheaper than ever, go and try,
Babb's (High Holborn).
That's the place,
To suit your *Purse*, and Charm your *Face*.
The Largest Stock in London's there,
The Newest Patterns, *rich* and *rare*.
Bonnets.
Tuscans, Dunstables, Silks and Straws.
Caps.
Lace, Tulle, Blond, Appliqué, and Gauze;
Habit shirts, Collars, Canzoves, Capes
Of every kind, and various shapes,
In English style, all British made,
As patronized by
Queen Adelaide.
An endless choice will there be found.
One shilling each, and some *One Pound*.
Then thither hasten, in a trice,
for now they sell at *Wholesale Price*.
Now *ladies*! *now* – your *attention fix*.
For Babb's 296,
HIGH HOLBORN.
Dealers and Milliners supplied on the very Lowest Terms.[22]

Like Babb's of High Holborn, many of the trade cards advertised the businesses of women engaged in dressmaking, millinery and clothing. It is clear from surviving collections, however, that the nature of the businesses in this sector varied enormously. Through their trade cards, businesswomen sent out very clear messages about the type of customer they hoped to attract. For example, Amelia Brady of Little Russell Street, Covent Garden, informed her 'ladies' of the availability of rich court and fancy dresses available in her rooms.[23] Mrs Bean informed prospective customers that she was a court dressmaker to 'Her Royal Highness, The Duchess of Kent and also the Princess Charlotte of Saxe Coburg by special appointment'.[24] Similarly, the trade card of Mrs Russell tells us that she was milliner and dressmaker 'to Her Majesty & Royal Family'.[25] Trade cards like these reveal that name-dropping was a vital component of nineteenth-century retail practice. This tactic, drawing directly on the cult of personality, conveyed not only messages about the standing of the clientele but also the respectability of the business and the proprietor. The cards portrayed intimate connections and confidences and articulated the standing of the proprietor in a hierarchical marketplace. Mrs Fraser of *Frasers' Patent Peruvian Hats, Bonnets, &c* of Sloane Square, Chelsea, was very keen to inform the public that she had displayed her wares for the benefit of Princess Charlotte, who 'was graciously pleased to express her entire Approval of them'.[26]

Meanwhile, other cards were pitched at quite a different audience – the woman aspiring to be the prudent financial manager. In order to create the right 'appearance', most middle-class women who struggled in the £150 to £300 income range needed to be functional and thrifty. If the economic ideal was the efficient direction of production, writes Loeb, then the womanly ideal was the 'beneficient ordering of consumption'.[27] For example, Susan Dolland's 'reasonable rates' indicate that her target clientele were probably from the more thrifty ranks.[28] Others conveyed the more modest quality of their clientele and products simply by the frugality of their cards – small, limited in detail and poorly printed.

Dressmakers and milliners were at the top of the needlework hierarchy in terms of both prestige and pay and their cards dominate the surviving trade card collections of female proprietors. In a period when the latest style or fit of a bonnet or garment, as opposed to merely its fabric or trimmings, distinguished the aspirational woman from the 'puckered, gaping, baggy masses', dressmaking and millinery were skilled trades.[29] *The Young Tradesman* advised:

> The Dress-Maker must be an expert anatomist; and must, if judiciously chosen, have a name of French [de]termination; she must know how to hide all defects in the proportions of the body, and must be able to mould the shape of stays that, while she corrects the body, she may not interfere with the pleasures of the palate.[30]

Not all proprietors went so far as to take up a French name but the successful dressmaker did require many skills, including not only talent but also tact as customers frequently expected more from a dress than it was capable of giving.[31] Milliners and dressmakers also needed to be able to keep up with the ever-changing fashions.[32] It is important to recognize that they were not all merely responding to the fancies of their customers. They themselves played an active part in the ever-changing fashion cycle, in order to generate a demand for their services. As *The Young Tradesman* wrote in 1839:

> Dress is a thing subject to almost daily fluctuation, so that a history of the ladies' dresses in England, for merely half a dozen years, would furnish matter for a bulky volume; we shall therefore not attempt it, but merely observe that the best, and, perhaps, the only excuse for such continual change in the empire of dress, is the opportunity which that change offers of employment to those persons who would otherwise have no immediate claim upon the rich and opulent.[33]

However, these trades had high start-up costs, particularly at the higher end of the market.[34] Campbell estimated that in the preceding century it had cost between £400 and £500 for a milliner to 'set up genteelly'.[35] One way to get around potentially prohibitive capital requirements was to form a partnership with another woman in similar circumstances, as in the case of 'Mess^{dms} Fisher & Dutton' of Great Castle Street.[36] It was also common for partnerships to be made between female relatives, as suggested by the trade cards of Ann and Jane Goulborn; 'Martha Wheatland and Sister' of Cheapside;[37] and 'A. Payne and Daughter', who promised 'the most respectful attention'. Perhaps the best known example is that of sisters Mary and Ann Hogarth, the siblings of engraver and painter William Hogarth.[38]

In an age of 'gentility', millinery and dressmaking were the most favoured trades for those in the class 'a little above the vulgar'. They were closely associated with the cultivation of a genteel appearance and manner. Hence in spite of seasonal unemployment and long hours at other times, they never lacked applicants.[39] Millinery and dressmaking, catering to an all-female clientele, were the main exceptions to the male dominance of the higher reaches of retailing.[40] In addition, more so perhaps than in any other trade, the female milliner-dressmaker was an aspiring woman. Engaging in an activity with perceived prospects, the proprietors in these trades were far less likely to have been forced into business by a calamity such as widowhood. Rather, these trades, requiring lengthy apprenticeships, provided a strategy not just for survival, but also for independence and social mobility. A good business head was essential for success, and even at mid-century the more enterprising milliner-dressmaker kept a woman agent in Paris who had 'nothing else to do but watch the Motions of the Fashions, and procure Intelligence of their Changes; which she signifies to her Principles (sic)'. Many London milliners also made trips to Paris themselves.[41] As was the case for men, reputation, both personal and professional, frequently underpinned a woman's business.[42]

By the 1840s the growth of outworking and casual labour practically destroyed the skilled end of the women's needle trades – competition from ready-made clothing was undermining all but the most exclusive dressmakers.[43] Nonetheless, these changes opened up opportunities for other women and some milliners and dressmakers also successfully adapted their businesses to meet the new demands for ready-made linens and fashion. As early as 1757, *Dawes*, run by Elizabeth Dawes, was advertising a variety of ready-made items, 'mass' produced on the premises in anticipation of future sales. A variety of cloaks, coats, caps, hoods, bonnets, children's clothes and linens were offered for sale.[44] Women in the retail drapery trade also picked up the expanding business in ready-made items. The trade card collections reveal that female proprietors of such outlets were numerous.

However, many women had to withstand fierce competition from the substantial draperies, which would eventually become the early department stores.[45] One area of intense rivalry was window-dressing. The effective display of goods in shop windows was essential for all retailers in the clothing and textile trades but especially so for the linen drapers, particularly those with establishments directed at a better class of customer. As one draper recalled:

> We used to be very lavish with our goods in window dressing. As for example, delicate goods, such as white or pink silks, which ought to have been kept inviolably fresh and nice, were often strung up for the sake of effect, resulting in creasing, and putting out of condition goods that afterwards needed 'tingeing' of another description before they could get sold.[46]

Indeed the whole shop front could be used to proclaim financial security and good taste, and became a focus of attention for retailers not just of linen and textile goods but of all sorts of different wares. The installation of glazed windows allowed the permanent display of goods and enticed the customer into the seclusion inside, away from the noise and bustle of the street. Once inside, the glazed window also enabled the shopkeeper to sell to a captive audience. This captive audience enabled London's drapers to transact so much daily business 'as almost to exceed belief'.[47] However, the importance of window-dressing, glazing and a plentiful stock meant that this trade could be costly to operate in. As *The Young Tradesman* warned, failure was common.[48]

Haberdashery usually attracted shoppers with a smaller purse than those who entered into the emporium of the draper. When an aspiring mid-nineteenth century draper opened a haberdashery section in his shop, he soon became concerned about the effects on the gentility of his establishment. He wrote:

> But there was rather an embarrassing drawback to this branch of trade. My object was to cultivate the trade generally, that we should do the best class possible; but as many of our new customers were of a ragged and dirty appearance, the shop, when several of this class of persons were in it, presented the appearance of one where the very lowest trade was carried on.[49]

Yet for women, haberdashery remained a genteel trade. Pinchbeck concluded from her survey of advertisements and trade directories that such businesses, along with stationery, grocery and the provision trades, provided opportunities for the female proprietor. 'Notices from haberdashers, who traded in stuffs and drugs as well as small wares, silk mercers, woollen and linen drapers are common', sometimes with two or more of these branches combined in the one shop.[50] Indeed, trade card evidence reveals that hosiery items frequently found their way into haberdashers.[51] Hosiers like Elizabeth Dent and Mary Rippon dealt in stockings, braces, belts, purses, watch chains, waistcoats, drawers and petticoats and sometimes combined with hatters and gloves.[52] The rather elaborate trade card of Ann James, a Soho-based 'Hosier, Haberdasher and Worsted Maker', although probably not a limited edition but rather one chosen from a printer's pattern book, would nonetheless have been picked to convey a visual message about the respectable and extensive establishment that Ann saw herself as running. Such was the scale of her enterprise that she offered both wholesale and retail services on a broad stock. However, the business of pins, ribbons, threads and hosiery could also be carried on at a smaller scale, especially along the minor streets, where rents were cheaper. The materials were familiar to every woman and if she chose not to engage in wholesale herself, she could restrict her sales to an essentially, although not totally, female economy.

For some women, the business of fancy dress or masquerade clothing provision was a viable venture, particularly during the London Season – roughly the period from late March until early August, which coincided with the sitting of Parliament, when the wealthy and influential came to the capital for a hectic round of social engagements. For example, Anne Dawson of Pall Mall combined millinery with fancy dress provision and counted Her Royal Highness the Princess of Wales amongst her clientele. Based on Pall Mall, two of her receipts have survived, one for £5 6s 6d and another for £9 2s 8d, both substantial sums for Seasonal party-wear.[53] It would seem that the trade for this specialist clothing was plentiful enough to support entire establishments devoted to the particular demands of the London Season and other important dates in the social calendar. The trade card of Mrs Sowden of 8 Gerrard Street, Soho, reveals that the partygoer could there delight in the choice of the 'most farcical, comical, droll unaccountable, inimitable and irresistible MASKS by the REAL MAKER, a stock which she had only recently replenished'. Her shop, *Opera House Masquerade,* claimed to entice even the nobility and gentry with its breadth of costumes, shepherd's crooks, flower baskets, forks, rakes, hat feathers and promotional poetry:

> Come ye Sons of glee and Fun,
> See all other Shops out done;
> Fie for Shame why must we press ye,
> To come to such a Shop to dress ye
> The Charge is small which must entice,
> You'll ne'er complain of Sowden's Price.[54]

As the nineteenth century progressed, haberdashers and hosiers, like the milliners, dressmakers and drapers, also increasingly stocked ready-made items of clothing (although their main function was to provide materials for the home production of clothing, for the clothing and footwear production trades, and for household furnishings). These businesses, particularly those located in the wealthy West End of London, had to be robust enough to survive the fluctuations in demand in the London marketplace caused by the Season.

Trade cards suggest women were also active in a range of other retail trades. Sarah Hind, for example, was one of a number of 'Wax, Spermaceti & Tallow Chandlers'.[55] In addition, pastry cooks, confectioners and a great variety of other food-related activities are common among the trade card collections. The strong association of women with domestic victuals provision secured them a niche where they exploited the commercial value of such skills.[56] No doubt many ventures of this kind were small-scale, targeting a very local clientele. Nonetheless, examples of the more ambitious female proprietors can be found and here, as with the superior clothing enterprises, the trade cards indicate a keen concern for establishing the reputation and respectability of the business. For example, cook and confectioner Elizabeth Debatt crammed on to her small trade card her extensive production range: 'Soups, French Pies, Made Dishes, Savoury Patties, Jellies, Blancmanges ... NB. Dinners & Turtles Dress'd at Home & ABROAD. Ice Creams, Soups sent out. Routs & Ball Suppers Served up in the Greatest Perfection'.[57] In so doing, she clearly outlined both her range and by default her target clientele.

Although primarily retailers by this time, grocers retained some processing responsibilities – blending, sorting and cleaning. As dealers in bulk, in addition to breaking down consignments of products for their own shop or branch of shops, trade cards suggest that they often acted as wholesalers for other shops. Even those grocers dealing only in a retail capacity would have processed and packaged goods into small amounts ready to sell to their customers.[58]

Until the mid-nineteenth century, because many of the grocers' goods were imported, the customers of grocers tended to be restricted to the middling and higher income groups, making this a particularly attractive trade to the more class-conscious proprietor. Tea, coffee, sugar and cocoa were luxury goods, only gaining a foothold in the wider urban diet as the nineteenth century progressed. From mid-century, sweetened tea became the main form of liquid refreshment, altering the clientele of the grocer. In addition, the second half of the nineteenth century brought mass production and semi-processing of common foodstuffs. This also brought competition from the plethora of general shopkeepers who could then stock packages of tea and other products.[59] Blackman writes:

> All sorts of shopkeepers took on some of the grocer's lines ... Shopkeepers took advantage of the almost daily sales they could make of some items, particularly sugar and tea

... The advent of blended and packaged teas enabled many shopkeepers, large and small, to stock one or two types or brands of tea without having themselves to be a specialist in tea blending and carry large stocks of several teas.[60]

In London, some women opted to specialize in the retailing of particular grocery products. An example of this is the 1812 trade card of Madame Rose promoting her chocolate, cocoa and coffee retail business.[61] It was most common to specialize in tea and coffee, as in the case of Helena Noble, a 'Tea Dealer and Grocer', based at 209 High Holborn. Her business, probably inherited from her late husband William Noble, was in a prime location. A major thoroughfare like this must have meant significant passing trade in addition to her regular customers.[62]

Different specialisms such as these were regarded as conferring different levels of gentility.[63] However, from a practical point of view, the range of goods grocers or specialist dealers carried probably largely depended on the location of their premises. On the major thoroughfares there was sufficient trade and variety of custom to permit a grocer to specialize, and thereby attract a particular type of customer. Grocers also increasingly stocked other provisions such as dairy products and Italian warehouse goods (sago, gelatines, tapioca, macaroni, vermicelli).[64] Tobacco retailers also crossed over into this market. For example, Elizabeth Gallaway sold tobacco and snuff followed by 'perfumery; turnery; candles; soap; starch; blue &c. on the most reasonable terms'.[65]

In London there were also numerous little pamphlet shops, often located on important thoroughfares, that were frequently kept by women. They sold all kinds of newspapers and journals, almanacks, parliamentary speeches, plays and pamphlets.[66] For example, Elizabeth Dartnell's shop near St. Martin's Lane and Elizabeth Fielding's on Broad Street, 'behind the Royal Exchange', were both well positioned.[67] In addition, Sophia Sewell's shop on the Norland Road included music and toys alongside stationery.[68] The trade cards suggest that the sale of print-based media was a popular and potentially profitable niche for women.

Conclusion

The analysis of trade cards reveals London women to have been active in a range of retail trades, operating at different levels and catering to a very varied clientele in terms of both taste and budget. These enterprising females clustered in the markets for which they were the best prepared, particularly textiles and provisions – areas in which they had received some training, formally or informally, or in which their experience in the household had schooled them. Particularly in the textile trades but to some extent in other areas too, they were able to harness the ideology of separate spheres to their own advantage. They offered a genteel shopping environment, laden with ritual and symbolic meaning, where their predominantly female clientele could exercise consumption choices and, through the act of purchasing goods, bolster an air of respectability for themselves. The retailing activities of London's independent women thus provided for the economic agency of other women as well their own social status and mobility. The trade cards designed to attract these customers were expensive to produce and operated as a very targeted form of advertising. Hence, the relative absence of these women in other forms of historical record may well in part reflect the proprietors' own desire to entertain a restricted audience of customers. In this feminized marketplace, London's independent women were able to sustain an appearance unsullied by the stormy seas of wider commerce. This research lends support to a growing historiography on metropolitan women and consumption which suggests a more public life than hitherto imagined.[69]

Notes

This research was made possible by the financial assistance of the Economic and Social Research Council, UK.

1. Nenadic, 1988, p. 626.
2. Clark, 1919; Pinchbeck, 1930.
3. Vickery, 1991.
4. Davidoff and Hall, 1987, p. 315.
5. Alexander, 1983.
6. Vickery, 1998, pp. 288, 290–91.
7. Peterson, 1984, p. 708.
8. See Higgs, 1987; Hill, 1993.
9. The 5 per cent sample of men's policies for each sample year yielded 51, 144, 413 and 511 policies respectively.
10. For further discussion see Kay, 2004.
11. Duplicate policies have been removed for these calculations.
12. Those aged 40 to 60 exceeded men by 116 to every 100 and those aged 60 to 80 by 137 to every 100. British Parliamentary Papers. Session 4, November 1852–August 1853. Vol. LXXXVIII, Part 1: 1852–1853 Accounts and Papers, p. xxvii.
13. Milne, 1857, p. 129.
14. Wakefield, 1798, pp. 9–10.
15. Cox, 2000, p. 46.
16. Winstanley, 1983, pp. 55–6.
17. The total abolition of this advertisement duty did not take place until 1853. Sampson, 1874, p. 9.
18. Rickards, 2000, p. 334.
19. Ibid.

20. Parley, 1855, p. 115.
21. Loeb, 1994, p. ix.
22. London Guildhall Library (hereafter LGL) Trade Card Collection. Box 1 Aar–Bar. c.1830.
23. Bank Collection, LGL, 86.16. Dated 1804.
24. Heal Collection, LGL, 86.5. Dated 1819.
25. Heal Collection, LGL, 86.69. No date.
26. Bank Collection, LGL, 86.44. Dated 1816.
27. Loeb, 1994, p. 21.
28. Heal Collection, LGL, 86.26. No date.
29. Gamber, 1997, p. 5.
30. Anon, 1839, p. 222. In spite of the obvious gendering of its title, publications like *The Young Tradesman* would have been read by women as well as men. Given the significant female presence in London's retail trades, it is likely that women were a key target audience of such advice literature.
31. Ibid., p. 224.
32. Ibid., p. 222.
33. Ibid.
34. Anon, 1806, pp. 37–8.
35. Ibid. p. 287. Campbell, 1747, p. 336.
36. Bank Collection, LGL, 86.42. No date.
37. Heal Collection, LGL, 86.87. Dated 1761.
38. Bank Collection, LGL, 86.61. Dated 1807.
39. Pinchbeck, 1930, p. 289.
40. Davidoff and Hall, 1987, p. 302.
41. Pinchbeck, 1930, pp. 287–8; Campbell, 1747, pp. 207–8.
42. Simonton, 1991, p. 153.
43. Ibid. p., 153.
44. Heal Collection, LGL, 86.23. Dated 1757.
45. See Rappaport, 2000.
46. Anon, 1876, p. 30.
47. Anon, 1839, pp. 227–29.
48. Ibid. pp. 230–31.
49. Ibid. pp. 146–147.
50. Pinchbeck, 1930, p. 294.
51. Alexander, 1970, pp. 143–4.
52. Bank Collection, LGL, 72.61 and 72.190. Dated 1805 and 1807 respectively.
53. Heal Collection, LGL, 86.24 and 86.25. Dated 1800 and 1804 respectively.
54. Bank Collection, LGL, 40.16. No date.
55. Heal Collection, LGL, 33.51a. Dated 1813.
56. Simonton, 1991, p. 158.

57. LGL, Trade Card Collection, Box 7, Cra-Der.
58. Blackman, 1976, p. 149; Alexander, 1970, p. 112.
59. Blackman, 1976, pp. 149, 150–1.
60. Ibid. p. 153.
61. Bank Collection, LGL, 38.7. Dated 1812.
62. Bank Collection, LGL, 68.90. Dated 1785.
63. Pinchbeck, 1930, p. 295.
64. Blackman, 1976, p. 151; Alexander, 1970, p. 115, 123–4.
65. LGL, Trade Card Collection, Box 10.
66. Pinchbeck, 1930, p. 295.
67. Heal Collection, LGL, 111.47. No date; Bank Collection, LGL, 86.44. Dated 1816.
68. Sophia Sewell: Sun Fire 639/1653468.
69. Rappaport, 2000; Walker, 1995.

–12–

Hidden Professions?
Female 'Placers' of Domestic Servants in Nineteenth-century Dutch Cities

Marlou Schrover

Introduction

In 1852, Helena Wolsing married Robertus van Altena. Van Altena's first wife had died less than a year earlier and he was left to care for their five children aged between 2 and 9. At the time of his second marriage, Van Altena was 39; Wolsing was 50. In the marriage certificate, he was registered as a 'commissioner', which meant that he received commissions for transactions he facilitated between merchants. Later he was the owner of a removal firm. Wolsing was registered as a woman without a profession. Marriage certificates, however, frequently registered women as jobless when other sources suggest that they were employed.[1] Wolsing may have been without a job at the time of her wedding, but immediately after her marriage she was registered as a placer of domestic servants; and from 1852 until her death aged 78 in 1880 she worked as a 'placer'. She was a widow for the last twelve years. In terms of the length of her working career, her age at marriage and the profession of her husband, Wolsing was typical of the women who worked as placers.

Placers were intermediaries between domestic servants looking for work and women seeking domestic help. In England and in France there were agencies that placed servants with their employers, and they were known as employment bureaus, register offices or placing agencies. They were mostly formal institutions, sometimes controlled or sanctioned by the government.[2] The Dutch placers – *besteedsters* – worked alone. The word was always used in the Dutch feminine form and no real equivalent word exists in English.[3]

This chapter examines the activities of placers in the Dutch town of Utrecht in the nineteenth century.[4] The number of women working as placers was small: in Utrecht there were never more than eleven at any one time. In Amsterdam (a much larger town), there were over sixty placers. The profession of placer is interesting for two reasons. First, the profession has unjustly been depicted as a marginal economic activity. This marginalization fits the stereotyped image of the economically active woman of the nineteenth century. Women were portrayed as either single, young and working-class, employed as factory workers and domestics, or as old and widowed, eking out a meagre income from marginal retail shops. Placers were neither. They were usually middle-class women and the majority were married. Moreover, they managed to circumvent the legal restrictions that curtailed the economic activities of married women.

Second and perhaps most importantly, the profession is interesting because of the light it sheds on the relationship between public and private spheres. Mediating between women looking for domestic employment and those looking for servants had been women's work for centuries. The activity was carried out from the home of the placer and within the sphere of the household.[5] The work of a placer therefore fitted perfectly into what is referred to as the 'feminine realm'. However, at the end of the century the profession shifted from the private to the public sphere as employment agencies, rather than individual female placers, took on the role of matching servants with employers. As a consequence, men began to enter the placing business. Ultimately, however, both the placers and the agencies were made redundant by the growth of newspaper advertisements, in which employers made a direct appeal to servants or vice versa. By 1900, placers had all but disappeared.[6]

The placers are but one example of a substantial group of working and middle-class women in nineteenth-century Dutch cities. According to the 1849 Utrecht census, 12 men and five women ran a soup-kitchen, 62 men and 13 women were registered as innkeepers, 88 men and 90 women were registered as publicans, 1 man and 26 women were brothel keepers, and 37 women worked as 'fashion makers'. There were other economically active women, whose activities went largely unrecorded. Amelia Padberg, for instance, kept a boarding house for many years.[7] Other females kept a 'dinner table', which was run from the woman's private house and attended on a regular basis by students and other single men. A tapster, who served gin in the front room of her own house, was a similar profession. These trades were run by females independently of their husbands, and provided a valuable income. The employment of these women went unrecorded in the censuses even though they worked in their professions for many years and paid taxes in their own right. Like the placers, these were women who could be economically active because of, rather than in spite of, the domestic centredness of their lives.

Placers tried to match women looking for help with women looking for a position as a servant. They competed with the informal networks through which servants also found employment. Placers could only compete if they had a good reputation. They needed to be good judges of character; they had to have insight into what employers were looking for, or what women seeking employment had to offer. Networks were crucial, and the whole trade was underpinned by trust: both from women seeking employment and from women looking for help. On the one hand, women hiring help wanted somebody they could trust with the family silver, who would not spread the family's secrets, or gossip about domestic affairs. On the other hand, servants had to be sure that they would be put into a respectable household. It was considered a difficult and sensitive trade and placers had to mediate within a personal and intimate sphere.[8] Placers exploited two key advantages when building up their networks. First, they used their own – often extensive – previous experience as domestics. Second, they used the connections of their husbands, who worked in the middle-class professions that brought them into contact with people from different ranks. The local origins of the placers and their religion proved to be of lesser importance to these networks. These characteristics of the placer's job explain why women often worked in the trade for many years; networks took a long time to build. Placers who went out of business because they were too old were succeeded by women who took up residence in the same house. It was important that a placer could be found easily by women who were relatively unacquainted with the town, such as newly arriving servants.

Unlike in many other professions, changes in the nature of the placer's work itself cannot explain its disappearance.[9] Furthermore, the profession was relatively insensitive to changes in supply and demand. If fewer women offered themselves for domestic work, families looking for help would be in greater need of the placer's services. If fewer households looked for domestics to hire, the services of the placers would be more sought after by domestics looking for a position. The demand for domestics increased in the second half of the nineteenth century, and the growth of the cities made the labour market for domestics less transparent. This increased the need for the agency of placers. All this makes the disappearance of the independent placer even more intriguing. Why did women leave this profession towards the end of the nineteenth century, or why and how were they forced out? In this chapter it is argued that it was not male competition but rather changes in the price of newspaper advertisements that led to the disappearance of the profession. The substantial decrease in costs of newspaper advertising made it possible for servants and those seeking help to communicate with each other without the need for an intermediary.

Women's Economic Agency and Domestic Labour

In the nineteenth century, domestic service was the most important profession for women. In 1849, 44 per cent of the female labour force in Utrecht were employed as domestic servants. In 1889 the figure was 57 per cent. In terms of the absolute figures, the numbers of women grew from 2,576 in 1849, to 3,659 in 1889, and to

4,822 in 1899. The demand for servants increased in the second half of the nineteenth century as more families could afford domestic help. In 1800, in Amsterdam, there were between 12,000 and 13,000 servants.[10] In London there were at that time over 90,000 servants.[11] Most women worked as servants from the age of 14–18 until their marriage at around the age of 25. Domestic service was therefore highly age-specific. In England, in 1852, 52 per cent of the servants were aged between 15 and 24.[12]

In 1976, the historian Theresa McBride complained that little had been written about domestic servants.[13] Although the situation improved, David Kent could still argue ten years later that many aspects of the most important female profession were little understood.[14] Bridget Hill began her 1996 book with a similar observation.[15] While the literature on domestic servants remains limited, even less is known about the mechanisms through which women found such employment.

The profession of placer is mentioned in Dutch sources from the early modern period. At this time there were many complaints about placers. Potential employers believed that placers and servants conspired against them. Placers were accused of supplying servants without ascertaining their good character and of luring away servants from their employers before their contracts expired. To remedy these problems, the Dutch cities of Leiden and Rotterdam made the profession into a monopoly. In each town, twelve women were selected; only they were allowed to work as placers and they had to swear that they would uphold the law and maintain certain standards. They had to fix a sign to their doors indicating that they were 'recognized' placers. Other cities soon followed.[16] In 1759, the Dutch city of Deventer ruled that all placers were to check if domestics were honest, faithful and decent. If the servants proved not to have these qualities, the placer was liable to pay a fine of ten golden guilders – an immense sum at the time. Placers were also required to pay a penalty if they assisted women seeking new employment who had left their previous employer without fulfilling their contracts.[17] The many complaints from this earlier period indicate that the profession was important and that it had been women's work for centuries. Government attempts to regulate the profession reinforced the position of placers, effectively sanctioning their activities.

In the nineteenth century, as in earlier periods, servants spent a large part of their working lives finding a position. Most domestics left their employers within one year.[18] November 11 (Martinmas) and May 1 were the days when servants' contracts expired. In the Netherlands, domestics were officially employed for six weeks. Short contracts, prevalent in other countries too, allowed employers to rid themselves of lazy or incompetent servants.[19] The contracts were verbal agreements and if neither the employer nor the servant indicated that the contract was terminated after six weeks, the assumption was that it had been renewed.[20] The employer was to pay the servant for the next six weeks and could not terminate the contract before that term expired, without having to pay the servant for the full period. The servant could not leave without losing her right to the pay.

The majority of servants changed employment each May. However, there were also frequent changes in the months in between. In Utrecht, 1,500 servants would have been looking for a new position every half year, and an equal number of mistresses would have been seeking domestic help. In Amsterdam the number was four times higher. In London there would have been over 40,000 domestics on the lookout for a new position. Complaints surrounded the hiring of servants at these times. The demand for a fair and transparent system of job placement for servants was the most common grievance in the nineteenth century.[21]

In the early nineteenth century, servants and their mistresses could resort to an open labour market. Intended primarily for hiring agricultural labour, these markets also included household servants. Such markets could be found throughout France in the early nineteenth century. In England in the eighteenth century annual hiring or 'Mop' fairs were widespread. By the middle of the nineteenth century they were in disrepute because of the slave-market atmosphere they engendered and because of the widespread drunkenness that followed the closing of deals.[22] At the end of the eighteenth century, Utrecht had an annual fair which functioned as a domestic labour market.[23] The market disappeared in the first decades of the nineteenth century.[24]

Domestics looking for work relied upon information passed on by family or friends who were already in service.[25] Many found work by recommending themselves to bakers, grocers and butchers. Mistresses asked merchants, traders and shopkeepers for advice, or sought domestics through friends and acquaintances.[26] Local clergy could also help out.[27] Servants looking for work in England called in at the large country estates to offer their services.[28] In towns, where most of the households only had one servant, such a strategy was too time consuming to be effective. In France servants could turn to municipal employment offices and in England to registry offices. McBride argues that these agencies became an important aspect of servant life in the nineteenth century, when the enormous increase in urban migration and the high frequency of job-changing necessitated some kind of intermediary help.[29]

Observations in the literature on how domestics found employment, and on how mistresses found servants, spring more from logic than from evidence. Not much is known about the work of domestics, and even less about how they found work. On the whole, we know little about the economic activities of married middle-class women. In England, census enumerators were instructed not to record irregular work of married women done in conjunction with domestic tasks. As a consequence, the work of many women, such as lodging-house keepers, went largely unrecorded.[30] Because placing work was erratic – busy times alternated with periods of relative leisure – it was also an activity not commonly recorded in the censuses.[31] Placers left few traces in the archives.

Sources: Population Registers, Address Books and Tax Registers

Three different sources were used to investigate the role of placers in nineteenth-century Utrecht: population registers, tax registers and address books. Population registers were introduced in the Netherlands in 1850 and form the basis for a continuous registration of all people.[32] The registers were kept locally and were based on censuses that were held every ten years. The population registers list name, address, date and place of birth, religion, marital status, occupation and date of death. The records state the relationship between the members of the household: head of the household, spouse, children, grandchildren, parents, in-laws, domestic servant, pupil or lodger. Unfortunately, the population registers are not reliable sources of information on the professions of women, especially married women. The registrars made the assumption that married women were without a profession.[33] Only a few of the placers – known to us from other sources – were recorded as such in the population registers. Most were registered as being without a profession. Thus, the population registers cannot be used to trace women working as placers, but they do inform us about the households and families of placers known to us from other sources.

Information about placers is more forthcoming from tax registers. The most important tax, levied on income, was known as the *patentbelasting*, which was paid yearly or twice yearly.[34] Registers of the *patentbelasting* show that many married women who were recorded in the population registers as being without a profession did in fact have employment, and consequently paid the tax. Women who, for example, kept a boarding house, a boarding school, a dinner table or worked as a tapster, and who went unrecorded in the census and population registers, do appear in the *patentbelasting* registers. The *patentbelasting* was not paid by all professions. Men and women who worked in professions that were assumed not to be profitable were exempted from the tax. The fact that placers were included in the tax therefore indicates that their profession was considered profitable. In the course of the nineteenth century more and more professions were exempted from the tax. When the *patentbelasting* was abolished in 1893, there were only a few professions left for which the tax still had to be paid; the profession of placer was among these.[35]

In Utrecht the *patentbelasting* registers comprise over a thousand volumes.[36] They contain the name and address of the taxpayer, the number of employees and the class and category in which people were taxed. In most professions the registration of taxpayers was by neighbourhood, not by profession. This makes placers hard to find in the registers. Taking a sample would be of little use, because of the small number of women involved. In order to extract information from the tax registers it was necessary to consult the address books.

Address books were the forerunners of trade and telephone directories. They were compiled by the urban authorities and consisted of two sections. One section listed people alphabetically by name with their address and profession. Another section listed people by profession, without an address. Women are recognizable in the address books because of the prefix Miss, Mrs or Widow. Address books were published yearly throughout the nineteenth century. They only included inhabitants of a town who wanted to advertise their profession, but placers were among these.

Throughout the nineteenth century the address books had a separate heading for placers. Until 1880, the feminine form of the word placer (*besteedster*) was used. After 1880, the label was changed to Domestic Servant Agencies. This name not only sounded more formal and professional, it was also less associated with women. With the information from the address books, the placers could be looked up in the tax and population registers. All placers who were listed in the address books were found in the tax registers. Two additional placers, who were not in the address books, were found in the tax registers more or less by accident. This indicates that the number of placers was probably higher than the address books show. Without going through the tax registers systematically – which would be an arduous task – it is not possible to say how much higher. However, it is likely that the women who appeared in the address books were the ones who were in business for many years and ran enterprises with some continuity.

Married Women's Employment Opportunities

Many of the women working as placers were married. As a result they encountered legal restrictions in their attempts to earn an independent income.[37] Under the Civil Code, married women were deemed incapable of economic action. Under common law, a married woman was bound by the rules of coverture, which vested her legal rights in her husband. A husband controlled his wife's earnings, as well as the property she acquired before or after marriage. Married women were prohibited from entering into contracts without the consent of their husbands. They could not sell or buy, pawn or give away anything, or hire workers, without their husbands' consent. Similar restrictions existed in other countries.[38] Married women could buy commodities necessary for running a household, such as bread and groceries, but only as long as these remained within the range of normal daily spending. The purchase of furniture, for instance, had to be approved by the husband.

Restrictions were not as rigid as they may seem at first glance. A woman became capable of independent action from the age of 23. Before that her father or guardian was legally responsible. When she married, 'disability of coverture' set in, but she regained her rights when she was widowed. The consequences of 'disability of coverture' must not be exaggerated. In the nineteenth century, half of the women in the age group 25 to 29 were not married; in the age group 30 to 34 a third were not married; in the age group 40 to 44 a quarter were without a husband.[39] Of those who did marry, more or less a third became a widow before the age of 45.[40] More importantly, 'disability of coverture' did not apply to married independent female traders. The assumption was that an independent female trader had been granted permission by her husband to make all agreements and contracts necessary for her work. His permission did not have to be given in writing. It was evident, according to the law, in all cases where a female trader who had been economically active before marriage continued her business after entering into wedlock. An independent female trader was not to be regarded as an assistant to her husband, and her husband was not to act in her name or to make purchases with her money. Such women were allowed to continue as traders until their husbands officially withdrew his permission, giving notice of this both in a daily newspaper and at the Chamber of Commerce. The court of law could, however, grant a married female trader her independent rights if her husband was unable or unwilling to give them to her, thus harming her economic activities.[41] The law does not define who precisely falls under the exemption for married traders. However, since married placers worked independently from their husbands and paid taxes in their own right, it is clear that they were included in the exemption.

Continuity and Income

According to the census of 1849, there were 132 women who worked as placers in 78 different cities.[42] Of these, 63 worked in Amsterdam. The Hague and Groningen had only one a piece and Maastricht, a town of considerable importance, had none. The absence or near absence in other important cities indicates that many placers went unrecorded. The number of placers in Utrecht reached a maximum in the years 1854–9, with eleven placers working concurrently (Table 12.1). Eleven is close to the number (twelve) that we find set as a maximum by the local governments in several towns in the early modern period. Although official restrictions had been lifted, tradition may have continued, perhaps as a consequence of the hereditary nature of the profession. The number for the earlier years (1839 to 1849) is probably too low due to under-registration. The data after 1869 are more accurate and signify a real decrease.

Especially striking is the length of time that placers were officially in business. On average, they were registered for twenty-three years. Many would have worked unofficially for some years before setting up business on a formal basis. An example is Maria Bucher, who was born in 1800.[43] In 1843, at the age of 43, she married a shoemaker, Jacobus Schadee. He was a widower, 38 years old, with two daughters (aged 14 and 11) from his previous marriage. The marriage certificate states that Maria Bucher was a domestic servant. Indeed, Maria had been working as a servant for over twenty years prior to her marriage. Immediately after she got

Table 12.1 Number of Placers in Utrecht According to Address Books and Census Data

Year	Number
1839	1
1844	2
1849	7
1854	11
1859	11
1864	9
1869	10
1874	3
1879	5
1884	4
1889	3
1899	1

married, she was registered as a placer. As an experienced domestic servant, it is likely that she had also been functioning informally as a placer before her wedding. She continued to work as a placer for another twenty-nine years, until her death, aged 72, in 1872.

Some women, such as Maria Rippé, were already officially registered as a placer prior to their marriage. As in the case of Helena Wolsing (discussed at the start of the chapter) and Maria Bucher, there was a considerable age difference between Rippé and her husband. She married Henri Bernhardi in 1845; she was 35 years old, he was 25. Bernhardi was the illegitimate son of a seamstress. He had served in the army for seven years, become a tailor, and later a district messenger and postman. The couple remained childless. The late age at which many of the placers married is striking. It meant that most placers had been working and gaining an independent income for some twenty years prior to their marriage. All women who became placers after marriage either worked as domestics prior to their marriage – usually for a considerable period of time – or already worked as a placer. This must have stimulated them to continue their careers after entering wedlock.

Most of the placers were married for at least a part of their working lives. Of the twenty placers operating before 1879, thirteen women were married, two were unmarried, and four were widowed. One placer was a man. After 1870 there were five married placers, three widows and four men. The husbands of the married placers were in professions that supplemented the activities of their wives. Van Altena, discussed at the start of the chapter, would have had contacts with many people through his work as a commissioner, and through the removal firm he operated. The husband of the placer Geertruida Wijland was a trader. The husbands of Wilhelmina Zuiderdorp and Maria Bucher were both shoemakers. Maria-Christina Vlak and Maria Rippé had postmen for husbands. The husband of Anna Maria van der Linde kept a boarding house, and Clara Weevers was married to an undertaker. These were middle-class professions that offered ample opportunities for hearing about job openings. The networks of women and men did not operate in separate spheres. The placers had their own domestic-oriented networks, but these interlocked with the networks of their husbands.

The labour market for domestic servants in Utrecht was segregated according to religion. Protestant families had a preference for Protestant servants, but frequently also hired Catholic servants. The preference for Protestant servants became stronger after 1853. In this year, the pope installed the first archbishop in the Netherlands since the time of the Reformation. This led to serious opposition from the Protestants. In pamphlets it was argued that Protestant mistresses should not employ Catholic domestics, or should send away their catholic servants even if they had been in their employment for many years.[44] Of the seven placers active in 1849, one was Catholic and six were Protestant. The population of Utrecht was equally divided between Protestantism and Catholicism. The higher number of Protestant placers can be explained by the fact that the Protestant half of the population was generally richer than the Catholic half, and therefore more likely to hire servants. A Catholic servant had an advantage if she came with the recommendation of a Protestant placer.

Before 1870 the majority of the placers (fourteen out of twenty) came from Utrecht. After 1870 there was a shift. Several of the placers who had been in business for a long time died or retired, and new women replaced them. Maria Bucher died in 1872, Maria Rippé in 1878, and Helena Wolsing in 1880, all after working for more than thirty years in the business. From 1870 only three out of fourteen placers came from the town itself. Most originated from neighbouring villages. The servants also came in greater numbers from neighbouring villages than they had in the years before 1870. This change reflected the increased mobility of this period as a whole. Wilhelmina Betmann was the only placer who came from Germany. She originated from the same region as many of the immigrant German servants present in Utrecht. These German servants were all Catholic, however, while Betmann was Protestant. She lived in Utrecht with her Dutch husband for many years – from 1848 until her death in 1875 – but she was only recorded as a placer for one year during this period. There was one other woman who had a German connection: Dina Weever worked as a placer for twenty years – from 1853 until 1873. She died in 1878 aged 75. Dina was born in Utrecht, but she was married to a German coppersmith who worked for the railways.

It could be argued that German servants would be in greater need of the services of a placer, since they might have had fewer contacts in Utrecht. Furthermore, data from the population registers shows that Utrecht-born servants who were temporarily out of work frequently returned to the houses of their parents until a new position became available. It might be assumed that foreign servants who became unemployed could rely less on family. In reality, however, many of the German domestic servants did have family in Utrecht. It was common for German servants coming to Utrecht to have older sisters, aunts and cousins already living in the town. Furthermore, the number of German servants was not large. Unlike in the United States, most servants in the Netherlands were native born.[45] Less than 1 per cent came from Germany. If Wilhelmina Betmann and Dina Weevers had set themselves up in business in order to cater specially to the needs of German servants, the potential pool of individuals from which they could recruit would not have been large.

Both the mistresses looking for a domestic servant and the servants looking for a position paid for the services of the placer. From the servants, the placer received a percentage of their earnings. This percentage varied but was often considerable: if the servant was hired for six months or more, the placer frequently demanded the full pay for the first three months. The incomes of the servants varied considerably.[46] How much money they earned depended on their position in the household, their skills and the size of the town. Cooks and chambermaids got more than second maids. Servants in The Hague made 110 to 175 guilders yearly. Servants in Utrecht generally got less: 150 guilders was a maximum.[47] For 18-year-old servants 26 guilders yearly (50 cents per week) was common. If the placer did indeed get full pay over the first three months, this would amount to 13 guilders for 18 year olds.

We can get more information by looking at the *patentbelasting*. This tax was divided into seventeen classes. Class one paid the highest rate, class seventeen the lowest. Placers were in the classes six to fourteen. The tax was not based on real incomes, but on an assessment of the income that was usually earned within a certain profession. The size of the town also made a difference. Some professions were considered to be more profitable in larger towns. The job of placer was regarded as such a profession and, accordingly, placers in larger towns paid higher taxes. Apart from the assessment of the average income for a certain profession, an assessment was also made of the placer's personal income. On average they paid between 1.9 and 9 guilders in tax per year. This was comparable to the amount paid by shopkeepers. Small shopkeepers paid 1.25 guilders per year. Larger shopkeepers with thirty or more employees paid as much as 270 guilders per year. With a tax of 1.9 to 9 guilders, placers ranked alongside the better-off shopkeepers and earned around 4,000 guilders yearly. To raise this income, a large percentage of servants would have to have found employment through the placers. As noted above, in Utrecht 1,500 domestics sought a new position every half year, equating to 3,000 women per annum. If we take twelve placers as a maximum – reflecting the tradition from the early modern period – this would result in 250 servants per placer. If the placer got the maximum of 15 guilders from every servant, this would result in a 3,750 guilder income on a yearly basis, or 72 guilders weekly. For the sake of comparison, in 1870 male cigar makers between the ages of 16 and 40 earned 5 to 15 guilders weekly. Female cigar makers between the ages of 20 and 40 got between 3 and 7.5 guilders. Seamstresses got 3 to 4 guilders a week.[48] As was noted above, servants aged 18 earned 25 to 50 cents weekly, plus free board and lodging. The income of the placers is similar to that of female shopkeepers. Women working as shopkeepers in their own right in this period had a turnover of 4,000 to 10,000 guilders yearly.[49] An income of 4,000 guilders yearly fits more or less with the taxes the placers paid, but this estimate of their income is probably on the high side. Even if the placers got only a third of the fee and found employment for only half of the women, they would still earn good money. Information is too scarce to confirm all the assumptions made here, but from these calculations it is clear that placers did play a significant role in finding employment for servants and finding domestics for middle-class employers. Moreover, this work was lucrative and earned placers a substantial income.

Newspaper Advertisements

In 1878 a newspaper advertisement appeared in the Utrecht daily newspaper in which domestic servants were offered for hire. Families looking for domestic help did not have to pay in advance for any services. What made the advertisement stand out was that it used the word 'company' (*Maatschappij*) instead of 'placer' (*besteedster*) to describe the service offered. The head of this company was referred to as the 'director'.[50] The director was a man: Antonie de Kreek. He was born outside Utrecht and had come to the town less than half a year before. The company appears not to have been a success; de Kreek disappeared shortly after his advertisement was printed and the firm was not listed in the address books. A few years later other men were trying their luck at this business and similar developments are evident in other towns.[51]

There was, however, a concurrent change that was more significant. After 1870 newspaper advertisements became more important for servants and their potential employers.[52] The tax on newspapers had been abolished in 1867. This made newspapers much cheaper. There followed new techniques in the production of paper and in printing. Newspapers became thicker and more informative and were more widely read. Women, both domestics and mistresses, were actively buying and reading them, as well as placing advertisements.

The placers had based their profession on trust. They could allocate good servants to good households. With contacts via newspaper advertisements there were no such guarantees. Surprisingly there were no stories about servants ending up in a 'bad house' through a newspaper advertisement, but there were frequent rumours that some of the placers were directing young women into prostitution.[53] The newspapers, for whom the advertisements were an important source of income, may have played a role in this propaganda and contributed to the placer's professional demise. But probably more significant was the fact that advertisements were a cheaper method of matching servants and employers. In the second half of the nineteenth century the ratio between the number of 'help-wanted' advertisements and the number of 'work-wanted' advertisements was between 2 to 1 and 4 to 1. Certainly the servants could save on expenses by bypassing the placers.

The reduction in the number of placers coincided with a rise in the number of advertisements. In 1850 the most important Utrecht newspapers had 23 advertisements in which servants were requested and 12 in which servants offered themselves for employment.[54] Ten years later this number had risen to 103 advertisements for 'help wanted' and 27 servants asking for work. In 1870 there were 542 advertisements in which servants were requested to apply and 148 women asking to be employed. In 1880 there were 6,000 'help-wanted' advertisements and 3,000 women applying for a position.[55] In other towns there were similar developments. A newspaper in Amsterdam had 80 advertisements for domestics in 1860. In 1898 there were 1,271 advertisements from servants asking for work in the month of January alone.[56] It was newspaper advertisements, rather than male competition, that put placers out of business.

Conclusion

By the end of the nineteenth century placers had become a rarity. The profession had sat securely within the private sphere of women, making use of domestic-centred networks based on trust and information. In building up these networks the placers had profited from the fact that this was a largely female realm. Their long careers, usually starting as servants themselves, enabled them to build up their own networks, but they also used the networks of their middle-class husbands, whose jobs brought them into frequent contact with all kinds of people.

The disappearance of the profession cannot be attributed to its transfer from the private to the public sphere, nor to competition from men, who, for a short time, tried to set up formal employment agencies for domestic servants. Cheaper newspaper advertising was the main reason for the demise of the placers. In view of the considerable cost reductions, women seeking help and women seeking work were willing to accept the risks that this mode of doing business involved.

Placing was a profession for which few administrative records have survived. Contracts between servants and their mistresses were verbal. Since census takers in the Netherlands and elsewhere were instructed not to record erratic and domestic-based work, we know little about women working independently in these middle-class professions. In Utrecht we can combine information from population registers, tax data and address books. This makes it possible to gain some insight into the profession of placers, middle-class women whose work was more important than is commonly believed, and whose income was substantial. The placers were part of a much larger group of economically active middle-class women, who worked in mostly hidden professions and whose contribution to the economic life of nineteenth-century European cities has yet to be fully understood. As has been demonstrated in this chapter, there are ways in which historians can begin to address these important historiographic deficiencies.

Notes

1. Walhout and van Poppel, 2003.
2. McBride, 1976, pp. 82–98.
3. In German the profession was *Gesindemäkler*, but, unlike the Dutch word, the German word was not feminine.
4. In this chapter I have made extensive use of de Jong, 1983. A copy of this paper can be found at the Utrecht Archief library.
5. For further discussion see Hill, 1996, p. 36.
6. See also the poem of Eduard Jacobs, 'Het arbeidscontract', in de Haas, 1958, p. 150. The poem was originally published in 1911.
7. Compare with Kay, 2003a.
8. Poelstra, 1996, p. 255.
9. For an overview of the literature see de Groot and Schrover, 1995, pp. 1–16.
10. Diederiks, 1982 p. 68.
11. Kent, 1989. There is much speculation about the precise number of domestic servants in nineteenth-century England. For an overview of this discussion see Schwarz, 1999, p. 246.
12. Schwarz, 1999, p. 250.
13. McBride, 1976.
14. Kent, 1989, pp. 111–28.
15. Hill, 1996.
16. de Vos van Steenwijk, 1870.
17. *Ordonnantie ende regelement betreffende dienstbooden, en der zelver besteederen of besteedsters te Deventer 1759*, deposited in Leiden University library.
18. Bras, 2002, p. 80. See also Bras, 1998.
19. Kent, 1989, p. 120.
20. de Pinto, 1839, p. 274.
21. McBride, 1976, p. 70.
22. Horn, 1975, p. 38; Hecht, 1980, p. 27.

23. Brugman, Buiter and van Vliet, 1995, p. 75.
24. Andriessen, 1871, p. 158.
25. Horn, 1975, p. 37.
26. Horn, 1975, p. 38.
27. McBride, 1976, p. 75
28. Hill, 1996, pp. 160–1.
29. McBride, 1976, p. 77.
30. Davidoff, 1979.
31. Hatton and Bailey, 2001, p. 91.
32. Schrover, 2002b. Utrecht has particularly rich archival sources; in other Dutch towns not all records have been preserved.
33. van Eijl, 1994, p. 49.
34. Wijne, 1853; the job tax was also levied in Belgium, see Alter, 1988, pp. 105–10.
35. Schrover, 2002a, p. 74.
36. Utrecht Archive, Stadsarchief V inv. no. 246 Registers der patenten over de twaalf wijken der stad 1851–1864 and 1875–1894.
37. Braun, 1992.
38. Khan, 1996, p. 357.
39. van Eijl, 1994, p. 74.
40. van Poppel, 1992, p. 355.
41. Petit, 1930, pp. 42–5.
42. Dutch census, 1849.
43. The examples given here are based on information from the population registers.
44. Schrover, 2002a, pp. 55–7.
45. Lintelman, 1995, pp. 249–65.
46. Bras, 2002, p. 46.
47. Ibid.
48. de Groot, 2001, pp. 65 and 105.
49. Schrover, 1997, p. 65.
50. *Utrechtsch Provinciaal en stedelijk dagblad*, 8–5–1878.
51. Poelstra, 1996, p. 134.
52. Poelstra, 1996, p. 72.
53. Staatscommissie over de werkloosheid IX eindverslag, The Hague, 1914, p. 606.
54. These data have been collected by Ank de Jong. See de Jong, 1983, p. 40.
55. Gewin, 1898, pp. 281–3.
56. Poelstra, 1996, p. 184.

–13–

The Business of Sex
Evaluating Prostitution in the German Port City of Hamburg

Julia Bruggemann

Introduction

Prostitution is often called the world's oldest profession, and most societies have sanctioned, explicitly or otherwise, the exchange of sex for money or favours.[1] Yet the organization, economic structure and socio-cultural implications of prostitution for those involved in the trade have varied considerably over time and by place. Whereas medieval towns tolerated and sometimes even profited from the existence of brothels, officials in some nineteenth-century European cities aspired to eradicate organized prostitution, which was often a thriving business.[2] More recently, several European states have begun to create legal frameworks within which prostitutes enjoy the benefits of other professionals, including the right to participate in social insurance, the right to sue clients for payment, and the right to refuse service.[3] These diverse approaches to prostitution reflect changing attitudes towards gender and sexuality. The economic organization of prostitution in any period – whether licit or illicit – sheds light therefore on the prevailing gender relations governing that society. By examining the legal and cultural norms that structure the business of prostitution, the historian can investigate not only the ways in which gender functioned but also how it was constructed and contested.

Like most of Europe, nineteenth-century Germany confronted prostitution as neither a new nor a unique phenomenon. Nevertheless, prostitution was a central issue in Germany, perhaps because it had become more visible but certainly because it had become crucial to the self-definition of bourgeois society. Most contemporaries thought of prostitutes as physical and moral threats. And whereas some considered them to be physically degenerate and beyond redemption, others hoped for their salvation and reintegration into what they considered to be honourable society. Scholars have focused on the sexist and exploitative aspects of regulated prostitution that existed across Europe at the end of the nineteenth century. Yet the history of prostitution has never fitted neatly into the paradigm of 'separate spheres', because the women involved (and to some extent the men as well) – whether prostitutes, procuresses or madams – defied prescribed gender stereotypes. In fact, their very existence destabilized the clear-cut notions of what gendered behaviour and sexuality should be. Not only did prostitutes work outside the home, but their activities offended contemporary bourgeois stereotypes of desirable female social and sexual behaviour. Many contemporaries used the vocabulary of 'separate spheres' (especially the defenders of regulated prostitution), but their description of the prostitute as a 'public woman' defied the logic of this ideology.

Although many municipalities attempted to enforce specific regulatory systems, they were increasingly unable to control the phenomenon of prostitution. More and more women evaded registration and practised prostitution secretly outside official regulation. After 1900 significantly more women sold sex illicitly than did so within the regulatory structures established by many German cities. Studying regulated prostitution remains important, however, not least because contemporaries demanded the control that it presumably provided. Taking the business of prostitution and its regulation more seriously will force us to abandon the notion that gender in the nineteenth century functioned within the clear-cut categories of 'separate spheres'. Whether regulated or secret, prostitution reveals a more complicated picture: it afforded some opportunity but also created repression and it ultimately both reinforced and undermined the ideology of 'separate spheres'.

This chapter investigates prostitution in Imperial Germany using the port city of Hamburg as a case study. It considers the history and organization of Hamburg's official regulation of prostitution as well as the persistence of secret prostitution. It also evaluates the social background of the prostitutes and their possible reasons for joining the profession. Finally, the chapter considers the roles played by women in other aspects of the profession, as madams or brothel-keepers and as procuresses.

Legal Parameters

The new German Imperial Criminal Code (*Reichsstrafgesetzbuch*) came into effect in 1871 and formed the legal basis for the regulation of prostitution.[4] Two sections of the Code, both taken almost verbatim from the Prussian Code of 1851, dealt primarily with prostitution. The most important section, the so-called 'prostitution-paragraph', legalized prostitution that conformed to specific regulations: '§ 361,6: The following shall be liable on conviction to detention: Any common prostitute under police supervision who acts contrary to the police regulations for the preservation of health, public order and decency, and also any prostitute not under police supervision.'[5] The second relevant paragraph dealt with the procurement and facilitation of prostitution and was therefore nicknamed the 'procurement-paragraph' (*Kuppeleiparagraph*): '§ 180: Anyone who makes a practice of assisting or for his own benefit assists immorality by acting as an intermediary or providing opportunity therefore shall be guilty of procuration and liable to confinement.'[6]

The tension between these paragraphs is immediately apparent. The 'prostitution-paragraph' established that prostitution itself was to be tolerated – albeit within specific, locally defined regulations. According to the 'procurement-paragraph', however, any kind of facilitation of prostitution, pimping or procurement was to be prosecuted. This legal ambiguity created problems for local governments and police forces, since the prostitution trade was dependent on pimps and procurers. This legal ambiguity also reinforced the multiple and confusing notions of gender roles in Imperial Germany, which were likewise codified in law. The criminalization of prostitution might have indicated some consensus on female sexuality and behaviour. But its legal sanction instead reflected contemporary uncertainty about these issues. Prostitutes constituted an evil insofar as they offered a vision of female sexuality incompatible with bourgeois morality. But the law treated them as a 'necessary' evil, and the state attempted to control rather than prohibit them.

Officials and jurists developed a standard legal interpretation of the relationship between the two sections of the Code. But remaining ambiguities were left for local authorities to resolve, which they did according to their specific social and political circumstances. According to the legal parameters of the Criminal Code, German municipal authorities created regulatory systems that defined and restricted prostitution and helped in turn to control male and female sexual behaviour.[7] With these regulations, authorities constructed categories of 'proper' and 'deviant' female sexuality while making it acceptable for men to have relations with both kinds of women. Like their counterparts in other German cities, Hamburg's officials designed their regulatory system to reflect and reinforce these specific gender expectations.

Hamburg's administration did not condemn men who patronized prostitutes, but instead assumed responsibility for providing healthy women free from infectious diseases such as syphilis, which was still essentially untreatable. While virginity was fetishized in women – especially bourgeois women – men were not expected to abstain from extra-marital sex.[8] Contemporary doctors supported this double standard by claiming a scientific basis for both the uncontrollable male sex drive and the natural sexual passivity of women.[9] The city's regulation of prostitution thus reflected not only an understanding of female sexuality but also contemporary perceptions of male sexuality.

Regulated Prostitution in Hamburg

The Imperial Criminal Code provided no more than the legal parameters for the treatment of pimps and prostitutes, whose regulation local municipal authorities all over Germany were forced to improvise. As a city-state, Hamburg had a long tradition of political autonomy, and this independence found expression in the type of regulatory system enforced in the port city. The municipal leaders insisted on a system of control different from that in the majority of other German municipalities – a type of regulation known as 'brothelization' (*Bordellierung*). After registering with the police, 'official' prostitutes were assigned to live and work in specific brothels and were not allowed to choose their places of residence. Brothel-keepers received licences and in return helped officials police the women and the milieu.[10] The other system of regulation, which became customary elsewhere in Imperial Germany (most famously in Berlin), was called 'casernation' (*Kasernierung*). With this method police restricted registered prostitutes to specific streets or neighbourhoods but did not rely on brothel-keepers for control. In the latter system, prostitutes had a direct relationship with the police. Over time casernation became the pre-eminent system of regulation in Imperial Germany, since operating without the assistance of brothel-keepers seemed to be in closer compliance with § 180 of the Criminal Code.

Almost immediately upon joining the new *Reich* in October 1871, Hamburg's municipal authorities issued new regulations for the prostitution trade.[11] The new law confirmed Hamburg's preference for brothelization since it emphasized that the regulatory system included not only the prostitutes but also the men and women who profited from the trade as landlords or brothel-keepers.[12] Local activists contested the legality of Hamburg's insistence on brothelization, arguing that its reliance on brothel-keepers was irreconcilable with § 180. Hamburg's government fought this claim in a protracted legal battle that led all the way to the Imperial Federal Council, which found in favour of the plaintiffs and in 1876 ordered Hamburg's government to close all existing brothels.[13] Hamburg's government seemingly complied by issuing new regulations, which avoided explicit mention of brothel-keepers. But in practice the local police continued to assign registered prostitutes to specific brothels and the system of brothelization remained intact.[14] In other words, the state determined who entered the profession and controlled where, how and when prostitutes, procurers and clients interacted. Moreover, the state retained the right to punish prostitutes or brothel-keepers at any time.[15] Officially regulated prostitution was a business that continued to be conducted under the watchful gaze of the police. The city changed its regulatory system merely in terms of semantics. Municipal leaders favoured brothelization because it gave them control over a business at the margins of legality and respectability that might otherwise have eluded the official gaze.

More than the system of casernation, brothelization maximized the state's oversight and intruded into the day-to-day affairs of prostitutes. Already in 1869 police had begun the practice of compulsory registration. But after 1876 women were forced to register only if they had previously been registered in Hamburg or elsewhere. This curb on involuntary registration was abandoned temporarily in the 1880s. But by 1894 all women who were 'obviously' engaged in prostitution were again compelled to register, though many who worked as prostitutes managed to evade the dreaded inscription. By forcing suspicious women to register, the police hoped to shunt as many potential prostitutes as possible into the regulatory system and therefore into the visible and hence controllable segment of the prostitution business.

Once registered, the regulations prescribed all aspects of the women's professional and personal lives.[16] They had to submit to frequent, usually fortnightly, medical examinations, and a city physician had to declare them healthy before they could legally return to work in a brothel. But the regulations went beyond precautions for health and hygiene. By means of routine police inspections of women's ledger books, which recorded earnings and expenses, municipal authorities monitored the prostitutes' economic situations and work environments. Many women were perpetually indebted to their landlords or brothel-keepers and the police were well aware of these structures of dependency.

Registration also subjected the women's residences and living conditions to state surveillance and regulation. For example, the prostitutes and their brothel-keepers were not allowed to employ female servants below the ages of 30 and 25, respectively, or they risked prosecution for promoting illicit prostitution. The front doors of the brothel were to be kept closed; the windows facing the street were to be kept shut and covered, unless opaque; the rooms on the first floor were to be kept dark at night and in the evenings, and price lists for beverages and sexual services were to be posted visibly in all rooms.

Professional conduct was prescribed as well. It was illegal for a prostitute to undress unless she and her client were in a separate room other than the main guest room or lounge. Nor were prostitutes allowed to perform so-called 'unnatural' acts, although men who demanded and paid for such services were not troubled by the police. Additionally, music, dancing and card or other games were banned from brothels. Police regulations extended beyond the walls of the brothels and further restricted the women's conduct in public. A registered Hamburg prostitute, for example, was not allowed to promenade on the Jungfernstieg, the local main boulevard, or ride in an open carriage. She did not have the right to go to the theatre (unless she was out of sight of the general public) or walk along the Alster, an inner-city lake with cafés and terraces on its banks. It was illegal for her to walk in public after 11 p.m. without an escort or address men in any way in the streets. The official rationale for these intrusions, *Polizeiherr* Petersen argued in 1871, was to protect the women from the exploitation that was perpetuated and institutionalized by the women's financial dependence on their brothel-keepers. However, these measures ensured instead that the police retained a firm grasp on the definition and control of prostitutes.

To what extent these strict rules were enforced is difficult to determine, but the number of women cited throughout the period for breaking the regulations increased. According to internal reports, the police imposed only 250 prison sentences on registered women who violated the regulations in 1875. By 1877 the number of sentences had risen to 1,312, and in the following years it averaged over 2,000 annually.[17] In 1890 registered prostitutes were sentenced 1,942 times. In 1906 the police amended their policies since expenses for these incarcerations were high and their effectiveness questionable. In one report a police officer remarked that 'the execution of these police punishments occasioned annual costs of about 15,000 marks [in 1906]. ... Nevertheless, one cannot claim that the work of the morals police was promoted in any palpable way.'[18] But the police did not abandon their vigilance and instead issued warnings to prostitutes who violated the regulations and jailed only repeat offenders. According to one investigating officer, the new policies had remarkably positive effects: 'As an outward sign, we must recognize that prostitutes have begun to behave more courteously and respectfully. ... Now the girls willingly and politely answer questions. Their comportment in the office is changed. Often they ask for a mild evaluation of their cases and promise to "be more careful" in the future.'[19] Thus the punishments decreased, but they did not stop altogether. In 1907 the police issued 1,469 warnings, 181 sentences, and turned 58 cases over to the courts. This trend stabilized and the police attributed the new policies' apparent success to the fact that repeat violations were punished with stiffer sentences (8–14 days). The police thus watched registered prostitutes closely. The regulations did not protect women from police interference, but instead made their actions visible and controllable. Although regulated prostitution was officially tolerated, the women involved in the business preserved very little independence and remained under the constant gaze of the police.

By decreeing which women were to be registered and under which circumstances, Hamburg's police defined and created the prostitute. Prostitutes were women who led so-called immoral lives, were homeless and sick, previously registered, or otherwise marginal to bourgeois society.[20] The power to force women to register and submit to official controls granted the state the power to marginalize them further and to monitor their behaviour. More generally, it gave the state the power to define both deviance and respectability. Through the strict regulations and multiple layers of control, the government actively separated 'public' women from all other aspects of middle-class sociability and amusement and restricted them to a life in the brothel milieu. Once designated a prostitute, the 'public' woman could scarcely participate in mainstream Hamburg society. She was stigmatized and forced outside the boundaries of her contemporary world.

In defence of their policies, the Hamburg authorities often couched their regulations in the language of fear. To our modern eyes, it might seem obvious that prostitutes were victims of the strict regulatory system, since their freedom of movement and economic pursuits were seriously curtailed. According to city officials, however, prostitutes were not victims but predators who threatened to undermine contemporary morality. Respectable society required protection lest it become influenced by the prostitution milieu and all its negative effects. One Hamburg politician wrote: 'If the police are no longer able through the localization of prostitution, through unfettered supervision of their establishments [brothels], and through the broad support of their brothel-keepers, to contain these elements [prostitutes], murder, rape, and other crimes and excesses of all kinds will increase to unfathomable degrees.'[21] Another one claimed: 'The vast incompleteness of control brings with it pimping, elegant courtesans and the demimonde. They are responsible for the ruin of the root of morality, as they grow wild and confuse imperceptibly the sense of what is morally tolerable and intolerable. In their extreme degeneration they form a veritable nursery for crime and the subversion of public order.'[22] These comments by municipal officials reveal the perceived stakes in the prostitution trade. While the state saw the need to tolerate prostitution, officials were deeply troubled by the confusion over gender roles which seemed to emerge from prostitution. Tellingly, the officials created explicit links between the confusion of 'what is morally tolerable and intolerable' and the threat of 'crime and the subversion of public order'. Prostitution was a business that could not be left unregulated since the very safety of public order and morality was at stake.

After 1876 the morals police in Hamburg divided registered women into two distinct categories: those who worked under so-called strict control and those who were subject to modified control. Strict and modified control differed in the terms of level of supervision to which women were subjected. Women under modified control were examined less frequently and also had somewhat more freedom in their choice of residence. Originally, modified control was a category designed to ease the transition of women out of the brothel milieu by relaxing the more onerous rules and allowing women more freedoms to pursue other employment or marriage, which enabled some women to re-enter respectable society.

In the years leading up to 1914, Hamburg's police kept statistics on the women inscribed in the regulatory system. While the number of prostitutes under strict supervision remained remarkably constant – 770 in 1877, 977 at its high point in 1893, and 876 in 1914 – those working under modified supervision grew enormously.[23] Between 1879 and 1895 the figure increased only modestly from 30 to 45, but after 1895 the number grew dramatically, reaching a record high of 394 in

1905, before falling again to 244 in 1914.[24] In the first period modified control remained a way to ease women out of the brothel milieu and back into mainstream society. After the middle of the 1890s, however, the category began to be used differently. If deemed unsuitable for a life in the brothel milieu, because of age, occupation, family or marital status, women were registered immediately under modified control. The expanded use of modified control reflected the government's attempt to extend its grasp over the growing number of part-time prostitutes, who might otherwise have escaped inscription.

A large percentage of the women who worked as registered prostitutes in Hamburg's brothels had not been born in the city and either immigrated to Hamburg or were recruited by pimps and procurers from elsewhere. For example, only 118 of the 770 women who worked under strict supervision in 1877 had lived in Hamburg prior to their inscription. Of these, 99 were foreigners (the largest group, 53 women, came from the Austrian Empire, and most of the rest came from other German states).[25] This trend continued throughout the Imperial period. In 1907 only 10.8 per cent of the women who lived in brothels had been born in the city, while 50.2 per cent of the city's overall population were natives. In contrast to the women under strict supervision, most women under modified control were locally born. These numbers suggest that brothelization targeted non-native women. Local women who had grown up in the city and had familial or social networks were less likely to be forced out of respectable society and into brothels. They might have worked as prostitutes temporarily but were not banished to the brothels and forced to give up their social relations completely.[26] Local women in periods of financial distress tended to slide in and out of prostitution more easily. They could use their knowledge of the city and the police, as well as their support networks, to escape the shame of the brothel. Foreigners, especially women who came to the city on their own and lacked such networks, were more likely to end up in a brothel under strict supervision. Without a family close by to vouch for them, they often had few hopes of finding 'respectable' employment. As social newcomers and outsiders, they were easier victims for the police and the cunning brothel-keepers who were always on the lookout for new faces.

Although youth was coveted by clients and brothel-keepers alike, the police were not supposed to register women who were younger than 18 years of age. Some minors always found their way into the registry, however, causing occasional outcries among critics of the regulatory system. In June 1907 11 women who lived in brothels were under the age of 21, 290 were between the ages of 21 and 30, 96 were between 31 and 40, and 11 were over 41.[27] Most women who worked in brothels were thus adults in their twenties or early thirties. It has been argued that prostitution was a temporary or transitional occupation for women who had fallen on hard times or who could not find other reasonable employment.[28] The large number of young prostitutes seems to bear out this interpretation, but the age distribution of registered prostitutes mirrored the age distribution among Hamburg's women more generally. Prostitutes – at least registered prostitutes in Hamburg – were thus not disproportionately young women who later re-entered respectable society and left the brothel milieu behind them. At least a small number of women seem to have spent their entire working lives as registered full-time prostitutes.

The total number of women who were registered as prostitutes in Hamburg in both categories fluctuated minimally during the three decades before the First World War. On average it was below 1,000 from 1879 to 1914.[29] For a city approaching the million mark, this number was negligible and meant that on average there was only one registered prostitute for every 1,000 inhabitants.[30]

Registered and Secret Prostitutes

Because the regulatory system relied on a specific definition of prostitution, its statistics account for only a fraction of the women who made their bodies available for sex. Traditionally, an official prostitute was a woman who sold her body on a regular, professional and full-time basis. She lived and worked outside the boundaries of respectable society; in fact, her existence helped establish those boundaries. Unlike other women, official prostitutes were allowed to have premarital or extramarital sex, but they paid for it with their exclusion from mainstream sociability. As the government in Hamburg clung to the traditional regulatory system, it retained the traditional definitions of prostitution, as well as traditional assumptions about its milieu and role in society. These assumptions, however, clashed increasingly with the reality in Hamburg.

As Germany industrialized in the second half of the nineteenth century, Hamburg's importance as a port city grew, and so did its population. The economic boom drew thousands of men, women and children to the city, hoping to find work and new lives. Especially for women, however, the realization of dreams often remained elusive. Many could not find adequate work and were vulnerable to slipping into – or being tricked into – prostitution.[31] Once a woman had entered the world of the brothel, it was hard for her to escape, not least because she had lost her honour. Contemporaries often asserted that 'a person who has fallen into prostitution is generally lost and cannot be saved, because she quickly loses the ability to muster enough strength for a respectable occupation'.[32]

Many bourgeois contemporaries stereotyped prostitutes as lazy, idle or obsessed with dressing up (*Putzsucht*), but unwilling to work at honest jobs. Others saw them as victims of their own desires and heightened sexuality, for which prostitution and other forms of illicit sexuality were necessary outlets. These commentators identified the causes of the growing prostitution milieu with the moral degeneracy or inadequacy of the women themselves.[33] But women's work in Imperial Germany was limited, often insecure and poorly remunerated, and many women if forced to earn a living had few alternatives.[34] Many women balanced work with childcare, but this was particularly difficult since the occupations open to them, such as waiting tables, factory work or dressmaking, were often insecure. In periods of economic trouble, female employees were often the first to be let go.[35] Contrary to contemporary opinions, prostitution was often a 'matter of rational choice rather than … of moral degeneracy or outright compulsion'.[36]

Under economic duress more and more women became involved in occasional, unregulated and secret prostitution. Most of their stories have vanished with them, but a few contemporary descriptions of secret prostitution have survived. They point to a phenomenon that was already significant in the middle of the nineteenth century, when it outpaced the development of Hamburg's official prostitution. Writing in 1848, one chronicler described secret prostitution in Hamburg as follows: 'Street prostitution is exorbitantly well developed in our city. As soon as the sun goes down, the main streets and the Jungfernstieg [the main promenade along the Alster lake] is teeming with prostitutes and whores. … In some parts of the city … it is often impossible to avoid harassment by these girls in the evening, scores of them approach one in the streets.'[37] Women who solicited sexual services in the streets were almost always secret prostitutes. Registered women had to work in the brothels, and the police could rely on the brothel-keepers to keep their prostitutes off the streets after 11 p.m. While brothelized prostitution stagnated, secret street prostitution flourished as the numerical gap between registered prostitutes and the women who practised prostitution outside official regulation widened during the Imperial period. In 1895 the chief of police estimated that at least 4,000 non-registered prostitutes worked in Hamburg, and this was probably a conservative guess.[38]

Registered prostitutes came from diverse social and occupational backgrounds, but many had switched jobs repeatedly, probably in desperate attempts to secure some kind of employment.[39] Nevertheless, one of the largest feeder jobs for prostitution was domestic service. Many, if not most, young women who came to the city found work as domestic servants, and an equally large percentage of these ended up in the prostitution milieu.[40] This trend was helped by the fact that relationships between masters and young servants were hierarchical, and male members of households often used their servants sexually. Even if a servant had had no sexual relations within the household but with someone of her own social milieu instead, she was often dismissed immediately upon becoming pregnant, and possibly rejected by her own family as well. She thus became easy prey for pimps and procurers. As a result, a ready supply of women were either forced or made willing to work as prostitutes by difficult circumstances.

Other Opportunities for Women?

Most women involved in the prostitution business worked as prostitutes. A small number played other roles, however. Although most of these appear only rarely in the archival record, there is clear evidence of women working as procuresses, especially in the mid-nineteenth century.[41] These so-called *Verschicksfrauen* recruited unsuspecting young women and sold them to brothel-keepers. For a fee, these *Verschicksfrauen* also arranged with the brothel-keepers for the transfer of prostitutes between brothels in Hamburg and across borders. The new landlord paid the debt of the prostitute to the previous brothel-keeper and the procuress received a cut of this payment. The prostitutes themselves had little or no say in these trades, and they were bought and sold like property. The statistics about fluctuations of women in and out of the regulatory system (between 1857 and 1862 there were between 400 and 610 new inscriptions while the number of women leaving the system ranged from 399 to 573) as well as those documenting address changes (there were between 813 and 1,646 annual relocations between 1857 and 1866) all indicate that these procuresses must have had steady income streams.[42]

The public priority for a stable system of prostitution discouraged interference with the large-scale procurement by the *Verschicksfrauen*. Consistent with their preference for regulating public practice rather than coping with a secret one, the city authorities turned a blind eye to these dealings. In 1859 they went even further when they acknowledged the existence of large-scale procuring by issuing an official pricing scale for procuresses, ostensibly in order to avoid the overcharging and abuse of prostitutes.[43] The scale was incorporated into the regulations of 1860 and remained in effect until 1876. The scale regulated the amount procuresses could charge for individual transactions according to the debt of the prostitute involved.[44] Because the procuresses stabilized the system of brothelized prostitution, they too, were included in the city's policy of toleration. *Verschicksfrauen* disappeared from the official documents after 1876, but there is reason to believe that some women continued to play similar roles in the prostitution business.

Archival references to female brothel-keepers or madams are even rarer, but these women, too, most likely existed. In one unusual document from 1908, self-described prostitute Mathilde Schween wrote about the actions of an infamous Hamburg madam.[45] Her story not only attested to the existence of madams in Hamburg but also illustrated the close relationship between brothel-keepers and the police. According to Schween, 'there was a madam here in Hamburg, who made officer Froman her heir. When Senator Kuhnhardt, who was wise and fair, found out about this, he dismissed the officer from public service. He became a coffee trader and then all the madams and brothel-keepers with whom he was on good terms bought coffee from him.' If true, Schween's accusations exposed a pattern of bribery, profiteering and co-operation between brothel-keepers and the police officers that would warrant an intense internal investigation. However, a police report that considered Schween's charges dismissed even the possibility that officers had engaged in such abusive behaviour and merely answered her accusations as follows: 'Officer Freeman (not Froman) was discharged dishonourably on March 1, 1884.'[46] The police did not dispute, however, the existence of the madam or her relationship with the police department.

Conclusion

Although prostitution allowed some women to escape traditional sexual and domestic roles, it did not function like other contemporary trades or services. Most prostitutes were not empowered by their profession and could rarely assert any agency in their situations. Instead, regulated prostitutes were marginalized both financially and socially and continued to be subject to the control of men (police officers, doctors, judges, brothel-keepers and customers or patrons). These women existed in highly marginalized if regulated spaces and could not profit from their actions. Their bodies had value only in the context of the sexual act and even then they were treated as objects, not independent agents. They were dependent on brothel-keepers, forced to conform to specific rules, and unable to make decisions about when and where to work. In addition to officially registered prostitutes, some women also sold sex secretly. But the very secrecy into which they were forced negated the empowerment of gainful employment. Women who were active in other capacities, such as madams and procuresses, were relatively rare. And while they may have experienced greater independence than the prostitutes, they also remained subject to extensive systems of regulation and control.

The function of commodified female sexuality in Imperial Germany precluded the possibility of any independence for prostitutes. While prostitution was a visible and integral part of Germany's society and economy, involving thousands of women and many more men, it was in no sense emancipatory for the women who earned their livings as prostitutes. The regulation system did force contemporaries to question their understanding of gendered behaviour and sexuality, however, and provides historians with an opportunity to explore the multi-faceted and contested character of gender roles. A simple bourgeois ideology based on 'separate spheres' could not begin to describe the phenomenon of prostitution, especially as a business or an occupation for lower-class women. At the same time, state officials and bourgeois moralists insisted on explaining prostitution in gendered and bourgeois terms. They posited notions that evoke a 'separate spheres' ideology. But the lived experiences of the prostitutes and the marginal roles they played surely prove otherwise. Whether prostitution might have been less stigmatizing from the perspective of the women involved eludes the historian. Regardless, gender was never a static category in nineteenth-century Hamburg.

Notes

1. Bassermann, 1993.
2. On medieval and early modern brothels see B. Schuster, 1991 and 1995; P. Schuster, 1992; and Roper, 1985. The literature on nineteenth-century prostitution is even richer: for England, Walkowitz, 1980; Finnegan, 1979; and Mahood, 1990; for France, Corbin, 1990; and Harsin, 1985; for Italy, Gibson, 1986; for Imperial Russia see Bernstein, 1995; and Engelstein, 1992; for Switzerland, Ulrich, 1985; for Vienna, Jusek, 1995; for Sweden, Swanström, 2000; for the Netherlands, de Vries, 1997; and for Germany, Evans, 1976a; and Schulte, 1979. Some newer works include Hilpert-Fröhlich, 1991; Stallberg, 1992; and Jenders and Müller, 1993. For a sophisticated and imaginative analysis of the Bavarian capital's struggle with its prostitution milieu, see Krafft, 1996, who structures her analysis of the interaction between the prostitution milieu and the local authorities around the concept of a prostitution market. For a good overview of recent publications on prostitution in Europe and elsewhere, see Gilfoyle, 1999.
3. Schelzig, 2002.
4. Bargon, 1982.
5. Translation cited in *Imperial German Criminal Code*, 1917, pp. 93–4.
6. Ibid.
7. Municipal authorities had other reasons for enforcing the regulations, such as concerns over public health and public safety. The regulations often fell short of expectations, however, in providing the expected control.
8. On the fetishization of virginity, see Lamott, 1992.
9. Hill, 1994, p. 288.
10. This system was amended in 1876 to rely less overtly on the brothel-keepers and come into closer compliance with § 180, but its tenor remained essentially the same throughout the period.
11. Hamburg had been a member of the North German Confederation since 1867 and therefore subject to its Criminal Code, which also included a paragraph outlawing procurement. These new regulations were issued in the context of a new local law of 1869 to bring Hamburg into compliance with the new legal context.
12. The Regulations of 1871 are cited in *Das Deutsche Strafgesetzbuch* (hereinafter St GB), 1877, pp. 55ff.
13. For documents concerning this legal battle, see *Das Deutsche Strafgesetzbuch*, 1877. The originals can be found in Staatsarchiv Hamburg (hereinafter StaHH): 111–1 Senat, Cl. I Lit. T. Nr. 7, Vol. 6, Fasc. 9, Inv. 1 and Inv. 2, 352–3 Medizinalkollegium II P 1 Band 1, as well as in the Bundesarchiv, Reichsjustizamt (hereinafter RJA) R 3001 5779 Abänderungen von

Vorschriften des StGB gegen Sittlichkeitsverbrechen (StGB §§ 180–184) Band 1 Dez. 1872–Juni 1890 (FilmSig 21765).
14. Urban, 1927, pp. 86 ff.
15. StaHH, 111–1 Senat, Cl. VII Lit. Lb Nr. 28a, Vol. 136, Fasc. 5; 'Verzeichnis derjenigen Wirthe welche wegen Verkehrs liderlicher Frauenzimmer verwarnt oder mit Entziehung der Concession bedroht sind, bezw. denen die Concession entzogen ist'.
16. The text of the Regulations of 1876 can be found in Urban 1927, pp. 86ff., 99. See also StaHH 241–1 I Justizverwaltung II D b 2 Vol. 1 [4] 'Polizeiliche Vorschriften für unter Controlle der Sittenpolizei stehende Frauenzimmer', April 1, 1889
17. StaHH 111–1 Senat Cl. I Lit. T Nr. 7, Vol. 6, Fasc. 9, Inv. 3; 'Polizeibericht der früher in Hamburg geduldeten Bordelle vom 28.11.1891.' See esp. the attached 'Übersicht über die wegen Übertretung der polizeilichen Vorschriften vehängten Haftstrafen gegen sittenpolizeilich controllierte Frauenzimmer, 1875–1890'.
18. StaHH 331–1 I Polizeibehörde I 195; 'Polizeibericht vom 31.12.1907'.
19. StaHH 331–1 I Polizeibehörde I 195; 'Polizeibericht vom 31.12.1907'.
20. Urban, 1927, p. 99.
21. Bundesrath Session 1874 No. 12, Bericht des Ausschusses für Justizwesen, 5
22. StaHH 352–3 Medinzinalkollegium II P 1 Band 1 'Prostitution Allgemeines,' 1847–1907 S. 108–112 Gutachten des Chefs der Polizeibehörde, 6.5.1873.
23. Urban, 1927, pp. 95, 98.
24. Ibid., p. 98.
25. Ibid., pp. 104–5.
26. Abrams, 1988.
27. Urban, 1927, p. 105.
28. See, for example, Evans, 1998, pp. 194–5.
29. The average number of women registered as official prostitutes in Hamburg between 1879 and 1914 was 945. See also Urban, 1927, p. 98.
30. Urban, 1927, p. 111.
31. Schulte 1979, pp. 68–113; and Krafft, 1996, pp. 97–122.
32. StaHH 111–1 Senat Cl. I Lit. T Nr. 7, Vol. 6, Fasc. 9, Inv. 3 'Bericht von Engel-Reimers vom 25.2.1880'.
33. Becker, 1994.
34. Frevert, 1989, pp. 83ff.
35. Adams, 1988. See also Bajor, 1981, and Abrams, 1992.
36. Evans, 1993, p. 179.
37. Urban, 1927, p. 59.
38. Ibid., p. 114.

196 • *Julia Bruggemann*

39. Contemporaries argued that most women were recruited from the lower classes. See Flexner, 1914, p. 64.
40. Walser, 1984.
41. Urban, 1927, p. 32.
42. Ibid., pp. 35–6.
43. Ibid., p. 32.
44. StaHH 111–1 Senat Cl VII Lit. Lb Nr. 28 a Vol. 50 Polizeiliche Vorschriften, 1860 § 34.
45. StAHH 111–1 Senat; Cl VII Lit. Lb Nr., 28a 2 Vol. 136 Fasc. 9. For a full analysis of this incident, see Bruggemann, 1998.
46. StAHH 111–1 Senat; Cl VII Lit. Lb Nr,. 28a 2 Vol. 136 Fasc. 9.

Bibliography

125 Jahre Henschel 1810–1935 (1935), Kassel: Henschel & Sohn.
Abram, L. (2002), *The Making of Modern Woman*, London: Longman.
Abrams, L. (1988), 'Prostitutes in Imperial Germany, 1870–1918: Working Girls or Social Outcasts?', in R. Evans (ed.), *The German Underworld*, London: Routledge, 189–289.
Abrams, L. (1992), 'Martyrs or Matriarchs? Working-class Women's Experience of Marriage before the First World War', *Women's History Review*, 1: 81–100.
Abrams, L. and Harvey, E. (1997, eds), *Gender Relations in German History: Power, Agency and Experience from the Sixteenth to the Twentieth Century*, Durham, NC: Duke University Press.
Adam, T. (2004), *Philanthropy, Patronage, and Civil Society: Experiences from Germany, Great Britain, and North America*, Bloomington: Indiana University Press.
Adams, C. E. (1988), *Women Clerks in Wilhelmine Germany: Issues of Class and Gender*, Cambridge: Cambridge University Press.
Adler, L. (1979), *A l'aube du féminisme. Les premières journalistes (1830–1850)*, Paris: Payot.
af Forsell, C. (1844), *Statistik öfver Sverige grundad på offentliga handlingar*, Stockholm: Bagge.
Agardh, C. A. (1857), *Försök till statsekonomisk statistik öfver, Sverige*, Karlstad: Publisher Unknown.
Ågren, M. (1992), *Jord och gäld*, Studia Historica Upsaliensa 166: Uppsala University.
Ågren, M. (1999), 'Fadern, systern och brodern. Maktförskjutningar genom 1800-talets egendomsreformer', *Historisk tidskrift*, 4: 683–708.
Aguado, A. (1993), 'Aproximació a l'estudi de le dones a través de la Prensa valenciana', in *Les Dones de l'Horta al llars del temps*, Valencia: Ideco, 101–55.
Aldaraca, B. (1982), 'El Ángel del Hogar', in G. Mora and K. S. van Hooft (eds), *The Cult of Domesticy in Nineteenth-Century Spain: Theory and Practice of Feminist Literary Criticism*, Ypsilanti, MI: Bilingual Press, 62–87.
Aldaraca, B. (1992), *El Ángel del Hogar: Galdós and the Ideology of Domesticity*

in Sapin, Chapel Hill, NC: University of North Carolina Press (Traducción española: *El Ángel del Hogar. Galdós y la ideología de la domesticidad en España,* Madrid: Visor, 1992).

Alexander, D. (1970), *Retailing in England during the Industrial Revolution*, London: Athlone Press.

Alexander, S. (1983), *Women's Work in Nineteenth-century London*, London: Journeyman Press.

Alter G. (1988), *Family and the Female Life Course: The Women of Verviers, Belgium, 1849–1880*, Madison: University of Wisconsin Press.

Alvarez Quintana, C. (1995), 'La marquesa de Argüelles, promotora inmobiliaria y turística de la costa oriental de Asturias (1890–1936)', in I. Carrera, R. Cid and D. Molina (eds), *Mujer e investigación*, Oviedo: Universidad de Oviedo.

Andersson, B. (1983), 'Early History of Banking in Gothenburg Discount House Operations 1783–1818', *Scandinavian Economic History Review*, 31: 49–67.

Andriessen, P. J. (1871), *Iets anders. Bevattende een beschrijving van de provincien Zuid-Holland en Utrecht*, Deventer: A.J. v.d. Sigtenhorst.

Anon. (1806), *The Book of Trades or Library of the Useful Arts. Parts 1, 2 and 3 Combined*, 3rd Edition, London: Tarbart & Co.

Anon. (1839), *The Young Tradesman; or, Book of English Trades: Being a Library of the Useful Arts, for Commercial Education*, London: Whitaker & Co.

Anon. (1876), *Reminiscences of an Old Draper*, London.

Anon. (1916), 'Berufsstatistik nach den Ergebnissen der Volkszählung vom 31. Dezember 1910', *Österreichische Statistik*, 3: 38–44.

Arbaiza, M. (1996), *Familia, Trabajo y Reproducción Social. Una perspectiva microhistórica de la sociedad vizcaína del Antiguo Régimen*, Bilbao: Universidad del País Vasco.

Aresti Esteban, N. (2000), 'El ángel del hogar y sus demonios. Ciencia, religión y Género en la España del siglo XIX', *Historia Contemporánea*, 21: 363–94.

Armstrong, N. (1987), *Desire and Domestic Fiction: A Political History of the Novel*, New York: Oxford University Press (Traducción española: *Deseo y ficción doméstica*, Madrid: Cátedra, 1991).

Arranz, M. (2001), *La menestralia de Barcelona al segle XVIII. Els gremis de la Construcció. Arixu Històric de la Ciutat-Proa*, Barcelona: Arxiu Històric de la Ciutat.

Artaeus, I. (1992), *Kvinnorna som blev över. Ensamstående stadskvinnor under 1800-talets första hälft – fallet Västerås*, Uppsala: Uppsala University.

August, A. (1999), *Poor Women's Lives: Gender, Work, and Poverty in Late-Victorian London*, London: Fairleigh Dickinson University Press.

Augustine, D. (1994), *Patricians and Parvenus: Wealth and High Society in Wilhelmine Germany*, Oxford: Berghahn.

Bajor, S. (1981), 'Uneheliche Mütter im Arbeitermilieu: Die Stadt Braunschweig

1900–1933', *Geschichte und Gesellschaft*, 7: 474–506.
Ballarín, P. (2001), *La educación de las mujeres en la España Contemporánea (Siglos XIX y XX)*, Madrid: Síntesis, 2001.
Bandhauer-Schöffmann, I. (1997), 'Wiener Geschäftsfrauen um die Jahrhundertwende', in I. Bandhauer-Schöffmann (ed.), *Auf dem Weg zur Beletage: Frauen in der Wirtschaft*, Vienna: Sonderzahl Verlag, 145–78.
Bandhauer-Schöffmann, I. (2003), 'Innovation und Männlichkeit: Schumpeters Unternehmer—ein österreichisches Muster?', in R. Pichler (ed.), *Innovationsmuster in der österreichischen Wirtschaftsgeschichte*, Innsbruck: Studienverlag, 103–18.
Banik-Schweitzer, R. (1979), 'Zur Entwicklung der Berufs- und Betriebsstruktur in Wien, 1870–1934', *Summa-Wirtschaftberichte*, 8: 22–9.
Banik-Schweitzer, R. and Meißl, G. (1983), *Industriestadt Wien: Die Durchsetzung der industriellen Marktproduktion in der Habsburgerresidenz*, Vienna: F. Deuticke.
Banker's Daughter (1864), *Guide to the Unprotected in Every-day Matters Relating to Property and Income*, 2nd edition, London: Macmillan and Co.
Bar, J. (1903), 'Frère-Orban intime' (interview de ses anciens domestiques), *La Chronique*, 20 janvier.
Bargon, M. (1982), *Prostitution und Zuhälterei: Zur kriminologischen und strafrechtlichen Problematik mit einem geschichtlichen und rechtsvergeleichenden Überblick*, Lübeck: Verlag Max Schmidt-Röhmhild.
Barth-Scalmani, G. (1996), 'Salzburger Handelsfrauen, Frätschlerinnen, Fragnerinnen: Frauen in der Welt des Handels am Ende des 18. Jahrhunderts', *L'Homme. Zeitschrift für feministische Geschichtswissenschaft*, 6: 23–45.
Barth-Scalmani, G. (2000), 'Frauen in der Welt des Handels vom 18. zum 19. Jahrhundert: Eine regionalgeschichtliche Typologie', in I. Bandhauer-Schöffmann and R. Bendl (eds), *Unternehmerinnen: Geschichte und Gegenwart selbständiger Erwerbstätigkeit von Frauen*, Frankfurt am Main: Peter Lang, 17–48.
Barth-Scalmani, G. and Friedrich, M. (1995), 'Frauen auf der Wiener Weltausstellung von 1873: Blick auf die Bühne und hinter die Kulissen', in B. Mazohl-Wallnig (ed.), *Bürgerliche Frauenkultur im 19. Jahrhundert*, Vienna: Böhlau Verlag, 175–232.
Bartsch, R. (1908), 'Die Reform des österreichischen Privatrechts', *Allgemeine Österreichische Gerichts-Zeitung*, 59: 1, 1–4; 2, 13–14; 3, 21–23; 4, 29–32.
Bassermann, L. (1993), *The Oldest Profession: A History of Prostitution*, New York: Dorset Press.
Baumann, C. (1985), *175 Jahre Henschel: Der ständige Weg in die Zukunft*, Düsseldorf: Steiger.
Beachy, R. (2001), 'Business Was a Family Affair: Women of Commerce in

Central Europe, 1680-1870', *Histoire sociale—Social History*, 34: 307–30.
Beachy, R. (2004), 'Women without Gender: Commerce, Exchange Codes, and the Erosion of Female Guardianship in Germany, 1680–1830', in D. R. Green and A. Owens (eds), *Family Welfare: Gender, Property and Inheritance since the Seventeenth Century*, Westport, CT: Praeger, 195–216.
Beauthier, R. and Piette, V. (2003), 'Egalité civile et société en Belgique. Evolution du Code civil dans sa dimension historique', in J.-P. Barriere and V. Demars-Sion (eds), *La femme dans la cité*, Lille: Centre d'Histoire Judiciaire, 141–63.
Becker, P. (1994), 'Kriminelle Identitäten im 19. Jahrhundert: Neue Entwicklungen in der historischen Kriminalitätsforschung', *Historische Anthropologie*, 2: 143–57.
Bell, G. M. (1846), *Guide to the Investment of Capital, or How to Lay out Money with Safety and Profit*, London: Mitchell.
Beller, S. (1989), *Vienna and the Jews 1867–1938: A Cultural History*, Cambridge: Cambridge University Press.
Benería, L. (1979), 'Reproduction, Production and the Sexual Division of Labour', *Cambridge Journal of Economics*, 3: 203–25.
Benería, L. and Sen, A. (1981), 'Accumulation, Reproduction and Women's Role in Economic Development', *Signs: Journal of Women in Culture and Society*, 7: 279–98.
Benson, J. (1983), *The Penny Capitalists: A Study of Nineteenth-century Working-class Entrepreneurs*, Dublin: Gill and Macmillan.
Berg, M. (1988), 'Women's Work: Mechanization and the Early Phases of Industrialization in England', in R. Pahl (ed.), *On Work: Historical, Comparative and Theoretical Approaches*, Oxford: Basil Blackwell, 61–94.
Berg, M. (1991), *Markets and Manufacture in Early Industrial Europe*, London: Routledge.
Berg, M. (1993), 'Women's Property and the Industrial Revolution', *Journal of Interdisciplinary History*, 24: 233–50.
Berg, M. (1996), 'Women's Consumption and the Industrial Classes of Eighteenth-century England', *Journal of Social History*, 30: 415–34.
Berg, M. and Hudson, P. (1992), 'Rehabilitating the Industrial Revolution', *Economic History Review*, Second Series, XLV: 24–50.
Bernstein, L. (1995), *Sonia's Daughters: Prostitutes and Their Regulation in Imperial Russia*, Berkeley: University of California Press.
Bieder, M. (1998), 'Women, Literature, and Society: The Essays of Pardo Bazán', in K. Glenn and M. Mazquiarán (eds), *Spanish Women Writers and the Essay: Gender, Politics and the Self*, Columbia and London: University Press, 25–54.
Biette C. (1987), 'Caroline Popp, première journaliste belge. Contribution à l'histoire de la condition féminine en Belgique', mémoire de licence Louvain-la-Neuve, UCL.

Biot, Lucien (1966), 'Famille Thiery', *Biographie nationale*, vol. XXXIII, Bruylant, Brussels: Académie Royale des Sciences, des Lettres et des Beaux-Arts de Belgique, col. 695–704.

Blackman, J. (1976), 'The Corner Shop: The Development of the Grocery and General Provisions Trade', in D. Oddy and D. Miller (eds), *The Making of the Modern British Diet*, London: Croom Helm.

Bladh, C. (1992), *Månglerskor. Att sälja från korg och bod i Stockholm 1819–1846*, Stockholm: Kommittén för Stockholmsforskning.

Blanco, A. (1998), 'Escritora, feminidad y escritura en la España del medio siglo', in I. Zavala (co-ord.), *Breve historia feminista de la literatura española en lengua castellana*, vol. V, Barcelona: Anthropos, 9–38.

Blanco, A. (2001), *Escritoras virtuosas. Narradoras de la domesticidad en la España isabelina*, Granada: Universidad, Feminae.

Bock, G. (1993), *Frauen in der europäischen Geschichte: Vom Mittelalter bis zur Gegenwart*, Munich: Beck. Traducción en español, *La mujer en la historia de Europa. De la Edad Media a nuestros días*, Barcelona: Crítica, 2001).

Bock, G. (2002), *Women in European History*, Oxford: Blackwell.

Bolognese-Leuchtenmüller, B. (1978), *Bevölkerungsentwicklung und Berufsstruktur, Gesundheits- und Fürsorgewesen in Österreich 1750–1918*, Vienna: Verlag für Geschichte und Politik.

Bolognese-Leuchtenmüller, B. and Mitterauer, M. (1993, eds), *Frauenarbeitswelten*, Vienna: Verlag für Gesellschaftskritik.

Borderías, C. (2002), 'Women Workers in the Barcelona Labour Market, 1856–1936', in A. Smith (ed.), *Red Barcelona: Social Protest and Labour Mobilization in the Twentieth Century*, London: Routledge.

Borderías, C., Carrasco, C. and Alemany, C. (1994), *Las Mujeres y el Trabajo. Rupturas Conceptuales*, Barcelona: Fuhem-Icaria.

Borrell, E. (1999), *Presoneres del progrés. Fragmentació i felicitat femenina*, Lleida: Pages Editors.

Botrel, J.-F. (1993), *Libros, prensa y lectura en la España del siglo XIX*, Madrid: Fundación Germán Sánchez Ruipérez.

Boyer, J. W. (1981), *Political Radicalism in Late Imperial Vienna: Origins of the Christian Social Movement, 1848–1897*, Chicago: University of Chicago Press.

Bras, H. (1998), 'Domestic Service, Migration and the Social Status of Women at Marriage: The Case of a Dutch Sea Province, Zeeland 1820–1935', *Historical Social Research*, 23: 3–19.

Bras, H. (2002), *Zeeuwse meiden. Dienen als levensloop van vrouwen, 1850–1950*, Amsterdam: Aksent.

Braun, M. (1992), *De prijs van de liefde. De eerste feministische golf, het huwelijksrecht en de vaderlandse geschiedenis*, Amsterdam: Spinhuis.

Breckman, W. (1991), 'Disciplining Consumption: The Debate About Luxury in

Whilhelmine Germany', *Journal of Social History*, 24: 485–505.

Brenan, J. (1849), *The National Debt and Public Funds*, London: Effingham Wilson.

Brewer, J. (1989), *The Sinews of Power: War and the English State 1688–1783*, London: Harper Collins.

Brewer, J. and Porter, R. (1993, eds), *Consumption and the World of Goods*, London: Routledge.

Brisman, S. (1923), *AB Göteborgs Bank (The Joint Stock Bank of Gothenburg)*, Gothenburg: AB Göteborgs Bank.

Brix, E. and Fischer, L. (1997, eds), *Die Frauen der Wiener Moderne*, Vienna: Oldenbourg.

Bruggemann, J. (1998), 'Selbst- und Fremdwahrnehmung einer Prostituierten in Hamburg 1908/1909', in M. Rheinheimer (ed.), *Subjektive Welten: Wahrnehmung und Identität in der Neuzeit*, Neumünster: Wachholtz Verlag, 293–305.

Brugman, J., Buiter, H. and van Vliet, K. (1995), *Markten in Utrecht van de vroege middeleeuwen tot nu*, Utrecht: Matrijs.

Brunner, O. (1968), 'Das "Ganze Haus" und die alteuropäische "Ökonomik"', in O. Brunner, *Neue Wege der Verfassungs- und Sozialgeschichte*, Göttingen: Vandenhoeck & Ruprecht, 103-27.

Buchholz, S. (1997), 'Das Bürgerliche Gesetzbuch und die Frauen: Zur Kritik des Ehegüterrechts', in U. Gerhard (ed.), *Frauen in der Geschichte des Rechts: Von der Frühen Neuzeit bis zur Gegenwart*, Munich: C. H. Beck, 670–82.

Buisiné, M. (2001), 'Estudio Socioeducativo de los Artesanos de Logroño capital (1751–1884)', in S. Castillo and R. Fernández (eds), *Campesinos, artesanos, trabajadores*, Lleida: Ed. Milenio.

Burdy, J. P., Dubesset, M. and Zancarini-Fournet, M. (1987), 'Rôles, travaux et métiers de femmes dans une ville industrielle, St Etienne, 1900–1930', *Mouvement social*, 140: 27–54.

Busto, L. (1994), *La Dote en el siglo XIX. Una estrategia social*, S.P. Diputación Provincial: Lugo.

Butel P. (1976), 'Comportements familiaux dans le négoce bordelais au XVIIIe siècle', *Annales du Midi*, 28: 139–57.

Butler, J. (1990), *Gender Trouble: Feminism and the Subversion of Identity*, London: Routledge.

Butler, J. (1993), *Bodies that Matter: On the Discursive Limits of 'Sex'*, London: Routledge.

Cabrera Boch, I. (2000), 'Ciudadanía y género en el liberalismo decimonónico español', in P. Pérez- Cantó, (ed.), *También somos ciudadanas*, Madrid: Universidad Autónoma, 171–214.

Cain, P. and Hopkins, A. (2001), *British Imperialism: Innovation and Expansion 1688–1914*, London: Longman.

Caine, B. (2001), 'Feminism in London, circa 1850–1914', *Journal of Urban History*, 27: 765–78.

Caine, B. and Sluga, G. (1999), *Gendering European History*, Leicester: Leicester University Press (Traducción en español, *Mujeres en el cambio sociocultural europeo, de 1780 a 1920*, Madrid: Narcea, 2000).

Campbell, R. (1747), *The London Tradesman, being a Compendious View of all the Trades, Professions, Arts, Both Liberal and Mechanic, now Practised in the Cities of London and Westminster*, London: T. Gardner.

Canning, K. (1992), 'Gender and the Politics of Class Formation: Rethinking German Labor History', *American Historical Review*, 97: 736–68.

Canning, K. (1996), *Language of Labor and Gender: Female Factory Work in Germany, 1850–1914*, Ithaca, NY: Cornell University Press.

Capel, R. (1982), *El trabajo y la educación de la mujer en España (1900–1930)*, Madrid: Instituto de la Mujer, Ministerio de Cultura.

Carlsson, S. (1977), *Fröknar, mamseller, jungfrur och pigor*, Stockholm: Almqvist and Wicksell International.

Carmona Gonzalez, Á. (1999), *Escritoras andaluzas en la prensa de Andalucía del siglo XIX*, Cádiz: Universidad.

Carter, A. C. (1968), *The English Public Debt in the Eighteenth Century*, London: The Historical Association.

Casas, N. (1989), *L'esmolet de la Barceloneta*, Barcelona: Museu d'Arts, Indùstries i Tradicions.

Cerdà, I. (1859), 'Monografía Estadística de la Clase Obrera de Barcelona en 1856', in *Teoría General de la urbanización. Reforma y Ensanche de Barcelona*, 3 vols, Madrid: Ildefons Cerdà.

Chacón, F. (1995), 'Hacia una nueva definición de las estructura social en la España del Antiguo Régimen a través de la familia y las relaciones de parentesco', *Historia Social*, 21: 75–104.

Chaloupek, G., Eigner, P. and Wagner, M. (1991), *Wien: Wirtschaftsgeschichte, 1740–1938*, Vienna: Jugend und Volk.

Charnon-Deutsch, L. (2000), *Fictions of the Feminine in the Nineteenth-century Spanish Press*, University Park: Pennsylvania State University Press.

Chassagne, S. (1981), *Une femme d'affaires au XVIIIe siècle*, Toulouse: Privat.

Chassagne, S. (1991), *Le coton et ses patrons en France, 1760–1840*, Paris: EHESS.

Clark, A. (1919), *Working Life of Women in the Seventeenth Century*, London: Routledge and Kegan Paul, reprinted 1982.

Clark, A. (1995), *The Struggle for the Breeches: Gender and the Making of the British Working Class*, Berkeley: University of California Press.

Clark, G. (1999), *Betting on Lives: The Culture of Life Assurance in England, 1695–1775*, Manchester: Manchester University Press.

Clark, J. G. (1981), *La Rochelle and the Atlantic Economy During the Eighteenth Century*, Baltimore: Johns Hopkins Press.

Codaccioni, F. P. (1976), *De l'inégalité sociale dans une grande ville industrielle, le drame de Lille de 1850 à 1914*, Lille: Presses de l'université de Lille.

Coffin, J. (1996), *The Politics of Women's Work: The Paris Garment Trades 1750–1915*, Princeton, NJ: Princeton University Press.

Colldeforns, F. (1951), *Historial de los Gremios del Mar de Barcelona (1750–1865)*, Barcelona: Gráficas Marina.

Colli, A. (2003), *The History of Family Business 1850–2000*, Cambridge: Cambridge University Press.

Collins, J. B. (1989), 'The Economic Role of Women in Seventeenth-Century France', *French Historical Studies*, 16: 436–70.

Comas d'Argemir, D. (1995), *Trabajo, género, cultura. La construcción de las desigualdades entre hombres y mujeres*, Barcelona: Icaria.

Corbin, A. (1987), *Les Filles de Noce. Misère Sexuelle et Prostitution aux 19ème et 20ème siècle*, Paris: Aubier Montaigne.

Corbin, A. (1990), *Women for Hire: Prostitution and Sexuality in France after 1850*, trans. Alan Sheridan, Cambridge, MA: Harvard University Press.

Coultrap-McQuin, S. M. (1990), *Doing Literary Business: American Women Writers in the Nineteenth Century*, Chapel Hill: University of North Carolina Press.

Cox, N. (2000), *The Complete Tradesman: A Study of Retailing, 1550–1820*, Aldershot: Ashgate.

Coyner, S. (1977), 'Class Consciousness and Consumption: The New Middle Class during the Weimar Republic', *Journal of Social History*, 10: 310–31.

Crafts, N. F. R. (1985), *British Economic Growth during the Industrial Revolution*, Oxford: Clarendon Press.

Craig, B. (1998), 'Salaires, niveaux de vie et travail féminin dans l'arrondissement de Lille au XIXe siècle', *Annales canadiennes d'histoire*, XXXIII: 215–48.

Craig, B. (2001a), 'Introduction: les affaires sont-elles affaires de femmes?', *Histoire Sociale/Social History*, 34: 277–81.

Craig, B. (2001b), 'Patrons mauvais genre: femmes et entreprises à Tourcoing au XIXe siècle', *Histoire Sociale/Social History*, 34: 331–54.

Craig, B. (2001c), 'Petites Bourgeoises and Penny Capitalists: Women in Retail in the Lille Area during the Nineteenth Century', *Enterprise & Society*, 2: 198-224.

Creighton, C. (1996), 'The Rise of the Male Breadwinner Family: A Reappraisal', *Comparative Studies in Society and History*, 38: 310–37.

Crossick, G. and Haupt, H.-G. (1984), *Shopkeepers and Master Artisans in Nineteenth-century Europe*, London: Routledge.

Crossick, G. and Haupt, H.-G. (1995), *The Petite Bourgeoisie in Europe 1780–1914, Enterprise, Family and Independence*, London: Routledge.

Crossick, G. and Jurmain, S. (1999, eds), *Cathedrals of Consumption: The European Department Store, 1850–1939*, Aldershot: Ashgate.

Cruz Valenciano, J. (2000), *Los notables de Madrid. Las bases sociales de la revolución liberal española*, Madrid: Alianza Editorial.

Curli, B. (2002), 'Women Entrepreneurs and Italian Industrialization: Conjectures and Avenues of Research', *Enterprise and Society*, 3: 634–56.

Cyganowski, C. K. (1988), *Magazine Editors and Professional Authors in Nineteenth-century America: The Genteel Tradition and the American Dream*, New York and London: Garland.

Daniel, U. (1989), 'Die Vaterländischen Frauenvereine in Westfalen', *Westfälische Forschungen* 39, 158–79.

Daumard, A. (1963), *La bourgeoisie parisienne de 1815 à 1848*, Paris: Sevpen.

Daumas, J.-C. (2004), *Les Territoires de la laine. Histoire de l'industrie lainière en France au XIXe siècle*, Lille: Septentrion.

Daunton, M. (1995), *Progress and Poverty: An Economic and Social History of Britain, 1700–1850*, Oxford: Oxford University Press.

Daunton, M. (2001), *Trusting Leviathan: The Politics of Taxation in Britain, 1799–1914*, Cambridge: Cambridge University Press.

Davidoff, L. (1979), 'The Separation of Home and Work? Landladies and Lodgers in Nineteenth- and Twentieth-Century England', in S. Burman (ed.), *Fit Work for Women*, London: Croom Helm, 64–97.

Davidoff, L. and Hall, C. (1987), *Family Fortunes: Men and Women of the English Middle Class, 1780–1850*, London: Hutchinson and Chicago: University of Chicago Press.

Davidoff, L. and Hall, C. (1994), *Fortunas familiars. Hombres y mujeres de la clase media inglesa, 1750–1850*, Madrid: Cátedra.

Davidoff, L. and Hall, C. (2002), *Family Fortunes: Men and Women of the English Middle Class, 1780–1850*, Revised Edition, London: Routledge.

Davis, N. (1986), 'Women in the Crafts in Sixteenth-century Lyon', in B. Hanawalt (ed.), *Women and Work in Preindustrial Europe*, Bloomington: Indiana University Press, 167–197.

de Groot, G. (2001), *Fabricage van verschillen. Mannenwerk, vrouwenwerk in de Nederlandse industrie (1850–1940)*, Amsterdam: Aksent.

de Groot, G. and Schrover, M. (1995),'General Introduction', in G. de Groot and M. Schrover (eds), *Women Workers and Technological Change in Europe in the Nineteenth and Twentieth Centuries*, London: Routledge.

de Jong, A. (1983), *Honderd jaar 'besteden' in Utrecht. Een onderzoek naar hen, die in de periode 1830–1930 bemiddelen op de dienstboden-arbeidsmarkt*, Paper Economic and Social History, Utrecht: Utrecht University.

de Pinto, A. (1839), 'Over het dienstboden-regt', *Themis, Regstkundig tijdschrift*, 271–91.

de Vos van Steenwijk, G. W. (1870), *Bijdrage tot het dienstbodenregt*, Leiden.
de Vries, P. (1997), *Kuisheid voor Mannen, vrijheid voor Vrowen. De Reglementering en Bestrijding von Prostitutie in Nederland, 1850–1911*, Hilversum: Verloren.
Denkschrift aus Anlass des hundertjährigen Bestehens der Maschinen- und Lokomotivfabrik Henschel & Sohn Cassel und der Vollendung der Lokomotive Fabriknummer 10,000 (1910), Kassel: Henschel and Sohn.
Dexter, E. A. (1924), *Colonial Women of Affairs: A Study of Women in Business and the Professions in America before 1776*, New York: Houghton Mifflin.
Dickson, P. G. M. (1967), *The Financial Revolution in England: A Study in the Development of Public Credit, 1688–1756*, London: Macmillan.
Die Entwicklung der Lokomotive im Gebiet des Vereins Mitteleuropäischer Eisenbahnverwaltungen (2 vols) (1937), vol. 2, *1880–1920*, Munich: Verein Mitteleuropäischer Eisenbahnverwaltungen.
Diederiks, H. (1982), *Een stad in verval. Amsterdam omstreeks 1800. Demografisch, economisch, ruimtelijk.* Amerstdam: Amsterdamse Historische Reeks 4.
Díez, F. (1990), *Viles y mecánicos. Trabajo y sociedad en la Valencia preindustrial*, Valencia: Ed. Alfons el Magnànim.
Duden, B. (1977), 'Das schöne Eigentum: Zur Herausbildung des bürgerlichen Frauenbildes an der Wende vom 18. zum 19. Jahrhundert', *Kursbuch*, 47: 125–40.
Ecker-Ertle, H. (1998) 'Sophie Henschel – Unternehmerin der Kaiserzeit', Unpublished PhD dissertation, University of Bonn.
Edgren, L. (1983), 'Hantverksänkor på äktenskapsmarknaden. "Änkekonservering" inom malmöhantverket 1816–1840', *Ale*, 4: 1–17.
Ehmer, J. (1980), *Familienstruktur und Arbeitsorganisation im frühindustriellen Wien*, Vienna: Verlag für Geschichte und Politik.
Ehmer, J. (1981), 'Frauenarbeit und Arbeiterfamilie in Wien: Vom Vormärz bis 1934', *Geschichte und Gesellschaft*, 7: 438–73.
Ehmer, J. (1996), 'Zur sozialen Schichtung der Wiener Bevölkerung 1857 bis 1910', in G. Melinz and S. Zimmermann (eds), *Blütezeit der Habsburgmetropolen: Urbanisierung, Kommunalpolitik, gesellschaftliche Konflikte (1867–1918)*, Vienna: Promedia Verlag, 73–83.
Ehmer, J. (2001), 'Family and Business among Master Artisans and Entrepreneurs: The Case of Nineteenth-century Vienna', *The History of the Family*, 6: 187–202.
Endel, E. (1915), 'Über die Rechtsstellung der Handels- und Gewerbefrau im 19. Jahrhundert', PhD Unpublished dissertation, University of Jena.
Engels, F. (1884), *The Origin of the Family, Private Property and the State*, London: Penguin (1986 edition).
Engelstein, L. (1992), *The Keys to Happiness: Sex and the Search for Modernity*

in Fin de Siècle Russia, Ithaca, NY: Cornell University Press.

Ent, H. (1979), 'Die Entgeltlichkeit der Mitwirkung eines Ehegatten im Erwerb des anderen', in E. Weinzierl and K. R. Stadler (eds), *Geschichte der Familienrechtsgesetzgebung in Österreich*, Vienna: Geyer Edition, 93–103.

Erickson, A. L. (1993), *Women and Property in Early Modern England*, London: Routledge.

Ericsson, E. (1983), *Den andra fackföreningsrörelsen. Tjänstemän och tjänstemannaorganisationer i Sverige före första världskriget*, Umeå: Institutionen för historiska studier.

Ericsson, T. (1988), *Mellan arbete och kapital. Småborgerligheten i Sverige 1850–1914*, Umeå: Umeå Studies in the Humanities 86.

Ericsson, T. (1997), 'Välstånd och välmåga. Sundsvalls borgerskap 1850-1900', in T. Lars-Göran (ed.), *Sundsvalls historia*, Vol. II, Sundsvalls Kommun: Stadshistoriska Kommittén, 137–54.

Ericsson, T. (2001), 'Women, Family and Small Business in Late Nineteenth-Century Sweden', *The History of the Family*, 6: 225–39.

Espigado Tocino, G. (1998), 'Precursoras de la prensa femenina en España: Mª Josefa Zapata y Magarita Pérez de Celis', in T. Vera Balanza (ed.), *Mujer, cultura y comunicación. Entre la historia y la sociedad contemporánea*, Málaga: Ediciones Málaga Digital, 171–5.

Evans, R. J. (1976a), 'Prostitution, State and Society in Imperial Germany', *Past and Present*, 70: 106-29.

Evans, R. J. (1976b), *The Feminist Movement in Germany, 1894-1933*, London: Sage Publications.

Evans, R. J. (1977), *The Feminist: Women's Emancipation Movements in Europe, America, and Australasia, 1840-1920*, London: Croom Helm.

Evans, R. J. (1991), 'Family and Class in the Hamburg Grand Bourgeoisie 1815-1914', in D. Blackbourn (ed.), *The German Bourgeoisie*, London: Routledge, 115-39.

Evans, R. J. (1998), *Tales from the German Underworld: Crime and Punishment in the Nineteenth Century*, New Haven: Yale University Press.

Fagerlund, S. (2002), *Handel och vandel*, Studia Historica Lundensia 8, Lund: Lund University.

Fairman, W. (1824), *An Account of the Public Funds Transferable at the Bank of England*, 7th edition, London: John Richardson.

Filton, R. S. and Wadsworth, A. P. (1973), *The Strutts and the Arkwrights, 1758–1830: A Study of the Early Factory System*, New York: A. M. Kelley.

Finn, M. (1996), 'Women, Consumption and Coverture in England, c. 1760–1860', *The Historical Journal*, 39: 703–22.

Finnegan, F. (1979), *Poverty and Prostitution: A Study of Victorian Prostitutes in York*, Cambridge: Cambridge University Press.

Fischer, W. (1978), 'Die Pionierrolle der betrieblichen Sozialpolitik im 19. und beginnenden 20. Jahrhundert', in H. Pohl (ed.), *Betriebliche Sozialpolitik deutscher Unternehmen seit dem 19. Jahrhundert*, Wiesbaden: Steiner.

Fishmann, J. (1992), 'Als Mann und Frau erschuf sie sie: Feminismus und Tradition', in A. Nachama, J. H. Schoeps and E. Van Voolen (eds), *Jüdische Lebenswelten: Essays*, Berlin: Suhrkamp, 86–107.

Flecha, C. (1996), *Las primeras universitaias en España*, Madrid: Narcea.

Flexner, A. (1914), *Prostitution in Europe*, New York: The Century.

Floßmann, U. (1992), *Österreichische Privatrechtsgeschichte*, 2nd Edition, Vienna: Springer Verlag.

Folbre, N. (1996), *The Economics of the Family*, Cheltenham: Edward Elgar.

Fout, J. (1984), *German Women in the Nineteenth Century: A Social History*, New York: Holmes & Meier.

Frader, L. L. and Rose, S. O. (1996), *Gender and Class in Modern Europe*, Ithaca, NY: Cornell University Press.

Fraisse, G. (1995), *Les Muses de la raison. Démocratie et exclusion des femmes en France*, Paris: Gallionard.

Frevert, U. (1989), 'Bürgerliche Meisterdenker und das Geschlechterverhältnis: Konzepte, Erfahrungen, Visionen an der Wende vom 18. zum 19. Jahrhundert', in U. Frevert (ed.), *Bürgerinnen und Bürger: Geschlechterverhältnisse im 19. Jahrhundert*, Göttingen: Vandenhoeck & Ruprecht, 17–48.

Frevert, U. (1990), *Women in German History: From Bourgeois Emancipation to Sexual Liberation*, Oxford: Berg.

Frevert, U. (1991), 'Classe et genre dans la bourgeoisie allemande au XIXe siècle', *Genèse*, 6: 5–28.

Frevert, U. (1995), 'Kulturfrauen und Geschäftsmänner: Soziale Identitäten im deutschen Bürgertum des 19. Jahrhunderts', in U. Frevert (ed.), *'Mann und Weib, und Weib und Mann': Geschlechter-Differenzen in der Moderne*, Munich: C. H. Beck Verlag, 133–65.

Frey, M. (1999), *Macht und Moral des Schenkens: Staat und bürgerliche Mäzene vom späten 18. Jahrhundert bis zur Gegenwart*, Zwickau: Fannei and Walz.

Friedrich, M. (1992), 'Versorgungsfall Frau? Der Wiener Frauen-Erwerb-Verein— Gründungsjahre und erste Jahre des Aufbaus', *Jahrbuch des Vereins für Geschichte der Stadt Wien* (1991/1992): 263–308.

Friedrich, M. and Urbanitsch, P. (1996, eds), *Von Bürgern und ihren Frauen: Bürgertum in der Habsburgermonarchie V*, Vienna: Böhlau Verlag.

Frölander, T. (1906), *Stockholm's Enskilda Bank 1856–1906*, Stockholm: Publisher Unknown.

Fuentes, J. F. and Fernández Sebastian, J. (1997), *Historia del periodismo español*, Madrid: Síntesis.

Galand, M. (2000), 'Dans les coulisses du pouvoir. La veuve Nettine (1706–

1775), banquière de l'Etat dans les Pays-Bas autrichiens', *Sextant*, 13–14: 69–80.
Gall, L. (1989), *Bürgertum in Deutschland*, Berlin: Siedler.
Gamber, W. (1992), '"A Precarious Independence": Milliners and Dressmakers in Boston, 1860–1890', *Journal of Women's History*, 4: 60–88.
Gamber, W. (1997), *The Female Economy: The Millinery and Dress Making Trades, 1860–1930*, Chicago: University of Chicago Press.
Gamber, W. (1998), 'A Gendered Enterprise: Placing Nineteenth-Century Businesswomen in History', *Business History Review*, 72: 219–24.
García-Maroto, A. (1996), *La mujer en la prensa anarquista. España, 1900–1936*, Madrid: Fundación de Estudios Libertarios Anselmo Lorenzo.
Garden, M. (1986), 'The Urban Trades: Social Analysis and Representations', in S. Kaplan and C. Koepp (eds), *Representations, Meanings, Organization and Practice*, Ithaca, NY: Cornell University Press.
Garrido, Elisa (1997, ed.), *Historia de las Mujeres en España*, Madrid: Síntesis.
Gasslander, O. (1962), *History of Stockholm's Enskilda Bank to 1914*, Stockholm: Publisher unknown.
Gerhard, U. (1978), *Verhältnis und Verhinderung: Frauenarbeit, Familie und Recht der Frauen im 19. Jahrhundert*, Frankfurt: Suhrkamp.
Gewin, B. (1898), *Arbeidsbeurzen*, Utrecht: Publisher Unknown.
Gibson, M. (1986), *Prostitution and the State in Italy 1860–1915*, New Brunswick: Rutgers University Press.
Gilfoyle, T. J. (1999), 'Prostitutes in History: From Parables of Pornography to Metaphors of Modernity', *American Historical Review*, 104: 117–41.
Gleadle, K. and Richardson, S. (2000, eds), *Women and British Politics, 1760–1860: The Power of the Petticoat*, Basingstoke: Macmillan.
Glenn, K. M. and Mazquiaran, M. (1998, eds), *Spanish Women Writers and the Essay: Gender, Politics and the Self*, Columbia and London: University Press.
Goldsmith, R. (1969), *Financial Structure and Development*, New Haven: Yale University Press.
Good, D. F. (1966), *The Economic Rise of the Habsburg Empire 1750–1914*, Berkeley: University of California Press.
Göransson, A. (1990), 'Kön, släkt och ägande', *Historisk Tidskrift*, 4: 525–44.
Göransson, A. (1993), 'Gender and Property Rights: Capital, Kin and Owner Influence in Nineteenth and Twentieth-Century Sweden', *Business History*, 35: 11–32.
Gordon, E. and Nair, E. (2000), 'The Economic Role of Middle-Class Women in Victorian Glasgow', *Women's History Review*, 9: 791–813.
Gordon, E. and Nair, E. (2002), 'The Myth of the Victorian Patriarchal Family', *The History of the Family*, 7: 125–38.

Gordon, E. and Nair, E. (2003), *Public Lives: Women, Family and Society in Victorian Britain*, New Haven: Yale University Press.

Gray, M. W. (2000), *Productive Men and Reproductive Women: The Agrarian Household and the Emergence of Separate Spheres during the German Enlightenment*, New York and London: Berghahn Books.

Green, D. R. (2000), 'Independent Women, Wealth and Wills in Nineteenth-century London', in J. Stobart and A. Owens (eds), *Urban Fortunes: Property and Inheritance in the Town, 1700–1900*, Aldershot: Ashgate, 195–222.

Green, D. R. and Owens, A. (2003), 'Gentlewomanly Capitalism? Spinsters, Widows and Wealth-holding in England and Wales, c. 1800–1860', *Economic History Review*, LVI: 510–36.

Guy, K. M. (1997), 'Drowning her Sorrows: Widowhood and Entrepreneurship in the Champagne Industry', *Business and Economic History*, 26: 505–14.

Habermas, J. (1989), *The Structural Transformation of the Public Sphere: An Inquiry into a Category of Bourgeois Society*, Cambridge, MA: The MIT Press.

Habermas, R. (2000), *Frauen und Männer des Bürgertums*, Göttingen: Vandenhoeck & Ruprecht.

Hafter, D. (1995, ed.), *European Women and Preindustrial Craft*, Bloomington: Indiana University Press.

Hafter, D. (1997), 'Female Masters in the Ribbonmaking Guild of Eighteenth Century Rouen', *French Historical Studies*, 20: 1–14.

Hagemann, K. (2002), *Mannlicher Muth und Teutscher Ehre: Nation, Militär und Geschlecht zur Zeit der Antinapoleonischen Kriege Preussens*, Paderborn: Schöningh.

Hahn, S. (2002), 'Women in Older Ages—"Old Women"?', *The History of the Family*, 7: 33–58.

Hall, C. (1992), *White, Male and Middle Class: Explorations in Feminism and History*, London: Routledge.

Hanawalt, B. (1986, ed.), *Women and Work in Preindustrial Europe*, Bloomington: Indiana University Press.

Hannes, J. (1965), 'L'histoire sociale. Problèmes de méthode et applications aux sources bruxelloises du XIXe siècle', *Cahiers bruxellois*, X: 240–67.

Hannes, J. (1973), 'De kleine producent en de kleinhandellar in de 19de eeuw', *Archives et Bibliothèques*, 10: 55–64.

Hannes, J. (1975), *De economische bedrijvigheid te Brussel 1846–47. Contrôle en aanvulling op de nijverheidstelling vn 15/10/1847*, Paris-Brussels: Nauwerlaerts

Harden Chenut, H. (1996), 'The Gendering of Skill as Historical Process: The Case of French Knitters in Industrial Troyes, 1880–1939', in L. Frader and S. Rose (eds), *Gender and Class in Modern Europe*, Ithaca, NY: Cornell University Press, 77–109.

Harnon-Deutsch, L. (2000), *Fiction of the Feminine in the Nineteenth-century*

Spanish Press, University Park: Pennsylvania State University Press.

Harsin, J. (1985), *Policing Prostitution in Nineteenth-century Paris*, Princeton, NJ: Princeton University Press.

Hartmann, H. (1981), 'The Family as the Locus of Gender, Class and Political Struggle: The Example of Housework', *Signs: Journal of Women in Culture and Society*, 6: 179–207.

Harty, S. (2002), 'Lawyers, Codification and the Origins of Catalan Nationalism, 1881–1901', *Law and History Review*, 20: 349–84.

Hasselberg, Y. and Matti, T. (2002), 'A Family of Owners? Ownership Networks in Stora Kopparberg, 1875–1917', Paper presented at the fifth annual meeting of the European Business History Association, Helsinki, August 2002.

Hatton, T. J. and Bailey, R. E. (2001), 'Women's Work in Census and Survey, 1911–1931', *Economic History Review*, Second Series, LIV: 87–107.

Haupt, H.-G. (1979), 'La petite bourgeoisie, une classe inconnue', *Le Mouvement social*, 108: 11–20.

Haupt, H.-G. (1982), 'Kleinhändler und Arbeiter in Bremen zwischen 1890 und 1914', *Archiv für Sozialgeschichte*, 22: 95–132.

Hausen, K. (1981), 'Family and Role Division: The Polarisation of Sex Roles in the Nineteenth Century', in R. J. Evans and W. R. Lees (eds), *The German Family*, London: Croom Helm, 51–83.

Hecht, J. J. (1980), *The Domestic Servant Class in eighteenth-century England*, Westport, CT: Hyperion.

Heindl, W. (1981), 'Frau und bürgerliches Recht: Bemerkungen zu den Reformvorschlägen österreichischer Frauenvereine vor dem Ersten Weltkrieg', in I. Ackerl, W. Hummelberger and H. Mommsen (eds), *Politik und Gesellschaft im alten und neuen Österreich: Festschrift für Rudolf Neck*, Vienna: Verlag für Geschichte und Politik, 133–49.

Heller, E. (1908), *Das österreichische Gewerberecht*, Vienna: Manz.

Heller, E. (1912), *Kommentar zur Gewerbeordnung und zu ihren Nebengesetzen*, Vienna: Manz.

Hellgren, H. (2002), 'Med säkerheten i centrum', Uppsala Papers in Financial History, no. 15, Uppsala: Department of Economic History, Uppsala University.

Hellgren, H. (2003), *Fasta förbindelser*, Uppsala Studies in Economic History 66, Uppsala: Department of Economic History, Uppsala University.

Herda, H. (1997), 'Recht und Rechtswirklichkeit für Unternehmerinnen und gewerbetreibende Frauen von 1859 bis heute', in I. Bandhauer-Schöffmann (ed.), *Auf dem Weg zur Beletage: Frauen in der Wirtschaft*, Vienna: Sonderzahl Verlag, 111–43.

Herda, H. (2000), 'Der Zugang von Frauen zum Gewerbe: Eine Analyse der rechtlichen Rahmenbedingungen von 1859 bis heute', in I. Bandhauer-Schöffmann and R. Bendl (eds), *Unternehmerinnen: Geschichte and*

Gegenwart selbständiger Erwerbstätigkeit von Frauen, Frankfurt am Main: Peter Lang, 135–159.

Hesse, C. (2001), *The Other Enlightenment: How French Women Became Modern*, Princeton, NJ: Princeton University Press.

Higgs, E. (1987), 'Women, Occupation and Work in the Nineteenth-Century Censuses', *History Workshop Journal*, 23: 59–80.

Hilger, S. (1996), 'Sozialpolitik und Organisation: Formen betrieblicher Sozialpolitik in der rheinisch-westf; alischen Eisen- und Stahlindustrie seit der Mitte des 19. Jahrhunderts bis 1933', *Zeitschrift für Unternehmensgeschichte*, 94: 445–47.

Hill, A. (1994), '"May the doctor advise extramarital intercourse?" Medical debates on sexual abstinence in Germany c. 1900', in R. Porter and M. Teich (eds), *Sexual Knowledge, Sexual Science: The History of Attitudes to Sexuality*, Cambridge: Cambridge University Press, 284–302.

Hill, B. (1993), 'Women, Work and the Census', *History Workshop Journal*, 35: 78–94.

Hill, B. (1996), *Servants: English Domestics in the Eighteenth Century*, Oxford: Oxford University Press.

Hill, B. (2001), *Women Alone: Spinsters in England, 1660–1850*, New Haven: Yale University Press.

Hilpert-Fröhlich, C. (1991), *Auf zum Kampfe wider die Unzucht: Prostitution und Sittlichkeitsbewegung in Essen 1890 bis 1914*, Bochum: SWI.

Hlawatschek, E. (1985), 'Die Unternehmerin (1800–1945)', in H. Pohl (ed.), *Die Frau in der deutschen Wirtschaft*, Stuttgart: F. Steiner Verlag, 127–46.

Hobsbawm, E. (1968), *Labouring Men: Studies in the History of Labour*, London: Weidenfeld and Nicolson.

Hofmann, F. (1874), 'Der Unterhaltsanspruch des überlebenden Gatten nach § 796 ABGB', *Zeitschrift für das Privat- und öffentliche Recht der* Gegenwart, 1: XVI, 547–69.

Holcombe, L. (1983), *Wives and Property: Reform of the Married Women's Property Law in Nineteenth-century England*, Toronto: University of Toronto Press

Holthöfer, E. (1997), 'Die Geschlechtsvormundschaft: Ein Überblick von der Antike bis ins 19. Jahrhundert', in U. Gerhard (ed.), *Frauen in der Geschichte des Rechts: Von der Frühen Neuzeit bis zur Gegenwart*, Munich: C. H. Beck, 670–82.

Honeyman, K. (2000), *Women, Gender and Industrialisation in England, 1700–1870*, Basingstoke: Macmillan.

Horn, P. (1975), *The Rise and Fall of the Victorian Servant*, New York: St. Martin's Press.

Horrel, S. and Humphries, J. (1993), 'Women's Labour Force Participation and the Transition to the Male Breadwinner Family, 1790–1865,' *Economic History*

Review, Second Series, VIII: 69–117.

Horrell, S. and Humphries, J. (1997), 'The Origins and Expansion of the Male Breadwinner Family: The Case of Nineteenth-century Britain', *International Review of Social History*, 42 (Supplement 5): 25–64.

Hörsell, A. (1982), 'The Economic Realities of Marriage: The "Free City" of Eskilstuna at the Beginning of the Nineteenth Century', in J. Rogers (ed.), *Marriage and Fertility: Local Patterns in Pre-industrial Sweden, Finland, and Norway*, Uppsala: Meddelande från Familjehistoriska Projektet, 3, Historiska institutionen, Uppsala University, 27–38.

Hörsell, A. (1983), *Borgare, smeder och änkor. Ekonomi och befolkning i Eskilstuna gamla stad och Fristad 1750-1850*, Uppsala: Studia Historica Upsaliensia 131, Uppsala University.

Howell, M. (1986), 'Women, the Family Economy, and the Structures of Market Production in Cities of Northern Europe during the Late Middle Ages', in B. Hanawalt (ed.), *Women and Work in Preindustrial Europe*, Bloomington: Indiana Univesity Press, 198–222.

Hudson, P. and Lee, W. (1990), *Women's Work and the Family Economy in Historical Perspective*, Manchester: Manchester University Press.

Hudson, S. (2001), 'Attitudes to Investment Risk amongst West Midland Canal and Railway Company Investors, 1760–1850', Unpublished PhD thesis, University of Warwick.

Hufton, O. (1992), *Women and the Limits of Citizenship in the French Revolution*, Toronto: University of Toronto Press.

Huget, R. (1990), *Els artesans de Lleida*, Lleida: Pagès Ed.

Humphries, J. (1990), 'Enclosures, Common Rights and Women: The Proletarianization of Families in the Late Eighteenth and Early Nineteenth Centuries', *Journal of Economic History*, 50: 17–42.

Humphries, J. (1991), 'The Sexual Division of Labor and Social Control: An Interpretation', *Review of Radical Political Economics*, 23: 269–96.

Humphries, J. (1995), *Gender and Economics*, Aldershot: Edward Elgar.

Hunt, Margaret (1996), *The Middling Sort: Commerce, Gender and the Family in England*, Berkerley: University of California Press.

Ighe, A. (2004), 'Minors, Guardians, and Inheritance in Early Nineteenth-Century Sweden: A Case of Gendered Property Rights', in D. R. Green and A. Owens (eds), *Family Welfare: Gender, Property and Inheritance since the Seventeenth Century*, Westport, CT, and London: Praeger, 217–42.

Imperial German Criminal Code (1917), translated by R. Captain, H. Gage and A. Waters, Johannesburg: W.E. Horton & Co.

Jacobs, E. (1958), 'Het arbeidscontract', in A. de Haas (ed.), *De minstreel van de mesthoop. Liedjes, leven en achtergronden van Eduard Jacobs: pionier van het Nederlandse cabaret, 1867–1914*, Amsterdam: De Bezige bÿ.

Jagoe, C. (1994), *Ambiguous Angels: Gender in the Novels of Galdós*, Berkeley: University of California Press.

Jagoe, C., Blanco, A. and Enríquez, C. (1998, eds), *La Mujer en los discursos de género*, Barcelona: Icaria.

Janssens, A. (1997), 'The Rise and Decline of the Male Breadwinner Family? An Overview of the Debate', *International Review of Social History*, 42 (Supplement 5): 1–23.

Jaumain, S. (1993), 'La boutique à la fin du XIXe siècle. Un univers féminin?', *Cahiers Marxistes*, 191: 113–26.

Jaumain, S. (1995), *Les petits commerçants belges face à la modernité (1880–1914)*, Brussels: ULB.

Jenders, A. and Müller, A. (1993), *'Nur die Dummen sind eingeschrieben': Dortmunder Dirnen- und Sittengeschichte zwischen 1870 und 1927*, Dortmund: Geschichtswerkstatt Dortmund.

Jiménez Morell, I. (1992), *La prensa femenina en España (desde sus orígenes a 1868)*, Madrid, Ediciones de la Torre.

John, M. (1989), *Politics and the Law in Late Nineteenth-century Germany: The Origins of the Civil Code*, Oxford: Oxford University Press.

John, M. and Lichtblau, A. (1993), *Schmelztiegel Wien – einst und jetzt: Zur Geschichte und Gegenwart von Zuwanderung und Minderheiten*, 2nd edition, Vienna: Böhlau Verlag.

Joyce, P. (2003), *The Rule of Freedom: Liberalism and the Modern City*, London: Verso.

Jusek, K. (1995), *Auf der Suche nach der Verlorenen: Die Prostitutionsdebatten im Wien der Jahrhundertwende*, Vienna: Löcker.

K. K. Statistische Zentralkommission (1908), 'Ergebnisse der gewerblichen Betriebszählung vom 3. Juni 1902 in den im Reichsrate vertretenen Königreichen und Ländern', *Österreichische Statistik*, 75: 3.

Kaplan, M. (1991), *The Making of the Jewish Middle Class: Women, Family, and Identity in Imperial Germany*, Oxford: Oxford University Press.

Kay, A. C. (2001), 'Small Business and the Sphere Switcher, Work Life Choices and the Redundant Woman in Nineteenth-century London', Paper presented to the XIII Economic History Congress.

Kay, A. C. (2003a), 'A Little Enterprise of Her Own: Lodging-house Keeping and the Accommodation Business in Nineteenth-century London', *The London Journal*, 28: 41–53.

Kay, A. C. (2003b), 'A Respectable Business: Women and Self Employment in Nineteenth-century London', Paper presented to the British Economic History Society Conference.

Kay, A. C. (2004), 'Small Business, Self Employment and Women's Work–Life Choices in Nineteenth-century London', in D. Mitch, J. Brown and M. H. D. van

Leeuwen (eds), *Origins of the Modern Career*, Aldershot: Ashgate, 191–206.

Kent, D. A. (1989), 'Ubiquitous but Invisible: Female Domestic Servants in Mid-eighteenth-century London', *History Workshop Journal*, 28: 111–28.

Kerber, L. (1988), 'Separate Sphere, Female Worlds, Women's Place. The Rhetoric of Women's History', *Journal of American History*, LXXV: 9–39.

Khan, B. Z. (1996), 'Married Women's Property Laws and Female Commercial Activity: Evidence from United States Patent Records, 1790–1895', *Journal of Economic History*, 56: 356–88.

Kirchner, L. (1921), 'Die industrielle Entwicklung der Stadt Kassel von 1866 bis 1914', Unpublished PhD dissertation, University of Cologne.

Kirkpatrick, S. (1989), *Las románticas: Women Writers and Subjectivity in Spain, 1835–1850*, Berkeley and Los Angeles: University of California Press. (Traducción en español, *Las Románticas. Escritoras y subjetividad en España, 1835–1850*, Madrid, Cátedra, 1991).

Kirkpatrick, S. (1990), 'La "hermandad lírica" de la década de 1840', in M. Mayoral (ed.), *Escritoras Románticas Españolas*, Madrid: Fundación Banco Exterior, 25–42.

Koch, E. (1997), 'Die Frau im Recht der frühen Neuzeit: Juristische Lehren und Begründungen', in U. Gerhard (ed.), *Frauen in der Geschichte des Rechts*, Munich: C. H. Beck Verlag, 73–93.

Kocka, J. (1996, ed.), *Les bourgeoisies européenes au XIXe siècle*, Paris: Belin.

Kocka, J. (1999a), 'Family and Bureaucracy in German Industrial Management, 1850–1914: Siemens in Comparative Perspective', in J. Kocka, *Industrial Culture and Bourgeois Society: Business, Labor, and Bureaucracy in Modern Germany*, New York: Berghahn, 27–50.

Kocka, J. (1999b), 'The Entrepreneur, the Family, and Capitalism: Examples from the Early Phase of German Industrialization', in J. Kocka, *Industrial Culture and Bourgeois Society: Business, Labor, and Bureaucracy in Modern Germany*, New York: Berghahn, 103–38.

Kocka, J. (1999c), 'Big Business and the Rise of Managerial Capitalism: Germany in International Comparison', in J. Kocka, *Industrial Culture and Bourgeois Society: Business, Labor, and Bureaucracy in Modern Germany*, New York: Berghahn, 156–173.

Komlos, J. (1983a, ed.), *Economic Development in the Habsburg Monarchy in the Nineteenth Century: Essays*, Boulder/New York: East European Monographs.

Komlos, J. (1983b), *The Habsburg Monarchy as a Customs Union: Development in Austria-Hungary in the Nineteenth Century*, Princeton, NJ: Princeton University Press.

Kowaleski-Wallace, E. (1996), *Consuming Subjects: British Women and Consumer Culture in the Eighteenth Century*, New York: Columbia University Press

Krafft, S. (1996), *Zucht und Unzucht: Prostitution und Sittenpolizei im München der Jahrhundertwende*, Munich: Hugendubel.

Kretschmer, S. (2000), *Wiener Handwerksfrauen: Wirtschafts- und Lebensformen von Frauen im 18. Jahrhundert*, Vienna: Milena Verlag.

Kurgan G., Jaumain, S. and Montens, V. (1996, eds), *Dictionnaire des patrons en Belgique*, Bruxelles: De Boek Université.

Kurgan-Van Hentenryk, G. (1979), 'Les patentables à Brussels au XIXe siècle', *Le Mouvement social*, 108: 63–88.

Kurgan-Van Hentenryk, G. and Jaumain, S. (1992, eds), *Aux frontières des classes moyennes. La petite bourgeoisie belge avant 1914*, Brussels:ULB.

Kwolek-Folland, A. (1998), *Incorporating Women: A History of Women and Business in the United States*, New York: Twayne Publishers.

Labouvie, E. (1993), 'In weiblicher Hand: Frauen als Firmengründerinnen und Unternehmerinnen (1600-1870)', in E. Labouvie (ed.), *Frauenleben – Frauen leben: Zur Geschichte und Gegenwart weiblicher Lebenswelten im Saarraum (17.–20. Jahrhundert)*, St. Ingbert: Röhrig, 88–131.

Lady (1854), *The Ladies' Guide to Life Assurance*, London: Partridge, Oakey and Co.

Lambert-Dansette, J. (1954), *Quelques familles du patronat textile de Lille-Armentières, 1789–1914. Origines et évolution d'une bourgeoisie*, Lille: Raoust.

Lamoreaux, N. R. (1994), *Insider Lending: Banks, Personal Connections and Economic Development in Industrial New England*, Cambridge: Cambridge University Press.

Lamoreaux, N. R. (2003), 'Rethinking the Transition to Capitalism in the Early American Northeast', *Journal of American History*, 90: 437–61.

Lamott, F. (1992), 'Virginität als Fetisch. Kulturelle Codierung und rechtliche Normierung der Jungfräulichkeit um die Jahrhundertwende', *Tel Aviver Jahrbuch für deutsche Geschichte*, 21, 153-70.

Landes, J. (1988), *Women in the Public Sphere in the Age of the French Revolution*, Ithaca, NY: Cornell University Press.

Lane, P. (2000), 'Women, Property and Inheritance: Wealth Creation and Income Generation in Small English Towns, 1780–1835', in J. Stobart and A. Owens (eds), *Urban Fortunes: Property and Inheritance in the Town, 1700–1900*, Aldershot: Ashgate, 172–94.

Laqueur, T. (1990), *Making Sex: Body and Gender from the Greeks to Freud*, Cambridge, MA: Harvard University Press.

Leclercq, E. (1864), *Histoire de deux armurières*, Paris.

Legrand, P. (1852), *La femme du bourgeois de Lille*, Lille.

Lehner, O. (1987), *Familie – Recht – Politik. Die Entwicklung des österreichischen Familienrechtes im 19. und 20. Jahrhundert*, Linz: Trauner Verlag.

Lemmens, P. (1987), 'De Brusselse middenstandvrouwen in de tweede helft van de 19d eeuw', *Tijdschrift voor Brusselse Geschiedenis*, 4: 111–32.
Lennander-Fällström, A. (1987), 'Kvinnor i lokalhistoriskt perspektiv. Levnadsvillkor i Örebro vid 1600-talets mitt', in B. Sawyer and A. Göransson (eds), *Manliga strukturer och kvinnliga strategier. En bok till Gunhild Kyle*, Gothenburg: Meddelanden från Historiska institutionen i Göteborg, 108–19.
Levi, L. (1862), 'On the Progress and Economical Bearings of National Debts in This and Other Countries', *Journal of the Statistical Society of London*, 25: 313–38.
Lewis, S. (1992), 'Female Entrepreneurs in Albany, 1840–1885', *Business and Economic History*, 21, 65–73.
Lewis, S. (1995), 'Beyond Horatio Algier: Breaking through Gendered Assumptions about Business "Success" in Mid Nineteenth-century America', *Business and Economic History*, 24: 97–105.
Lilja, K. (2000), 'Utav omsorg och eftertanke', *Uppsala Papers in Financial History*, no. 11, Uppsala: Uppsala University.
Lilja, K. (forthcoming), 'Household Savings and Investments in Falun, 1830–1914', Uppsala: Department of Economic History, Uppsala University.
Lincini, S. (2004), 'Women's Wealth in the XIXth Century: Some Evidence from the Probate Records of Milan, Italy (1862–1900)', unpublished paper.
Lindgren, H. (1997), 'The Influence of Banking on the Development of Capitalism in the Scandinavian Countries', in A. Teichova, G. Kurgan-van Hentenryk and D. Ziegler (eds), *Banking, Trade and Industry in Europe*, Cambridge: Cambridge University Press, 191–213.
Lindgren, H. (2002), 'The Modernization of Swedish Credit Markets, 1840–1905: Evidence from Probate Records', *Journal of Economic History*, 62: 810–32.
Lindgren, H. and Sjögren, H. (2002), 'Banking Systems as "Ideal Types" and Political Economy" The Swedish Case, 1820–1914', in D. Forsyth and D. Verdier (eds), *Gerschenkron Revisited. The Political Origins of Banking Structures*, Oxford: Oxford University Press.
Lindqvist, C. (1987), 'Kvinnor i tvåförsörjarfamiljen. Gifta krögerskor och månglerskor i Stockholm under första delen av 1800-talet', in B. Sawyer and A. Göransson (eds), *Manliga strukturer och kvinnliga strategier. En bok till Gunhild Kyle*, Gothenburg: Meddelanden från Historiska institutionen i Göteborg, no. 33, 136–41.
Lindsey, C. and Duffin, L. (1985, eds), *Women and Work in Preindustrial England*, London: Croom Helm.
Lintelman, J. (1995), 'Making Servants Serve Themselves: Immigrant Women and Domestic Service in North America, 1850–1920', in D. Hoerder and J. Nagler (eds), *People in Transit: German Migrations in Comparative Perspective, 1820–1930*, Cambridge: Cambridge University Press, 249–65.

Lipp, C. (1986), 'Frauen und Öffentlichkeit: Möglichkeiten und Grenzen politischer Partizipation im Vormärz und in der Revolution 1848/49', in C. Lipp (ed.), *Schimpfende Weiber und patriotische Jungfrauen: Frauen im Vormärz und in der Revolution 1848/49*, Moos: Elster, 270–307.

Liu, T. (1996), 'What Price a Weaver's Dignity? Gender Inequality and the Survival of Home-based Production in Industrial France', in L. Frader and S. Rose (eds), *Gender and Class in Modern Europe*, Ithaca, NY: Cornell University Press, 57–76.

Lluch, E. and Sevilla, E. (1978), 'La reducción del tamaño de las empresas. Un enfoque teórico a una paradoja histórica', *Hacienda Pública*, 55: 178–201.

Loeb, L. A. (1994), *Consuming Angels: Advertising and Victorian Women*, Oxford: Oxford University Press.

López, V. and Nieto, J. (1996, eds), *El trabajo en la encrucijada. Artesanos urbanos en la Europa de la Edad Moderna*, Madrid: Libros de la Catarata.

Lottin, A. (1988, ed.), *Histoire de Tourcoing*, Dunkirk: Edition des beffrois.

Lowe, J. (1823), *The Present State of England in Regard to Agriculture, Trade and Finance*, London: Longman, Hurst, Rees, Orme and Brown.

Lown, J. (1990), *Women and Industrialization: Gender and Work in Nineteenth-century England*, Cambridge: Polity.

Lunander, E. (1988), *Borgaren blir företagare. Studier kring ekonomiska, sociala och politiska förhållanden i förändringens Örebro under 1800-talet*, Studia Historica Upsaliensia 155, Uppsala.

Magnusson, L. (2000), *An Economic History of Sweden*, Routledge: London.

Mahood, L. (1990), *The Magdalenes, Prostitution in the 19th Century*, London: Routledge.

Maltby, J. and Rutterford, J. (2005), '"The Widow, the Clergyman and the Reckless": Women Investors before 1914', *Feminist Economics*, forthcoming.

Marín Corbera, M. (2001), *Joan Sallarès i Pla. Industrial i polític*, Sabadell: Bosch Cardellach.

Martin, J.-C. (1980), 'Le commerçant, la faillite et l'historien', *Annales*, 35: 1251–68.

Martínez, C. (2000, ed.), *Mujeres en la Historia de España. Enciclopedia Biográfica*, Barcelona: Planeta.

Martínez, F. (1994), 'Disolución gremial y constitución societaria. Los términos del vínculo. Valencia, 1834–1868', in S. Castillo (ed.), *Solidaridad desde abajo. Trabajadores y Socorros Mutuos en la España Contemporánea*, Madrid: Ed. UGT.

Martinius, S. (1970), *Agrar kapitalbildning och finansiering 1833-1892 [Agrarian capital formation and financing 1833–1892]*, Gothenburg: Ekonomisk-historisk institut.

Massange, C. (1987), 'Jacqmotte, d'un négoce familial à une multinationale', *Les*

Cahiers de La Fonderie, 11: 21–30.
Mathelart, S. (1994), *Pour l'histoire des médias en Belgique. Bibliographie de 1830 à nos jours*, Brussels: ULB.
Matilla, M. J. (1995), *Las mujeres de Madrid como agentes de cambio social*, Madrid: Instituto Universitario de Estudios de la Mujer, Universidad Autónoma de Madrid.
McBride, T. (1976), *The Domestic Revolution: The Modernisation of Household Service in England and France 1820–1920*, New York: Holmes and Meier.
McCants, A. (1997), *Civic Charity in a Golden Age: Orphan Care in Early Modern Amsterdam*, Urbana: University of Illinois Press.
McDonogh, G. (1986), *Good Families of Barcelona: A Social History of Power in the Industrial Era*, Princeton, NJ: Princeton University Press.
McKendrick, N., Brewer, J. and Plumb, J. H. (1982), *The Birth of a Consumer Society: The Commercialization of Eighteenth-century England*, Bloomington: Indiana University Press.
McMillan, J. (2000), *France and Women, 1789–1914: Gender, Society and Politics*, London: Routledge.
Meillassuox, C. (1975), *Femmes, greniers et capitaux*, Paris: Maspero.
Meinhold, W. (1942), 'Das kurhessische Industriegeschlecht Henschel', in I. Schnack (ed.), *Lebensbilder aus Kurhessen und Waldeck 1830–1930*, Marburg: N. G. Elwert, 149–89.
Meißl, G. (1992–7), 'Gewerbe', 'Handel' and 'Industrie', in F. Czeike (ed.), *Historisches Lexikon Wien*, 5 vols, Vienna: Kremayr and Scheriau.
Meyer, S. (1987), 'The Tiresome Work of Conspicuous Leisure: On the Domestic Duties of the Wives of Civil Servants in the German Empire, 1871–1918', in M. Boxer and J. Quataert (eds), *Connecting Spheres: Women in the Western World, 1500 to the Present*, New York: Oxford University Press, 156–65.
Miles, M. (1981), 'The Money Markets in the Early Industrial Revolution: Evidence from the West Riding Attorneys, c. 1750–1800', *Business History*, 23: 127–46.
Milne, J. D. (1857), *Industrial and Social Position of Women in the Middle and Lower Ranks*, London: Chapman and Hall.
Mitchell, B. and Deane, P. (1962), *Abstract of British Historical Statistics*, Cambridge: Cambridge University Press.
Morris, R. J. (1983), 'Voluntary Societies and British Urban Elites, 1780–1850', *The Historical Journal*, 26: 95–118.
Morris, R. J. (1994), 'Men, Women and Property: the Reform of the Married Women's Property Act 1870', in F. M. L. Thompson (ed.), *Landowners, Capitalists and Entrepreneurs: Essays for Sir John Habakkuk*, Oxford: Clarendon Press, Oxford University Press, 171–91.
Morris, R. J. (1998), 'Reading the Will: Cash Economy Capitalists and Urban

Peasants in the 1830s', in A. Kidd and D. Nicholls (eds), *The Making of the British Middle Class: Studies in Regional and Cultural Diversity since the Eighteenth Century*, Stroud: Sutton, Stroud, 113–29.

Murphy, L. (1987), 'Her Own Boss: Businesswomen and Separate Spheres in the Midwest, 1850–1880', *Illinois Historical Journal*, 80: 155–76.

Murphy, L. (1991), 'Business Ladies: Midwestern Women and Enterprise, 1850–1880', *Journal of Women's History*, 3: 65–89.

Musgrave, E. (1993), 'Women in the Male World of Work: The Building Industries of Eighteenth-Century Brittany', *French History*, 7: 30–52.

Nandrin, J. (2001), 'Het juridich statuut van de vrouwelijke zelfstandige. De erfenis van Napoleon', in L. Van Molle and P. Heyrman (eds), *Vrouwenzakenvrouwen, Facetten van vrouwelijk zelfstanding ondernemerschap in Vlaanderen 1800–2000*, Gent: KADOC, 40–8.

Nandrin, J. (2002), 'L'évolution du statut juridique de la femme indépendante en Belgique', *Sextant*, 17–18: 271–83.

Nash, M. (1994), 'Experiencia y aprendizaje. La formación histórica de los feminismos en España', *Historia Social*, 20: 151–72.

Nead, L. (2000), *Victorian Babylon: People, Street and Images in Nineteenth-century London*, New Haven: Yale University Press.

Nenadic, S. (1988), 'The Social Shaping of Business Behaviour in the Nineteenth-century Women's Garment Trades', *Journal of Social History*, 31: 625–45.

Nieto, J. (1996), 'Asociación y conflicto laboral en el Madrid del siglo XVIII', in V. López and J. Nieto (eds), *El trabajo en la encrucijada. Artesanos urbanos en la Europa de la Edad Moderna*, Madrid: Libros de la Catarata.

Norlander, K. (1994), 'Women Capitalists and the Industrialization of Sweden', *Umeå Papers in Economic History*, no. 12, Umeå: Umeå University.

Norlander, K. (2000), *Människor kring ett företag*, Gothenburg: Ekonomiskhistoriska institutionen.

Norrman, R. (1993), *Konserverade änkor och kvinnor på undantag. Prästänkornas villkor i Uppsala stift 1720–1920 – från änkehjälp till änkepension*, Uppsala: Studia Historico-Ecclesiastica Upsaliensia 36.

Nygren, I. (1983), 'Transformation of Bank Structures in the Industrial Period: The Case of Sweden 1820–1913', *Journal of European Economic History*, 11: 575–603.

Öberg, L. (1989), 'Fosterhem i Stockholm vid 1800-talets slut', in S. Sperlings (ed.), *Studier och handlingar rörande Stockholms historia*, Stockholm: Statsarlisvet, 161–88.

O'Brien, P. (1988), 'The Political Economy of British Taxation, 1660–1815', *Economic History Review*, Second Series, XLI: 1–32.

Ögren, A. (2003), *Empirical Studies in Money, Credit and Banking: The Swedish Credit Market in Transition, 1834–1913*, Stockholm: Institute for Research in

Economic History.
Olivé Serret, E. (1998), *Els Moragas. Història íntima d'una familia de notables, 1750–1868. Privacitat i família en la crisi de l'Antic Règim a Catalunya*, Tarragona: Diputació de Tarragona.
Olsson, U. (1997), *In the Center of Development: Skandinaviska Enskilda Banken and Its Predecessors 1856–1996*, Stockholm: Institute for Research in Economic History.
Österreichisches Biographisches Lexikon, 1815–1950 (1954–), 44 vols, Graz and Cologne: H. Böhlau.
Owens, A. (2000), 'Property, Will Making and Estate Disposal in an Industrial Town, 1800–1857', in J. Stobart and A. Owens (eds), *Urban Fortunes: Property and Inheritance in the Town, 1700–1900*, Aldershot: Ashgate, 79–107.
Owens, A. (2001), 'Property, Gender and the Life Course: Inheritance and Family Welfare Provision in Early Nineteenth-century England', *Social History*, 26: 297–315.
Owens, A. (2002a), 'Backbone of the Nation: Women and Investment in Nineteenth-century Britain', Paper presented to the Third European Social Science History Conference, The Hague.
Owens A. (2002b), 'Inheritance and the Life-Cycle of Family Firms in the Early Industrial Revolution', *Business History*, 44: 21–46.
Oxaal, I. and Weizmann, W. R. (1985), 'The Jews of pre-1914 Vienna: An Exploration of Basic Sociological Dimensions', *Leo Baeck Institute Yearbook*, XXX, 495–532.
Oxaal, I., Pollak, M. and Botz, G. (1987, eds), *Jews, Anti-Semitism and Culture in Vienna*, London: Routledge and Kegan Paul.
Palazzi, M. (2002), 'Economic Autonomy and Male Authority: Female Merchants in Modern Italy', *Journal of Modern Italian Studies*, 7: 17–36.
Pammer, M. (1996), 'Umfang und Verteilung von Unternehmervermögen in Wien 1852–1913', *Zeitschrift für Unternehmensgeschichte*, 41: 40–64.
Parley, P. (1855), *The Book of Trades, Arts and Professions, Relative to Food, Clothing, Shelter and Ornament. For the Use of the Young*, London: Darton and Co.
Pascual, P. (1990), *Agricultura i industrialització a la Catalunya del segle XIX. Formació i desestructuració d'un sistema econòmic*, Barcelona: Crítica.
Peiró Arroyo, A. (2002), *Jornaleros y Mancebos. Identidad, organización y conflicto en los trabajadores del Antiguo Régimen*, Barcelona: Crítica.
Pellegrin, N. (1994), 'Las costureras de la historia. Mujeres y trabajo en el Antiguo Régimen en Francia. Un balance historiográfico', *Arenal. Revista de Historia de las Mujeres*, 1(1): 25–38.
Perinats, A. and Marrades, I. (1980), *Mujer, prensa y sociedad en España, 1800–1939*, Madrid: Centro de Investigaciones Sociológicas.

Peterson, M. J. (1984), 'No Angels in the House: The Victorian Myth and the Paget Woman', *American Historical Review*, 89, 667–708.

Petersson, C. (2001), *Lanthandeln. En studie av den fasta handelns regionala utveckling i Västmanlands län 1864-1890*, Uppsala Studies in Economic History, no. 57, Uppsala: Uppsala University.

Petersson, T. (2000), 'Playing it Safe? Lending Policies of the Savings Bank in Nyköping 1832–1875', in L. Fälting (ed.), *Both a Borrower and a Lender Be: Savings Banks in the Economic Development of Sweden 1820–1939*, Uppsala Papers in Economic History, no. 12, Uppsala: Department of Economic History, Uppsala University.

Petersson, T. (2001), *Framväxten av ett lokalt banksystem*, Uppsala Studies in Economic History, no. 56, Uppsala: Uppsala University.

Petit, J. J. M. (1930), *De burgerlijke rechtstoestand der gehuwde vrouw*, Zwolle: Tjeenk Willink.

Piette, V. (1996), 'Trajectoires féminines. Les commerçantes à Bruxelles vers 1850', *Sextant*, 5: 9–46.

Piette, V. (2000a), 'Artisanat et commerce féminin à Bruxelles au XIXe siècle. Sources, problèmes méthodologiques et perspectives de recherche', *Actes du Cinquième Congrès de l'Association des Cercles francophones d'Histoire et d'Archéologie de Belgique, Herbeumont*, actes II, 237–44.

Piette, V. (2000b), *Domestiques et servantes. Des vies sous condition. Essai sur le travail domestique en Belgique au 19e siècle*, Brussels: Académie royale de Belgique.

Pinchbeck, I. (1930), *Women Workers and the Industrial Revolution, 1750–1850*, London: Frank Cass & Co., reprinted 1969.

Playford, F. (1864), *Practical Hints for Investing Money, with an Explanation of the Mode of Transacting Business on the Stock Exchange*, London: Virtue Brothers & Co.

Poelstra, J. (1996), *Luiden van een andere beweging. Huishoudelijke arbeid in Nederland (1840–1920)*, Amsterdam: Het Spinhuis.

Poovey, M. (1988), *Uneven Developments: The Ideological Work of Gender in Mid-Victorian Britain*, London: Virago.

Poovey, M. (2002), 'Writing about Finance in Victorian England: Disclosure and Secrecy in the Culture of Investment', *Victorian Studies*, 45: 17–41.

Poovey, M. (2003, ed.), *The Financial System in Nineteenth-century Britain*, Oxford: Oxford University Press.

Poters, A. (1905), 'Caroline Popp', *Biographie nationale*, Brussels: Académie Royale des Sciences, des Lettres et des Beaux-Arts de Belgique, col. 33–8.

Pouchain, P. (1980), 'L'Industrialisation de la région lilloise de 1800 à 1860', Thèse de 3e cycle, Université de Lille III.

Pouchain, P. (1998), *Les maîtres du Nord du XIXe siècle à nos jours*, Paris: Perrin.

Prazák, K. (1898), 'Über die Reform des österreichischen Erbrechts', *Gerichtshalle*, 22: 17, 191–3.

Preda, A. (2001), 'The Rise of the Popular Investor: Financial Knowledge and Investing in England and France, 1840–1880', *The Sociological Quarterly*, 42: 205–32.

Prior, M. (1985, ed.), *Women in English Society 1500–1800*, London: Methuen & Co.

Prochaska, F. (1980), *Women and Philanthropy in Nineteenth-century England*, Oxford: Clarendon Press.

Quataert, J. (2001), *Staging Philanthropy: Patriotic Women and the National Imagination in Dynastic Germany, 1813–1916*, Ann Arbor: University of Michigan Press.

Qvist, G. (1960), *Kvinnofrågan i Sverige 1809–1846*, Gothenburg: Kvinnohistoriskt arkiv 2.

Qvist, G. (1977), 'Ett perspektiv på den sk. kvinnoemancipationen i Sverige', *Historisk Tidskrift*, 1: 145–80.

Qvist, G. (1980), 'Policy towards Women and the Women's Struggle in Sweden', *Scandinavian Journal of History*, 5: 51–74.

Rabuzzi, D. (1995), 'Women as merchants in Eighteenth Century Northern Germany: The Case of Stralsund, 1750-1830', *Central European History*, 28: 435–56.

Rabuzzi, D. (2001), 'Fading Images, Fading Realities? Female Merchants in Scandinavia and the Baltic', *Histoire sociale–Social History*, 34: 355–70.

Ramos, M.-D. (2002), 'Federalismo, laicismo, obrerismo, feminismo. Cuatro claves para interpretar la biografía de Belén Sárraga', in M. D. Ramos and T. Vera (eds), *Discursos, realidades, utopías. La construcción del sujeto femenino en los siglos XIX y XX*, Barcelona: Anthropos, 125–64.

Rappaport, E. (2000), *Shopping for Pleasure: Women in the Making of London's West End*, Princeton, NJ: Princeton University Press.

Rauchberg, H. (1893), *Die Berufsverhältnisse der Bevölkerung Wiens*, Vienna: Hölder.

Rauchberg, H. (1895), *Berufsstatistik nach den Ergebnissen der Volkszählung vom 31. Dezember 1890*, Vienna: Hölder.

Ravet-Anceau (1853–9, ed.), *Annuaire de l'arrondissement de Lille*, Lille.

Ravet-Anceau (1860-90, ed.), *Annuaire du commerce, de l'industrie, de la magistrature et de l'administration de l'arrondissement de Lille*, Lille.

Reagin, N. R. (1995), *A German Women's Movement: Class and Gender in Hanover, 1880–1933*, Chapel Hill: University of North Carolina Press.

Redlich, F. (1959), 'Unternehmer', in *Handwörterbuch der Sozialwissenschaften*, Göttingen: Vandenhoeck & Ruprecht, 10, 486-98.

Reed, M. C. (1975), *Investment in Railways in Britain, 1820–1844: A Study in the*

Development of the Capital Market, Oxford: Oxford University Press.

Reyerson, K. (1986), 'Women in Business in Medieval Montpellier', in B. Hanawalt (ed.), *Women and Work in Preindustrial Europe*, Bloomington: Indiana University Press, 117–44.

Richard, E. (1996), 'Femmes chefs d'entreprises à Marseille, une question de visibilité', *Sextant*, 5: 47–58.

Richardson, S. (2000), '"Well-Neighboured Houses": The Political Networks of Elite Women', in K. Gleadle and S. Richardson (eds), *Women and British Politics, 1760–1860: The Power of the Petticoat*, Basingstoke: Macmillan, 56–73.

Rickards, M. (2000), *Encyclopaedia of Ephemera*, London: British Library.

Rigler, E. (1976), *Frauenleitbild und Frauenarbeit in Österreich vom ausgehenden 19. Jahrhundert bis zum Zweiten Weltkrieg*, Vienna: Verlag für Geschichte und Politik.

Riot-Sarcey, M. (1994), *La Démocratie à l'épreuve des femmes. Trois figures critiques du pouvoir (1830–1848)*, Paris: Albin Michel.

Robert, E. (1984), *A Woman's Place: An Oral History of Working-Class Women, 1890–1940*, Oxford: Blackwell Publishers.

Roemer, J. (1982), *A General Theory of Exploitation and Class*, Cambridge, MA: Harvard University Press.

Roig, M. (1977), *La mujer y la prensa desde el siglo XVII a nuestros días*, Madrid: Mercedes Roig.

Romero-Marín, J. (1997), 'La Maestría Silenciosa. Maestras artesanas en la Barcelona de la primera mitad del siglo XIX', *Arenal. Revista de Historia de las Mujeres*, 2: 275–94.

Romero-Marín, J. (2001), 'Familial Strategies of Artisans during a Modernization Process: Barcelona, 1814-1860', *The History of the Family*, 6: 203–24.

Roper, L. (1985), 'Discipline and Respectability: Prostitution and Reformation in Augsburg', *History Workshop Journal*, 19: 3–28.

Rose, S. (1992), *Limited Livelihoods: Gender and Class in Nineteenth-century England*, Berkeley: University of California Press.

Rose, S. (1993), 'Gender and Labor History: The Nineteenth-century Legacy', *International Review of Social History*, 3 (Supplement 1): 145–62.

Rozenblit, M. L. (1983), *The Jews of Vienna, 1867–1914: Assimilation and Identity*, Albany: State University of New York Press.

Rubinstein, W. D. (1992), 'Cutting up Rich: A Reply to F. M. L. Thompson', *Economic History Review*, Second Series, XLV: 350–61.

Rückblick auf die Entwicklung der Maschinenfabrik Henschel & Sohn Cassel (1899), Kassel: Henschel and Sohn.

Ruiz Guerrero, C. (1997), *Panorama de escritoras españolas*, 2 vols, Cádiz: Universidad.

Rule, J. (1987), 'The Property of Skill in the Period of Manufacture', in P. Joyce (ed.), *The Historical Meanings of Work*, Cambridge: Cambridge University Press, 99–118.

Ryan, M. (1992), 'Gender and Public Access: Women's Politics in Nineteenth-century America', in Craig Calhoun (ed.), *Habermas and the Public Sphere*, Cambridge: MIT Press, 259–88.

Sabel, C. and Zeitlin, J. (1985), 'Historical Alternatives to Mass Production: Politics, Markets and Technology in Nineteenth-century Industrialization', *Past and Present*, 108: 133–76.

Sachbe, C. and Tennstedt, F. (1988), *Geschichte der Armenfürsorge in Deutschland*, vol. 2, *Fürsorge und Wohlfahrtspflege 1871 bis 1929*, Stuttgart: Klett-Cotta.

Sampson, H. (1874), *A History of Advertising from the Earliest Times*, London: Chatto and Windus.

Sánchez Llama, I. (2000), *Galería de escritoras isabelinas. La prensa periódica entre 1833 y 1895,* Madrid: Cátedra.

Sánchez Llama, I. (2001), *Antología de la prensa periódica isabelina escrita por mujeres (1843–1894),* Cádiz: Universidad.

Sandberg, L. (1978), 'Banking and Economic Growth in Sweden before World War I', *Journal of Economic History*, 38: 650–80.

Sarasúa, C. (1995), 'La industria del encaje en el Campo de Calatrava', *Arenal. Revista de Historia de las Mujeres*, 2: 151–74.

Saurer, E. (1993), 'Frauengeschichte in Österreich. Eine fast kritische Bestandsaufnahme', *L'Homme*, 4: 37–63.

Schelzig, E. (2002), 'Perks for the Oldest Profession; German Law Offers Prostitutes Union Rights, Profit Sharing', *The Washington Post*, 12 May, 2002, Sunday, A13.

Schimmer, G. A. (1874), *Die Bevölkerung von Wien und seiner Umgebung nach dem Berufe und der Beschäftigung*, Vienna: Ueberreuter.

Schötz, S. (2004), *Handelsfrauen in Leipzig: Zur Geschichte von Arbeit und Geschlecht in der Neuzeit*, Cologne: Böhlau Verlag.

Schrover, M. (1997), 'De affaire wordt gecontinueerd door de veduwe. Handelende vrouwen in de negentiende eeuw', *Geld and Goed: Jaarboek voor Vrouwengeschiedenis*, 17: 55–74.

Schrover, M. (2002a), *Een kolonie van Duitsers. Groepsvorming onder Duitse immigranten in Utrecht in de negentiende eeuw*, Amsterdam: Aksant.

Schrover, M. (2002b), 'Registratie van vreemdelingen in hetbevolkingsregister (1850-1920)', M. Schrover (ed.), *Bronnen betreffende de registratie van vreemdelingen in Nederland in de negentiende en twintigste eeuw*, The Hague: Instituut voor Nederlandse Geschiedenis, 93–111.

Schulte, R. (1979), *Sperrbezirke: Tugendhaftigkeit und Prostitution in der bürgerlichen Welt*, Frankfurt am Main: Syndikat.

Schulz, G. (1991), 'Betriebliche Sozialpolitik in Deutschland seit 1850', in H. Pohl (ed.), *Staatliche, städtische, betriebliche und kirchliche Sozialpolitik vom Mittelalter bis zur Gegenwart*, Stuttgart: Franz Steiner, 137–76.

Schumpeter, J. (1928), 'Unternehmer', in *Handwörterbuch der Staatswissenschaften*, Jena: G. Fischer, 8, 476–87.

Schuster, B. (1991), 'Frauenhandel und Frauenhäuser im 15. und 16. Jahrhundert', *Vierteljahresschrift für Sozial- und Wirtschaftsgeschichte*, 78: 172–89.

Schuster, B. (1995), *Die Freien Frauen*, Frankfurt am Main: Campus.

Schuster, P. (1992), *Das Frauenhaus*, Paderborn: Schönigh.

Schwarz, L. (1999), 'English Servants and Their Employers During the Eighteenth and Nineteenth Century', *Economic History Review*, Second Series, LII: 236–56.

Schwarzmann-Tischler, M. (1906), 'Der Weg, wie ich Anstreicher-Meisterin wurde', *Der Bund*, 1: 5.

Scott, J. W. (1987), *Gender and the Politics of History*, New York: Columbia University Press.

Scott, J. W. (1996), *Only Paradoxes to Offer: French Feminists and the Rights of Man*, Harvard: Harvard University Press.

Scott, J. W. (1998), 'Comment: Conceptualizing Gender in American Business History', *Business History Review*, 72: 242–9.

Secretan, J. J. (1833), *Fortune's Epitome of Stocks and Public Funds*, London: Sherwood, Gilbert and Piper.

Segura, I. and Selva, M. (1984), *Revistes de Dones (1846–1935)*, Barcelona: Edhasa.

Seoane, M.-C. (1996), 'La prensa', in P. Lain Entralg (ed.), *La edad de Plata de la cultura española (1898–1936)*, vol. 2, *Letras. Ciencia. Arte. Sociedad y Cultura. Historia de España de Ramón Menéndez Pidal*, Madrid: Espasa Calpe, 701–30.

Shanley, M. L. (1989), *Feminism, Marriage and the Law in Victorian England, 1850–1895*, London: I. B. Tauris.

Sharpe, P. (1998, ed.), *Women's Work: The English Experience 1650–1914*, Oxford: Oxford University Press.

Sharpe, P. (2001), 'Gender in the Economy: Female Merchants and Family Business in the British Isles, 1600–1850', *Histoire sociale-Social History*, 38: 283–306.

Simón Palmer, C. (1990), 'Panorama general de las escritoras románticas españolas', in M. Mayoral (ed.), *Escritoras Románticas Españolas*, Madrid: Banco Exterior, 9–16.

Simón Palmer, C. (1991), *Escritoras españolas del siglo XIX. Manual biobibliográfico*, Madrid: Castalia.

Simonton, D. (1991), 'Apprenticeship: Training and Gender in Eighteenth-century England', in M. Berg (ed.), *Markets and Manufacture in Early Industrial Europe*, London: Routledge, 227–58.

Simonton, D. (1998), *A History of European Women's Work, 1700 to the Present*, London: Routledge.
Sinclair, T. (1991), 'Women, Work and Skill: Economic Theories and Feminist Perspectives', in N. Redclift and T. Sinclair (eds), *Working Women: International Perspectives on Labor and Gender Ideology*, London: Routledge, 1–24.
Sjöberg, M. (2001), *Kvinnors jord, manlig rätt*, Stockholm: Gidlunds.
Sjölander, A. (1995), 'Mariestads sparbank', unpublished paper, Uppsala: Department of Economic History, Uppsala University.
Sjölander, A. (1996), 'Sparbankens roll i den lokala ekonomin', unpublished paper, Uppsala: Department of Economic History, Uppsala University.
Smith, B. (1981), *Ladies of the Leisure Class: The Bourgeoises of Northern France in the Nineteenth Century*, Princeton, NJ: Princeton University Press.
Snell, K. D. M. (1981), 'Agricultural Seasonal Employment: The Standard of Living, and Women's Work in the South and East, 1690–1860', *Economic History Review*, Second Series, XXXIV: 407–39.
Söderberg, T. (1965), *Hantverkarna i genombrottsskedet 1870-1920*, Stockholm: Sveriges hantverks-och industriorganisation.
Solà Parera, A. (2000), 'Una burgesia plural', in B. Riquer (ed.), *Història, política, societat i cultura dels Països Catalans*, Vol. 6, Barcelona: Enciclopèdia Catalana, 196–211.
Solà Parera, A. (2002), 'Les puntaires del Baix Llobregat. Primeres notes per a un estudi socioeconòmic', in C. Borderías and S. Bengoechea (eds), *Les Dones i la Història al Baix Llobregat*, 2 vols, Barcelona: PAM, vol. 1, 315–36.
Spree, U. (1994), 'Die verhinderte "Bürgerin"? Ein begriffsgeschichtlicher Vergleich zwischen Deutschland, Frankreich und Grossbritannien', in R. Koselleck and K. Schreiner (eds), *Bürgerschaft: Rezeption und Innovation der Begrifflichkeit vom Hohen Mittelalter bis ins 19. Jahrhundert*, Stuttgart: Klett-Cotta, 274–308.
Stadin, K. (1980), 'Den gömda och glömda arbetskraften. Stadskvinnor i produktionen under 1600-1700-talet', *Historisk Tidskrift*, 3: 298–319.
Stallberg, F. W. (1992), *Eine Stadt und die (Un-)Sittlichkeit. 100 Jahre Prostitutionspolitik in Dortmund*, Dortmund: Projekt Verlag.
Staves, S. (1990), *Married Women's Separate Property in England, 1660–1833*, Cambridge, MA: Harvard University Press.
Steckzén, B. (1921), *Umeå stads historia 1588–1888*, Umeå: Umeistad.
'Stockholm's savings bank' (1946), unpublished manuscript prepared for the 125th anniversary, Stockholm.
Steinmetz, G. (1993), *Regulating the Social: The Welfare State and Local Politics in Imperial Germany*, Princeton, NJ: Princeton University Press.
Streller, V. M. (1989), 'Fleiß und Leichtsinn. Österreichische Unternehmer: ein

Querschnitt für das Jahr 1906', in R. Sandgruber (ed.), *Magie der Industrie. Leben und Arbeiten im Fabrikszeitalter*, Munich: Oldenbourg, 238–48.

Svanberg, M. (1999), *Företagsamhet föder framgång. Yrkeskarriärer och sociala nätverk bland företagarna i Sundsvall 1850–1890*, Umeå: Institutionen för historiska studier.

Svensson, P. (2001), *Agrara entreprenörer*, Lund Studies in Economic History 16, Stockholm: Almqvist & Wiksell International.

Swanström, Y. (2000), *Policing Public Women: The Regulation of Prostitution in Stockholm 1812–1880*, Stockholm: Atlas Akademi.

Sweets, J. (1995), 'The Lace Makers of Le Puy in the Nineteenth Century', in Daryl M. Hafter (ed.), *European Women and Preindustrial Craft*, Bloomington: Indiana University Press, 67–86.

Tavera, S. (1999), 'Feminismo y literatura en los inicios del periodismo profesional femenino. Carmen de Burgos y Federica Montseny', in C. Barrera (ed.), *Del gacetero al profesional del periodismo. Evolución histórica de los actores humanos del cuarto poder*, Madrid: Fragua, 327–40.

Thirsk, J. (1990), 'Popular Consumption and the Mass Market in the Sixteenth to Eighteenth Centuries', *Material History Bulletin*, 31: 51–8.

Thompson, F. M. L. (1992), 'Stitching it Together Again', *Economic History Review*, Second Series, XLV: 362–75.

Tiersten, L. (1993), 'Redefining Consumer Culture: Recent Literature on Consumption and the Bourgeoisie in Western Europe', *Radical History Review*, 57: 116–59.

Tilly, L., and Scott, J. (1978), *Women, Work and the Family*, New York: Holt, Rinehart and Winston.

Torstendahl, R. (1984), 'Technology in the Development of Society 1850–1980: Four Phases of Industrial Capitalism in Western Europe', *History and Technology*, 1: 157–73.

Toscas, E. (1999), *Família i Context. La Casa Papiol i la Vilanova de la Primera Meitat del Segle XIX*, Barcelona: El Cep i la Nansa.

Tosh, J. (1999), *A Man's Place: Masculinity and the Middle-Class Home in Victorian England*, New Haven: Yale University Press.

Trénard, L. (1977, ed.), *Histoire d'une métropole, Lille, Roubaix, Tourcoing*, Toulouse, Privat.

Trepp, A. (1996), *Sanfte Männlichkeit und selbständige Weiblichkeit*, Göttingen: Vandenhoeck & Ruprecht.

Treue, W. (1974), 'Henschel & Sohn – Ein deutsches Lokomotivbau-Unternehmen 1860-1912, Teil I', *Tradition: Zeitschrift für Firmengeschichte und Unternehmerbiographie*, 19: 3–27.

Treue, W. (1975), 'Henschel & Sohn – Ein deutsches Lokomotivbau-Unternehmen 1860-1912, Teil II', *Tradition: Zeitschrift für Firmengeschichte und*

Unternehmerbiographie, 20: 3–23.
Tuana, N. (1993), *The Less Noble Sex: Scientific, Religious and Philosophical Conceptions of Woman's Nature*, Bloomington: University of Indiana Press.
Ulrich, A. (1985), *Bordelle, Straßendirnen und bürgerliche Sittlichkeit in der Belle Epoque: Eine sozialgeschichtliche Studie der Prostitution am Beispiel der Stadt Zürich*, Zurich: Mitteilungen der Antiquarischen Gesellschaft in Zürich.
Ulvros, E. (1996), *Fruar och mamseller*, Lund: Historiska media.
Urban, A. (1927), *Staat und Prostitution in Hamburg vom Beginn der Reglementierung bis zur Aufhebung der Kasernierung (1807-1922)*, Hamburg: Verlag Conrad Behre.
Vaes, J. P. (1990), 'Wielemans-Ceuppens. Grandeur et décadence d'une brasserie', *Les Cahiers de la Fonderie*, 13–23.
Valenze, D. (1991), 'The Art of Women and the Business of Men: Women's Work and the Dairy Industry, c. 1740–1840', *Past and Present*, 130: 142–69.
Van Eijl, C. (1994), *Het werkzame verschil. Vrouwen in de slag om arbeid 1898–1940*, Hilversum: Verloren.
Van Molle, L. and Heyrman, P. (2001), *Vrouwen zaken vrouwen. Facetten van vrouwelijk zelfstandig ondernemerschap in Vlaanderen, 1800–2000*, Ghent: Museum van de vlaamse sociale strijd.
Van Neste, A.-S. (1989), 'De participatie van de vrouw in de kommerciële en ambachtelijke aktiviteiten 1829–1846. Een dynamische studie op basis van patenten in twee wijken van Brussel', mémoire de licence en histoire, Brussels, VUB.
Van Ortoy, F. (1905), 'Christian Popp (1805–1879)', *Biographie nationale*, Brussels: Académie Royale des Sciences, des Lettres et des Beaux-Arts de Belgique, col. 38–42.
Van Poppel, F. (1992), *Trouwen in Nederland. Een historisch-demografische studie van de 19e en vroeg-20e eeuw*, The hague: Stichting Nederlands Interdisciplinair Demografisch Instituut.
Varlez, L. (1901), *Les salaires dans l'industrie gantoise*, vol. 1, *Industrie cotonnière*, Brussels: Ministère de l'Industrie et du Travail, Office du Travail.
Verley, P. (1994), *Entreprises et entrepreneurs du XVIIIe siècle au début du XXe siècle*, Paris: Editions Hachette.
Vicens, J. (1958), *Industrials i polítics del segle XIX*, Barcelona: Vicens.
Vicente Valentín, M. (1994), 'Mujeres artesanas en al Barcelona Moderna', in A. Ibero, I. Pérez and M. Vicent (eds), *La mujer en el Antiguo Régimen. Imagen y Realidad*, Barcelona: Icaria, 57–90.
Vickery, A. (1991), 'The Neglected Century: Writing the History of Eighteenth-century Women', *Gender and History*, 3: 211–19.
Vickery, A. (1993), 'Golden Age to Separate Spheres? A Review of the Categories and Chronology of English Women's History', *Historical Journal*, 36: 383–414.

Vickery, A. (1998), *The Gentleman's Daughter: Women's Lives in Georgian England*, New Haven: Yale University Press.
Vogel, U. (1992), 'Property Rights and the Status of Women in Germany and England', in J. Kocka and A. Mitchell (eds), *Bourgeois Society in Nineteenth-century Europe*, Oxford University Press: Oxford, 241–72.
Wahrman, D. (1993), '"Middle-class" Domesticity Goes Public: Gender and Class Politics from Queen Caroline to Queen Victoria', *Journal of British Studies*, 32: 396–432.
Wakefield, P. (1798), *Reflections on the Present Condition of the Female Sex*, London: J. Johnson.
Waldenström, D. (1998), 'Early Bondholding in Stockholm 1881-1930', *Research Report no. 8*, Stockholm: Stockholm School of Economics.
Walhout, E. and van Poppel, F. (2003), 'De vermelding des beroeps. Eene ijdele formaliteit? Twee eeuwen vrouwelijke beroepsarbeid in Nederlandse huwelijksakten', *Tijdschrift voor Sociale Geschiedenis*, 3: 301–32.
Walker, L. (1995), 'Vistas of Pleasure: Women Consumers and Urban Space in the West End of London, 1850–1900', in C. C. Orr (ed.), *Women in the Victorian Art World*, Manchester: Manchester University Press, 70–85.
Walker, L. (2000), 'The Feminist Re-mapping of Space in Victorian London', in I. Borden, J. Kerr, J. Rendell and A. Pivaro (eds), *The Unknown City: Contesting Architecture and Social Space*, Cambridge, MA: MIT Press, 297–309.
Walkowitz, J. R. (1980), *Prostitution and Victorian Society: Women, Class, and the State*, Cambridge: Cambridge University Press.
Walser, K. (1984), 'Prostitutionsve dacht und Geschlechterforschung. Das Beispiel der Dienstmädchen um 1900', *Geschichte und Gesellschaft*, 11: 99–111.
Ward, J. C. (1974), *Finance of Canal Building in Eighteenth-century England*, Oxford: Oxford University Press.
Weatherill, L. (1988), *Consumer Behaviour and Material Culture in Britain 1660–1760*, London: Routledge.
Whitney, W. (1986), 'To Triumph before Feminine Tastes: Bourgeois Women's Consumption and Hand Methods of Production in Mid-nineteenth-century Paris', *Business History Review*, 60: 541–63.
Whyte, M. (1978), *The Status of Women in Preindustrial Societies*, Princeton, NJ: Princeton University Press.
Wijne, H. A. (1853), *De wet op het regt van patent uit een handels- en staathuishoudkundig oogpunt beschouwd*, Groningen: Wolters.
Willenbacher, B. (2003), 'Individualism and Traditionalism in Inheritance Law in Germany, France, England, and the United States', *Journal of Family History*, 28: 208–25.
Winstanley, M. (1983), *The Shopkeeper's World 1830–1914*, Manchester:

Manchester University Press.

Wiskin, C. (1999), 'Business Women and Entrepreneurial Networks in Late Eighteenth and Early Nineteenth-century England', Paper presented to the British Economic History Society Conference.

Wiskin, C. (2000), 'Women, Finance and Credit in England, c. 1780–1826', Unpublished PhD thesis, University of Warwick.

Wörner-Heil, O. (2002), '"Anstifterinnen": Frauenengagement in Kassel im 19. und frühen 20. Jahrhundert', *Ariadne – Forum für Frauen- und Geschlechtergeschichte*, 42: 34–42.

Wurzbach, C. (1856–1891), *Biographisches Lexikon des Kaiserthums Österreich*, 60 vols, Vienna: Zamarski.

Yernaux, J.-L. (1964), 'Les taux féminins d'activité. Leur évolution en Belgique 1866–1962', *Revue belge de sécurité sociale*, 1102–24.

Young, C. (1995), 'Financing the Micro-scale Enterprise: Rural Craft Producers in Scotland, 1840–1914', *Business History Review*, 69: 398–421.

Zlotnick, S. (1998), *Women, Writing and the Industrial Revolution*, Baltimore: Johns Hopkins University Press.

Index

abortion, 106
absolutism, Spain, 82
accountancy, 89
accounting books, 36
address books, *see* trade directories
advertising, 102, 130, 152–64 passim, 168, 178–80
advice literature, 165n30
Agardh, Carl Adolf, 139, 141
agency, 21, 37, 40, 50
agriculture, 39, 81, 126
alcohol, 53
Alexander, Sally, 153
Alter, George, 146, 150
Amsterdam, Netherlands, 167, 170–1, 174, 179
anarchism, Spain, 105–7
ancien régime, 81–2, 85, 129
  see also early modern period
angel in the house, 101, 106
Anglada, Juan, 89
annuities, 27, 28, 31
appraisers, 26
apprentices, 2, 83, 85, 87, 94n25, 113–15, 121
Armentière, France, 64
articles of association, 63
artificial flower makers, 113–19
Artigas, Dolores, 88
artisans, 13, 82, 83–93 passim, 148
  female, 81, 85–6, 140
  strategy, 85
Ashby de la Zouch, United Kingdom, 24
Asia, 68
assurance, *see* life assurance
attorneys, *see* solicitors
auctioneers, 26, 131
Augusta Victoria, Empress of Germany, 75–6
Austria, 110–125, 189
  Civil Code (1812), 111–15
  Civil Code (1914), 114
  Commercial Code (1862), 111
  Trades Regulations (1859), 111–13
Austro-Prussian War (1866), 71, 76

bakers, 56, 88, 92, 130, 132, 144, 171
Bank of England, 27–33
  will registers, 28–30
bankers, 132
banking, Sweden, 36, 39–50 passim
bankruptcy, 26, 88, 144
barbers, 128, 131
Barcelona, Spain, 81–95, 100, 105
  Commerce Board, 87
basket weaving, 87
beer, 53
Belgium, 14, 126–38
  Civil Code (1804), 128–9
  Commercial Code (1807), 129
  Revolution (1830), 135
Bell, G. M., 26
Benson, John, 149
Berlin, Germany, 76–7
Bertran, Juan, 89
billheads, 157
bills of exchange, 39, 155
Birmingham, United Kingdom, 24
Blackman, J., 162
blacksmiths, 57
blue-collar workers, 77
boarding-house keepers, 53
boiler operators, 60
Bonet, María, 89
bookbinders, 57
bookkeepers, 89
bookshops, 102
Borås, Sweden, 43
borrowing, 40, 44, 47
  British government, *see* national debt
  women and, 48–9

233

234 · Index

Borsig (German locomotive manufacturers), 74, 76–7
Boston, United States, 10
Bourbon dynasty, 83
bourgeois morality, 3, 70, 101, 184–6, 193
bourgeoisie, *see* middle class
boys, 87
branding, 156
breadwinner, *see* male breadwinner
Bremen, Germany, 70
brewers, 127, 129, 135
brides, 111–12
Britain, 39, 98, 148
　see also England
broadsides, 156
brokers, 24, 26, 27, 128, 131–2
brothelization, Hamburg, 185–90
brothels, 15, 185–93
　keepers, 168, 185, 189, 191, 193
brothers, 7, 100, 147
Brussels, Belgium, 97, 104, 126–37 passim
bureaucratization, *see* industrial bureaucratization
burghers, 38, 141
business, 6, 7, 8, 12, 13
　meetings, 74
　size, 117–118
　see also family firms
businessmen, 23, 98, 112, 120
businesswomen, 10, 14, 22, 37, 52, 53, 55, 62, 64–5, 116–22, 136, 156–64
butchers, 56, 130, 171
button makers, 87

cabinet makers, 131, 133
Cádiz, Spain, 98, 100, 103
Caesar, Friedrich Wilhelm, 70
calico printing, 83
Campbell, R., 159
canals, investment in, 24
candle making 88
capital markets, Sweden, 39
capital outlay, 150
capitalism, 4, 99, 140, 148
Carlsson, Sten, 146
carpenters, 84, 87, 90, 119
casernation, 185–6
casual labour, 159
Catalonia, 13, 86
Catholicism, 82, 96, 101–4, 119, 176
celibacy, 139–40, 149
censorship, 100

censuses, 8, 13
　Austria, 117–18
　Belgium, 128, 130–2, 136–7
　England, 153–4
　France, 53–4, 59, 62
　Netherlands, 171, 179
Cerdà, Ildefons, 87
chair-makers, 84, 87
champagne industry, 64–5
chandlers, 154
charity, *see* philanthropy
Chelsea, London, United Kingdom, 158
chemical-makers, 57
child care, 61, 110, 112, 118, 154, 191
children, 60, 61, 70, 89–90, 114, 120, 126, 146–8
　foster, 147
　illegitimate, 139, 146
chimney sweepers, 131
china manufacturing, 134
Christian Social Party, Austria, 113, 121
Christianity, 3, 104
　see also Catholicism, evangelical religion, Protestantism, religion
cigar makers, 178
citizenship, 4, 9
civil servants, 4, 5, 8, 101
Clark, Alice, 22, 152
class, 3, 4, 21
　see also working class, middle class
class formation, 3, 21, 153
　and consumption, 3, 4
clerks, 139
clothing industries, 16, 56, 59, 60, 116–18, 132–4, 157–8, 161–2
clubs and societies, 26
coffee-house keepers, 118, 134, 154
coffee traders, 192, 135
Cologne, Germany, 71, 72
colonial goods, 135
Colonies, Spanish, 83, 97
co-management, 82, 90
comb-makers, 84, 89
commercial banks, Sweden, 36, 39–50 passim
common law
　Castile, 86
　Catalonia, 86, 89
　England, 23
　Netherlands, 173–4
community of property, 111
competition, 83, 113, 160
confectioners, 131, 135, 162

consolidated annuities, 'consols', 28
  see also annuities
consumption, 6, 7, 8, 14, 23, 89, 155
  and class formation, 3, 4
  mass consumption, 9
contraception, 106
contractors of public works, 57
coopers, 57
corporate governance, 47–9
Cortez, Spanish (1812), 97–8
cottage property, England, 24
cotton industry
  factories, 83
  manufacturers, 86
  spinning, 55, 61–3
  twisting, 61–3
  weaving, 55, 62–3
  wholesalers, 55
court records, 120–1
Covent Garden, London, United Kingdom, 158
coverture, 23, 121, 130, 136, 173–4
craft industries, 5, 6, 36, 40, 54, 56, 60, 82, 84, 116, 126, 130, 139–43, 148–9
craftsmen, 2, 6, 13, 54, 81, 112, 126, 156
craftswomen, 82, 88–90, 139
credit, 40, 64, 155
credit markets
  Britain, 23
  Sweden, 12
    agrarian, 39–40, 45
    informal, 40–1, 49
    institutional, 39–41, 45, 49
    Sweden, urban, 40–1, 49
creditors, 29, 32, 40
creditworthiness, 155
Crossick, Geoffrey, 5, 10, 126
Cuba, 98, 100
cult of personality, 158
Curli, Barbara, 5, 7
custom, 26, 47

Darmstadt, University of, 74
daughters, 4, 12, 38, 53, 85, 87–9, 92, 114–15, 134, 137, 153
Davidoff, Leonore, 3, 4, 9, 10, 21, 37, 81, 153
death, 25, 86–7, 114, 176
debentures, *see* railway debentures
debt, 40, 88
  and women, 23, 63
debtors, 32
department stores, 10, 126, 160

dependency, 10, 15, 21
depositors,
  Swedish commercial banks, 45–6
  Swedish savings banks, 42–3, 46
didactic literature, 98
Diet, Prussian, 70–1
dinner table keeping, 168, 173
directories, *see* trade directories
discount houses, 39, 44
discourse, 3, 8, 10, 14, 17, 33, 53, 64–5, 101, 137
display of goods, 160
dividends, 27, 31
divisions of labour, 113
divorce, 75, 87, 112
dockers, 85
domestic labour, 61, 85, 99, 110, 112, 118, 154
  see also family reproduction
domestic servants, 31, 136, 167–81, 181
  contracts, 170
  employment fairs, 170–1
  sexual harassment of, 191
  wages, 177
domestic service, 6, 15, 116, 126, 136, 167–81
domestic sphere, *see* private sphere
domesticity, 2, 3, 4, 12, 14, 22, 31, 32, 70–2, 74, 81, 99, 101, 103, 119, 121, 127, 136, 152, 193
  'the cult of', 4, 5, 103
  see also private sphere
dowry, 86–8, 111–12
drapers, 154, 160–1
dress making, 53, 113, 119, 133, 153, 157–60, 162, 191
dyeing, 62

early modern period, 2, 52, 170, 178
  see also ancien régime
Ecker-Ertle, Heidmarie, 79n11
economic
  agency, 1, 12, 17
  development, 22–3, 36, 38, 93n11, 111
  growth, 22, 39, 63, 115–16
Edgren, Lars, 142
editors, 96–8, 134
education, 53, 96–7, 99, 102, 103, 110, 113
electrical industries, 116
embroidery, 83
emigration, 5
Empire, British, 27–8, 30

236 · *Index*

employment agencies (domestic servants), 167–8, 173
emulation, 6
Engels, Friedrich, 152
  see also Marxism
engineering, 67, 68, 70, 73, 75
England, 3, 5, 7, 11, 12, 14, 20–33 passim, 167, 170–1
  see also Britain
engraving, 156
Enlightenment, 98
Enskilda banks, *see* commercial banks, Sweden
entertainment, 98
entrepreneurs, 14, 22, 36, 68, 103
entrepreneurship, 7, 113, 122
equity, law of, 23
Eskilstuna, Sweden, 142
eugenics, 105
evangelical religion, 3, 101

factories, 6, 8, 14, 22, 60–1, 67, 74, 76, 88–9, 135, 140, 152, 191
Falun, Sweden, 41, 43
family, 20
  economy, 6, 36, 88
  farms, 7
  firms, 5, 7, 11, 12, 13, 41, 67–8, 82–5, 87, 89, 92–3, 98, 100, 110, 114, 137
  life course, 85
  management, 70, 72–6
  networks, 15, 26, 42, 46, 49, 84, 176, 189
  planning, 106
  property, 38, 47
  reproduction, 7, 53, 85–6, 118
  strategies, 47, 82, 86, 93, 126, 141
  trade groups, 84–5
fancy goods, 142–3
farmers, 39, 112
farms, 7, 40
fashions, 14, 98, 132, 159
  French, 158
fathers, 7, 8, 64, 86, 100, 133, 146–7
female-headed businesses, *see* businesswomen
females, *see* women, gender
femininity, 1, 2, 7, 9, 14, 69, 137, 154
feminism
  Austria, 110
  Spain, 96, 103–4
financial
  information, 12, 25, 26, 31

markets, 26
  women and, 11, 12, 23, 26
  see also investment markets
financial revolution
  Britain, 27, 34n49
  Sweden, 37
financial system
  Britain, 28, 30, 31, 34n27
  Sweden, 36–50 passim
finishing industries, 61–3
fire insurance records, 154–6
firms, *see* business, family firms
First Republic, Spain, 97
First World War, 53, 62, 106, 123n14, 190
fishmongers, 130
flexible specialization, 83
flour, 53
food and drink retailers, 6, 14, 53, 56, 57, 60, 90, 112, 117, 128, 131–2, 135–6, 148, 162–3
foremen, 60
Fourierism
  see Socialism, Utopian
France, 4, 7, 8, 13, 52–66 passim, 96, 98, 103, 150, 167
Franco-Prussian War, 76–7
free love, 105, 107
free market, 5
free professions, 110
freedom of expression, 99
freedom of trade
  Austria, 113
  Spanish Decrees on, 82, 84, 92
  Sweden, 139, 144–5
Freemasons, 104, 106
French Civil Code, 4, 111–12
French Revolution (1789), 4
friendly societies, Britain, 28
Funds, the, 27
  see also governments securities, Britain

Gambers, Wendy, 7
garment industries, *see* clothing industries
gender
  binary oppositions, 2, 17n1, 97
  concepts, 2, 9, 21, 182
  contested understandings, 182, 193
  discourse, 3, 10, 14, 17, 33, 97, 137
  and economic activity, 6, 7
  identity, 1, 2, 9, 16, 17n1, 97
ideology, 1–17 passim, 20, 22, 23, 31–3, 36–7, 50, 52, 64–5, 68, 70, 81, 102, 121–2, 149, 153, 182–3

management, 67, 70
relations, 2, 16
roles, 5, 11
and skill, 7
stereotypes, 10, 15, 37, 96, 121, 127, 183
gentility, 12, 32, 155, 157–8, 160–1, 163–4
German Imperial Criminal Code, 183–4
German Unification, 71
Germany, 4, 5, 15, 56, 67–80 passim, 111, 176–7, 182–93 passim
see also Prussia
girls, 87
Glasgow, United Kingdom, 10
glass-eye makers, 57
glass-makers, 91–2
glaziers, 84
glove-makers, 87, 90, 132
Gordon, Eleanor, 10, 11, 16
gossip, 26, 169
Göteborg, Sweden, 39, 44, 149
government policies, Sweden, 14
government securities, Britain, 12, 20, 27–33
granddaughters, 4, 6, 53, 63
grandmothers, 56
grave diggers, 116
Greece, 1
grocers, 60, 132, 162–3, 171
Groningen, Netherlands, 174
grooms, 111–12
guardianship, 5, 37–8, 43, 49, 111, 140
guilds, 5
abolition of, 13, 82, 87
Austria, 112–14, 119
Germany, 13
Spain, 13, 81–6, 90
Sweden, 142, 148
gunsmiths, 57
Guy, Kolleen, 64

haberdashers, 16, 60, 130, 132, 154, 160–2
Habermas, Jürgen, 96
Habsburg monarchy, 111, 115
Hague, Netherlands, 174
Hall, Catherine, 3, 4, 9, 10, 21, 37, 81, 52
Hamburg, Germany, 15, 16, 182–93 passim
Hanomag (German locomotive manufacturers), 74
harness makers, 57

Härnösand, Sweden, 141, 144–8
Hasselberg, Ylva, 46
hat and bonnet makers, 113, 133
hat and bonnet retailers, 158
Haupt, Heinz-Gerhard, 5, 10, 126
Henschell & Sohn, 67–78
Henschell family
Carl Anton, 67–9
Georg Christian, 70
Oskar, 67, 68, 70–4, 77–8
Sophie, 67–78
background and marriage, 70–1
domestic life, 70–2, 74
as firm manager and entrepreneur, 72–6, 78
images of, 68–9, 78
philanthropic work, 67–9, 76–8
Hesse, Germany, 70
heterosexuality, 2
Hill, Bridget, 170
Hinckley, United Kingdom, 24
Hohenzollern dynasty, Prussia, 76
Holborn, London, United Kingdom, 157, 163
Holland, *see* Netherlands
home, 2, 127, 136, 152, 154
homemaking, 127, 136
hosiery, 62, 154, 161–2
hospitality industry, 6
house painters, 129, 131
households, 10, 20, 37, 40, 42, 53, 61, 86, 110, 112, 121, 147, 163, 168–9
artisan, 84–6, 89, 93
nuclear, 53
housewives, 7
housework, 61, 99, 110, 112, 118, 128, 150
see also family reproduction
husbands, 5, 6, 7, 14, 25, 38, 40, 42, 52, 54, 58, 62, 65, 87, 100, 111–14, 126, 128–30, 133–4, 137, 148–9, 168, 174–5, 179

identity formation, 4
identity, *see* gender identity
illiteracy, 99
immiseration of women, 61
income, 31, 136
independent female traders, 174
individualism, 99, 101
industrial bureaucratization, 71, 72
industrial revolution
Britain, 22, 32

France, 64
Spain, 81
revolution, Sweden, 37
industrial training, 78
industrialization 3, 5, 96
   Austria, 115–16
   Belgium, 126
   Britain, 22
   Spain, 82–3
   Sweden, 12, 36–8, 140
information, *see* financial information
inheritance and succession, 8, 16, 25, 27, 37–8, 41, 69, 74, 90, 114–15, 120, 129–30, 142
   of firms, 13, 16, 62, 69, 74, 90, 92, 114–15, 120, 129–30, 142
   impartible, 86
   partible, 86
   see also wills
innkeepers, 117–18, 136, 140, 142, 149, 168
insider loans, 48
insolvency, 26, 39
institutional change, 38, 44
insurance, 132
   companies, 28, 154–6
   health, 68, 77
   see also life assurance
interdependence of public and private spheres, 20, 21, 27, 31–3
International Red Cross, 76
inventories, 36, 40–1, 124n42
investment, 75
   attitudes to women and, 20, 25, 26, 27
   in canals, 24
   in commercial banks, 44–7, 49–50
   economic, 25
   financial, 25
   in government securities, 27–33
   in joint stock companies, 24
   in life assurance, 25
   literature on, 22, 25
   passive 25–6, 47
   in real estate, 24
   rentier, 12, 25, 47, 54, 70
   risk, 25–7
   in savings banks, 42–7, 49–50
   women and, 12, 20–33 passim, 36–50 passim
   see also land ownership, shareholding
investors, 23, 25
Italian warehouses, London, 163

Italy, 5
Ixelles, Belgium, 134

Jews, 119–21
joint property, 38, 111, 114
joint sphere, 2, 10, 17
joint stock
   banks, 44
   companies, 24, 46, 73–4, 76
Jönköping, Sweden, 43
journalism, Spain, 97–107 passim
journals, *see* publishing, Spain, periodicals
journeymen, 83, 85, 89, 92, 114, 142, 148
journeywomen, 81

Kalamar, Sweden, 41
Karlplatz, Vienna, 119
Karlsruhe, Germany, 70
Kassel, Germany, 67–78 passim
Kekke, Stadin, 140
Kent, David, 170
kinship, 42, 49, 81, 93
Kirkpatrick, Susan, 100
Kocka, Jürgen, 71, 73
Kwolek-Folland, Angel, 7

labour
   associations, 81
   female, 22
   legislation, 140
   market segmentation, 82, 116
   relations, 68, 81
lace-makers, 83, 87, 128, 133
Lamoreaux, Naomi, 48
lamp makers, 131
land, *see* landownership, real estate
landownership, 23, 39, 54
laundering and ironing, 6, 56, 117–19
law
   commercial law, Austria, 14
   equity, 23
   property law
      Austria, 111–15, 121
      Belgium, 128–30
      England, 23
      Netherlands, 173–4
      Spain, 86, 89
      Sweden, 37–8, 139–40
   reform Sweden, 37–8
   and women, 4, 5, 68
      Austria, 111–15, 121
      Belgium, 128–30

England, 23, 29
  Netherlands, 168, 173–4
  Spain, 89–90, 99
  Sweden, 37–8, 139–40, 147, 149
lawyers, 8
  see also solicitors
leather industries, 84, 90–1
Leiden, Netherlands, 170
Lennander-Fällström, Ann-Marie, 140
letter press printing, 156
liberalism
  Austria, 113, 115
  economic, 4, 92, 113
  political, 4
    Spain, 81, 82, 107
life annuities, *see* annuities
life assurance, 25, 147
life course, 82, 90, 146, 148
life cycle, firms, 13
Lilja, Kristina, 41
Lille, France, 13, 53–64
lime makers, 57
limited liability, 88
Lindgren, Håkan, 40
Lindqvist, Christine, 140
linen drapers, *see* drapers
linen industry, 55, 59
  see also drapers
lithography, 156
Liverpool and Manchester Railway, United Kingdom, 24
locksmiths, 83, 133
locomotive manufacturing, 13, 67–76, 78
lodging-house keepers, 171–2
Loeb, Lori, 157–8
London Season, 161
London, United Kingdom, 10, 15, 74–5, 170–1
  West End, 161
Low Countries, 53
  see also Netherlands, Belgium
lower middle class, *see* petite bourgeoisie
lumber industry, 141
Lunander, E., 141, 147
luxury goods, 15, 16, 53, 99

Maastricht, Netherlands, 174
machine tool manufacturers, 57, 67, 70
madams, *see* brothel-keepers, 183, 191–2
Madrid, Spain, 82, 98, 105, 107
magazines, 97
majority, status, 4, 38, 45, 112
Malaga, Spain, 104

male breadwinner, 5–6, 60–1
Mallart, Antonio, 89
Malmö, Sweden, 142
management, 7, 13, 22, 37, 48, 53, 67, 68, 71–6, 78, 87–8, 91
  and attitudes to women, 69, 88
  family, 70–2, 92
  see also co-management
managerial revolution, 53
Mangot, Maria, 92
manufacturing, 13, 22, 52, 54, 59–63, 81–2, 127, 137
Marimon, Antonio, 89
markets, 2, 6, 26, 116
  see also financial markets
marriage settlements, 38, 54, 111–12, 114
marriage, 4, 5, 38, 60, 71, 75, 83, 85–8, 103, 111, 155, 167, 174
married women, 14, 43, 53, 54, 57, 58, 111–13, 118, 120, 127–8, 141–3, 147–50, 171–2
Marseilles, France, 52–3
Martí, Madrona, 90
Marxism, 7, 105, 110
masculinity, 1, 2, 6, 7, 37, 72, 137
mass consumption, *see* consumption
mass production, *see* production
masters, 82–5, 87, 90, 92, 115, 136, 142
Mathus, Thomas, 105
McBride, Theresa, 170–1
McDonogh, Gary, 81
mechanics, 60, 73, 133
Mediterranean, 5
Mercantilism, 83
merchants, 54, 62, 75, 127, 131, 135, 137, 171
metal working, 70, 84, 88, 116, 119
Middle Ages, 53, 111, 114
middle class, 3, 21, 25, 46, 59, 64, 81, 83, 101, 110, 119, 126, 134–7, 139, 147, 152–5, 168, 171, 179, 187
migration, 83, 115, 171, 189
military service, 112, 123n14
milk sellers, 16, 127
millinery, 10, 15–16, 53, 117, 133, 143, 154, 157–60, 162
mills, 22, 62, 64
Milne, J. D. 155
minority status, 4, 38, 128
modernity, 64
modernization, 44, 81–2, 93, 140
money lenders, 40, 49, 92
money, attitudes to, 26

morality, 3, 139
　see also bourgeois morality
mortality rates, sex differentials in, 13, 23
mortgage associations, 39, 41, 44
mortgages, 39–40, 129
motherhood, conscious, 106–7
mothers, 7, 8, 12, 64, 68, 98, 146–7
mutual aid societies, 85

Nair, Gwyneth, 10, 11, 16
Napoleonic Wars, the, 24, 27
National Bank of Sweden, 39, 45
national debt, Britain, 12, 27–3
　attitudes to, 28–9, 35n56
naturalism, 101, 104
needlework trades, 6, 117, 158–9
neoclassical theory, 7
Netherlands, 8, 15, 52–3, 167–81
networks
　business, 14, 87–8, 101, 168–9
　economic, 83
　family, 15, 26, 42, 46, 49, 84, 176, 189
　kinship, 26
　social, 15, 25, 36, 48, 168–9, 179, 189
newspapers, 26, 31, 67, 97–100, 102–3, 105, 134, 153, 163, 168
　advertising, 167–9, 178–81
　subscriptions, 99–100, 102
nieces, 134–5
nobility
　Prussian, 70
　Swedish, 38
Nocedal Law, Spain (1857), 100
Norfolk, United Kingdom, 25
Norlander, Kerstin, 46
North America, 5
North German Confederation, 76
Nyköping, Sweden, 43

occupations, 54–5, 60, 128, 141
oil, 53
old age, 25, 68, 169
Örebro, Sweden, 140, 147
orphans, 77

painters, 57, 133
　see also house painters
Palazzi, Maura, 5
pamphlet shops, 163
paper merchants, 131
Paris, France, 10, 63–4, 159
Parisian World Fair, 70
Parliament, Swedish, 38

partnerships, business, 24, 54, 62–3, 73, 119, 130
patentes, *see* tax registers
patents, 70
paternalism, industrial, 68, 77
patriarchy, 21, 22, 68, 94n25
patrimonialization of trades, 84, 93, 94n19
patrimony, 5, 13, 69, 85–8, 91, 93, 115
Patriotic Women's Association (Kassel, Germany), 69
peasantry, Swedish, 38
peddlers, 16
penny capitalism, 149
pensions 68
periodicals, *see* publishing
perpetuity, 27
petite bourgeoisie, 5, 16, 112–13, 118, 126, 137, 139, 144, 146, 150
philanthropy, 5, 7, 9, 67, 121
photography, 67
pimps, 184–5, 188, 191
Pinchbeck, Ivy, 22, 152, 161
placers, 15, 167–81
　career and earnings, 174–5, 177–8
　decline, 169
　government regulation of, 170
　marriage, 175–6
　origins and background, 176–7
　roles, 167–71
plasterers, 129
Playford, Francis, 31
poetry, 98–9, 106
political
　change, 3
　debate, 28–9, 35, 96
　participation, 97
　reform
　　and women, 9
　representation, 96
　see also suffrage
poor, 6
popular investor, Britain, 23
population registers, 135, 172–3, 180
　see also censuses
porters, 85
pottery and porcelain makers, 92
power relations, 1, 21, 22
pregnancy, 85, 191
pre-industrial societies, 140
preparatory industries, 61–3
press, financial, 26, 31
Primogeniture, 86
　see also inheritance and succession

printing, 108n10
private sphere, 2, 9, 12, 14, 21, 22, 26, 31–2, 36, 52, 81, 93, 96, 136, 137, 152–3, 168, 179
privatization of artisan trades, 86, 93
probate inventories, *see* inventories
procuresses (prostitution), 187, 191–2
  see also pimps
production
  mass, 22, 83, 160
  spatial organization of, 85–6, 147
professional status of women, 96, 113
profit, 7, 37, 41–2, 50, 172
property, 111
  see also family property, inheritance and succession, landownership, real estate
prostitution, 179, 182–93 passim
  Hamburg, Germany, 185–93
  and the law, 183–5
  middle-class attitudes to, 182, 184, 187–8, 190, 193
  regulation and policing, 182–3, 185–92
    modified control, 188–90
    strict control, 188–90
  secret, 190–3
Protestantism, 3, 120–1, 176
Prussia, 67–80 passim
Prussian Code (1851), 183
public creditors, Britain, 29
public finance, Britain, 12, 31
public houses, *see* innkeepers, victuallers
public sphere, 2, 3, 4, 9, 12, 14, 21, 22, 26, 31–2, 36, 69, 81, 89, 93, 96, 137, 140, 152–3, 155–6, 164, 168
public woman, 183, 187–8
publishing, 53, 134
  Belgium, newspapers, 134
  Spain, 13, 96–107
    books, 99–100, 106
    literary, 98
    magazines, 97, 102, 108n13
    newspapers, 97–100, 102, 103, 105, 108n10
    periodicals, 96–107
putting out, cotton industry, 61

Quataert, Jean, 76
Qvist, Gunnar, 140

rag-and-bone merchants, 131
railroads, *see* railways
railways, 64, 71, 76
  carriage manufacture, 70
  debentures, 24
  investment in, 24
  locomotives, 70–1
Ravet-Anceau, M. (publisher), 54–7, 59
real estate, 23, 24, 48, 92, 129
real property, *see* real estate
realism, 101, 104
Reformation, 176
religion, 53, 100, 119–22, 176
  see also evangelical religion, Catholicism, Christianity, Jews, Protestantism
remarriage of widows, 142–3, 148
rentier investments, 12, 25, 47, 54, 70
reproduction, *see* family reproduction
republicanism
  France, 4
  Spain, 103–6
reputation, 41, 86, 159, 168
  literary, 96, 100
respectability, 3, 15, 31, 155, 158, 164, 187–9
restaurant keeping, 41, 110, 117–18
  see also innkeeping
retailing, 5, 6, 13
  Austria, 117–19
  Belgium, 14, 126–32, 135–7
  feminization of, 56, 59, 62, 126, 143, 164
  France, 13, 53–5
  London, United Kingdom, 15, 152–66
  small-scale, 52, 61, 88, 113, 118, 126–7, 130, 132, 168
  Spain, 90
  Sweden, 14, 139–50
  see also shops, shopkeepers
retirement, 86, 176
revolution, proletarian, 105
  see also Marxism, Socialism
Richard, Eliane, 8, 52
risk, 12, 25–6, 31–2, 48
Romantic period, 97, 99, 101
Rome, Italy, 1
rope-makers, 84
Rothenditmold, Germany, 67, 74
Rotterdam, Netherlands, 170
Roubaix, France, 63
Royal Academy of Spanish Language, 100
Rule, John, 94n19

Sabel, Charles, 83
Saint Simonians, 103

Sala, Sweden, 41
salaries, 104
salesmen, 67
savings banks
    Britain, 28
    Sweden, 12, 36, 39–50 passim
Schäffer, August, 75
schoolteachers, *see* teachers
Schrover, Marlou, 8, 52
Schumpeter, Joseph, 7
Scott, Joan, 1, 10, 53
seamstresses, 103, 113, 116–19, 175, 178
second-hand-goods dealers, 117–19
Second Republic, Spain, 105
securities, 26, 31
    see also government securities
security
    domestic, 31
    financial, 25, 31
segmented sphere, 11, 17, 53, 116
self-employment, women, 13–4, 110, 116–22, 135, 150, 152
semolina makers, 84, 92
separate property, married women's, 54
separate spheres
    ideology, 1–17 passim, 20, 21, 23, 32, 37, 52, 53, 64–5, 69–70, 81–2, 97, 107, 110, 118–19, 152–5, 163, 193
    interdependence of, 20, 21, 27, 31–3
    thesis, 8, 9, 17, 20, 21, 29, 30, 33n3, 52, 81–2, 152–4, 183
        challenges to, 9, 17, 20, 21, 30, 32, 52, 69, 153, 183, 193
servants, *see* domestic servants, domestic service
Seville, Spain, 100
sewing, 7, 148
    see also needlework
sex, 1, 2, 17n1
sexual behaviour, 183–4, 190
sexuality, 2, 182, 184, 190, 193
sexually transmitted diseases, 184–5
shareholding, 12, 24, 61
    Britain, 23, 24, 25
    corporate, 24, 47
    politics, 47–8
    Sweden, 37, 46–7
shares, 76
Sheffield, United Kingdom, 24
shirt-making, 117
shoemakers, 84, 87, 89
shop fronts, 160
shop workers, 81, 148
shopkeepers, 6, 61, 113, 119, 127–9, 133, 140, 144, 148, 162, 171, 177–8
shops
    Belgium, 14, 126–37 passim
    department stores, 10, 126, 160
    France, 56, 57
    high end, 60
    low end, 60
    small, 52, 61, 88, 113, 118, 130, 132, 144, 168
siblings, 146–7
    see also brothers, sisters
silk mercers, 161
silk weaving, 89
single women, 12, 23, 29, 31–2, 54, 58, 111, 127, 142, 145, 147
sisters, 58, 135, 147
skill, 3, 6, 7, 8, 13, 25, 26, 57, 86, 89, 94n19, 101, 158
Smith, Bonnie, 4, 10, 53
soap manufacturing, 88
Social Democratic Party, Germany, 77
social mobility, 136, 148, 150
social policy, 77
Socialism
    Germany, 77
    Spain, 105–7
Socialism, Utopian, 103–4, 106–7
Soho, London, United Kingdom, 161
Solà Perera, Àngels, 81
solicitors, 24, 26
Sölvesborg, Sweden, 43
sons, 8, 16, 85, 88, 90, 115, 120, 135, 127
sources
    absence of women in, 54, 60, 64, 87, 92, 152–4, 171
    masculine bias, 8, 9, 54, 152–4
    for studying women, 8, 9, 52, 54, 60, 64, 130, 154–8
South America, 68
Spain, 5, 13, 14, 81–109
Spanish Civil Code (1889), 86
Spanish Civil War, 97, 105
Spanish War of Independence, 98
spinsters, 6, 23, 19, 42, 58, 62–3, 111, 139–40, 145–8
spiritualism, 104, 106
standard of living, 61
start-up costs, 159
state bureaucracy, Sweden, 14
state, the British, 27–33
stationers, 154, 132, 163

statisticians, 8, 153
stay makers, 133
steam power, 83
Stock Exchange, London, 30, 31
stock exchanges, England, 26, 27
stock market crash, Germany, 72
stockholders, 73
Stockholm, Sweden, 43–4, 46, 140–3, 147, 149
Stockport, United Kingdom, 24
stocks, 88
  see also shares, shareholding
stores, *see* shops
street vending, 127, 136, 140
succession, *see* inheritance and succession
suffrage
  men's, 129
  women's, 105–6
  see also feminism, women's movements
sugar refiners, 57
sugar, 53
Sun Fire Office, 154
Sundsvall, Sweden, 141, 145–6
surnames, 86, 100, 126
Sweden, 12, 14, 15, 36–51 passim, 139–50 passim
Swedish Banking Act (1864), 44
Swedish Code (1734), 37–8, 141
Swedish Free Trade legislation (1864), 139, 145

tailors, 83, 84, 88, 116, 133,
  see also clothing industries
tallow chandlers, 162
tanners, 85, 87, 90–1
tapsters, 168, 172
Tarafa, Maria, 92
taste, 3, 5
tavern keepers, *see* innkeepers, victuallers
tax registers, 13
  Belgium, 128–9, 133
  France, 53–5, 59–62
  Netherlands, 52, 172–4, 177–8, 180
  Spain, 90
tax rolls, *see* tax registers
teachers, 98, 103, 139, 152
telegraph operators, 139
testaments, *see* wills
textile industry
  Austria, 116–17
  Belgium, 14, 133

France, 13, 53–5, 61–4
textile retailing, 55–7
tobacconists, 131–2, 154, 163
Tourcoing, France, 53–5, 59–64
toy sellers, 163
trade and business cycles, 25, 63, 130
trade associations, 26
trade cards, 152, 156–64
  design, 156–8, 161
  functions, 156–7
  production, 156
trade corporations, 82,
  see also guilds
trade directories, 10, 13, 54–63, 120, 133, 153, 161, 172–4, 180
trade guilds, *see* guilds
trade manuals, 155
trade schools, 113
trade unions, 77
traders, 126–37 passim
Trades Regulation, Austria (1883), 113
training, 86
transgression, 9
transport infrastructure, 24
transportation, 24, 116, 120, 132
Treue, Wilhelm, 71, 74, 79n11
trust, 41, 44, 169, 178–9
trustees, 23
Tuyet, Pelegrin, 89

umbrella makers, 118
Umeå, Sweden, 141, 145–6
unemployment, 159
United States, 10, 52–3, 56, 87, 177
universal heir, 86
  see also inheritance and succession
universities, 99
unlimited liability, 39, 63
unmarried women, *see* spinsters, single women
usury, 44
Utrecht, Netherlands, 167–80 passim

Valencia, Spain, 82, 104
Vanackère, M. (publisher), 54–7, 59
venture capital, 36
Verviers, Belgium, 146, 150
Vicens, Jaume, 81
Vickery, Amanda, 9, 52, 82, 152
victuallers, 118, 154, 162, 168
Vienna, Austria, 14, 110–25
Viennese Commercial Court, 111
virginity, 184

watchmakers, 57, 131
wax-makers, 84
welfare, 5, 14, 31, 37, 68
West Midlands, United Kingdom, 24
Westphalia, Germany, 70
white-collar workers, 28, 77
wholesalers, 57, 59, 61–2, 127, 137
widowers, 123n28
widowhood, 25, 90, 114, 128, 130, 159
widows, 2, 5, 10, 12, 13, 16, 23, 29, 37, 40–4, 47–9, 52, 54, 58, 60–5, 68, 77, 83, 88, 90–2, 112–15, 118, 120–2, 127–30, 135, 137, 140–50, 167–8, 173, 175
will registers, *see* Bank of England will registers
wills, 23, 73–4, 114
see also inheritance and succession
window dressing, 160
wives, 7, 8, 12, 38, 40, 54, 89, 92, 111–13, 118, 126–30, 135, 137, 149, 153, 175
women
and business, 10, 22–3, 36, 52–63
economic agency, 1, 12, 17, 21, 32, 37, 40, 45, 50, 63, 114, 180
entrepreneurs, 14, 22, 36, 68, 72–8, 110, 121,163
independent, 152–64 passim
as inheritors of firms, 10, 16, 62, 69–70, 74, 90, 92, 114–15, 120, 129–30, 137, 142
instinct, 2, 7

and investment, 12, 20–33 passim, 39–50 passim
and law, 23, 28–9, 37–8, 69, 89–90, 99, 111–15, 121, 128–30, 139–40, 147, 149, 168, 173–4
managers, 22, 37, 68, 81, 88–93, 110–11, 119,
see also co-management
manufacturers, 57, 59–63, 81, 127
nature of, 9, 78, 94n25, 97
and philanthropy, 67–70, 76–8
representations of, 97, 153
and retailing, 10, 53–63
and self-employment, 13, 14, 116–22, 152
young, 42, 47, 168, 179, 189
women's movements, 96, 105, 110,
see also feminism
wool, manufacture, 53, 60, 62
work, 6–8, 97
workers' movements, Spain, 105, 107
working class, 3, 61, 104–5, 112, 118, 130, 133, 135, 147–9, 168
workshops, 62, 82, 83–6, 90–91, 142, 148, 152
writers and novelists, women 14, 96–107, 135

Young Tradesman, The, 158–60, 165n30

Zeitlin, Jonathan, 83
Zola, Emile, 104